WITH THE DEVIL'S HELP

WITH THE DEVIL'S HELP

A TRUE STORY OF POVERTY, MENTAL ILLNESS, AND MURDER

NEAL WOOTEN

PEGASUS CRIME

NEW YORK LONDON

WITH THE DEVIL'S HELP

Pegasus Crime is an imprint of
Pegasus Books, Ltd.
148 West 37th Street, 13th Floor
New York, NY 10018

First Pegasus Books cloth edition September 2022

Interior design by Maria Fernandez

Library of Congress Cataloging-in-Publication Data is available.

ISBN: 978-1-63936-240-0

10 9 8 7 6 5 4 3 2 1

Printed in the United States of America
Distributed by Simon & Schuster
www.pegasusbooks.com

To Mom, Uncle Doodle, my sisters and brother,
38 first cousins, and thousands of other kinfolk on the mountain.

CONTENTS

INTRODUCTION

In the fall of 1983, after graduating from Sylvania High School, I was attending Northeast Alabama Community College in Rainsville, only twelve miles from my parents' home. I was working at the Shell gas station on Main Street, Fort Payne, a block from the city park and within walking distance of Fort Payne Church of Christ.

One Sunday morning, while staring out the window wishing I was anywhere but at work, an old man walked over from the church. His slow gait told me that time had caught up with him years ago. His few remaining strands of white hair were trimmed close and circled his mostly bald head like a horseshoe. He walked in with his index finger tugging at his tie like it was a noose. "I snuck out of Sunday school to come get some candy. Don't tell my wife."

I smiled as he grabbed a handful of Peanut Logs. As he stood there savoring the sugar-laden treats out of his wife's sight—*and God's*—he struck up a conversation.

"What's your name?"

"Neal Wooten."

He seemed curious. "Wooten, huh? Where are you from?"

"Blake."

I wasn't sure if that was enough information. It's such a tiny place, some valley folks don't know about it, even though it's the first community atop Sand Mountain from the north end of town. Just drive up Sylvania Gap Road, a narrow, steep, winding, asphalt artery traversing through a sea of green vines and leaves where the DeKalb County Road Department has been waging a never-ending war against the burgeoning kudzu.

I always imagined that centuries after humans no longer inhabit Earth, the planet will become a huge ball of kudzu drifting through space.

Anyway, that's how you get to Blake. You can't really miss it . . . unless you blink. The only two upholders testifying to Blake's existence at all are the volunteer fire department and the small sign pointing the way to the Blake Community Center, where the elementary school once stood. The school closed just before I started kindergarten and burned down a few years later. Yes, I have an alibi.

That's why I began school at Sylvania, the closest real town to Blake on the mountain. The word Sylvania means "wooded area," so the town was aptly named. The town boasted a population of 1,900, but I think they might have counted the cows as well.

"That's where my parents lived," the old fellow said. "You didn't know a Pete Wooten, did you?"

I nodded. "Yeah, he was my grandfather."

"Oh my. He was the fastest runner I ever saw." He went on to give me accounts of my grandfather's speed, the same old stories I had heard many times growing up, only retold differently each time. Frankly, I had written them off as exaggerated folklore. Hearing older people from the mountain talk about it, you'd think my grandfather was supernatural. Then, the old man's face took on a solemn expression. "That was before he got in that trouble. Do you know about that?"

"Yes, sir." I had only known about it for five years. For some reason, I wasn't trusted with this information until I was thirteen. That's when the big secret of the family was revealed, and suddenly, all the little puzzles fell into place.

What I've learned in my life is this—and it took me *five-and-a-half decades* to fully appreciate: there is *no* normal. Behind the door of every family lurks a mystery we will never understand or be privy to. The only normal we will ever know comes from the perceptions created by our own experiences in our own little worlds.

Blake, Alabama, was my entire world. For me, it was an idyllic place to grow up with sprawling farms, rock churches, dirt roads, and great fishing holes. It hasn't changed much in a century. The area itself offers up perhaps the only fond memories of my childhood.

Growing up in a small rural area in the Deep South is no different from growing up on the West Coast or in New York City. Every location has its own idiosyncrasies that are just as foreign to those not from around there. The people could certainly be described as "backwoods," "hillbilly," or "redneck," and no one would care because those terms are not offensive here. But this story isn't about that. I do not write this from my "hillbilly" perspective, only from the perspective of a child's memory—a child not unlike every other in the world.

Sure, we had odd pronunciations: every two-syllable word that ended in *ow* came out sounding like it ended in *er*. (*See that feller in the yeller shirt? He lives in the holler near the shaller part of the crick and fishes with minners.*) We said "far" for "fire" and "mater" for "tomato" and "cheer" for "chair" to name a few others, but to focus on those things would be to distract from the story itself. I will keep the word "y'all" because, dang it, that's just proper.

I wrote this book to tell a story that will be lost forever once my mother and I are gone. It is the story of my grandfather, Pete Wooten, and my father, Travis Wooten—two men who shared the same struggles and battled the same demons in life. Each of these incredible men had uncanny physical ability, above-average mental acuity, and a mean streak more than a mile wide.

It is also the story of those who loved and feared them and the effects these men had on them, especially me. Both of these men spent their lives searching for the pot of gold at the end of the rainbow, the one big score that would make them a huge success in life. That success was something they forever craved but were never able to make a reality. They had intelligence, vision, and drive, but there was always something missing, something damaged about their psyche, a stray link in their DNA, or something just "off" to keep this goal just out of reach. I can't say for sure what was missing, because I was born without it too.

And, so, here I stand at the threshold of my childhood with the door swung wide open for you to come on inside and have a peek.

CHAPTER ONE

THE MEN IN BLACK SUITS

1969

Knock. Knock.

I jumped. We had been in our brand-new house less than a year, but we never got visitors, except our cousins who lived just up the little dirt road a piece from us—and they never knocked.

Mama's brother, Doodle Jackson, and his family lived the closest to us. Beyond them, closer to the paved road, was Mama's mother, Lela Jackson. We lived on Jackson Road. Actually, we lived well beyond the end of Jackson Road, down in the woods where the mailman and school bus wouldn't go.

Mama and my two sisters, Julene and Neenah, were in the kitchen preparing dinner. That's the midday meal on Sand Mountain. Mountain folks have three daily meals: breakfast, dinner, and supper.

I hopped off the couch and ran to the door. It almost felt like Christmas morning as I struggled to turn that old knob. The house was new; the door was ancient. The door finally opened, and there at the base of several cinderblocks we used for steps stood those two men, tall, slender, and mysterious. Like statues they stood, rigid, intimidating, their hands crossed in front of their waists. The light coming around them made it look like that scene from *War of the Worlds*. Maybe they were robots.

The odd thing was, neither their clothes nor themselves gave off any odor. Daddy always smelled of cheap aftershave, sweat, and Camel cigarettes—not independently, but his scent was always a medley of all three. Quite the contrast to my uncles on my mama's side, who reeked of Red Man chewing tobacco and Miller High Life.

In the yard behind them, I saw the long black car, the same one they always seemed to be driving. I really wasn't sure if it was the same car or if, in fact, the two men were always the same either. But the suits were always the same: black dress pants, black dress jackets, and black ties. They dressed like they were always heading to or coming from a funeral. Maybe that's why they wore sad faces. If I knew as many jokes as Daddy, I could have cheered them up.

But I knew something was off. I stared up at them in disbelief, not so much because they normally just watched us from a distance but because it was ninety degrees in the shade and they still wore those jackets. I wasn't well educated in the ways of the world. I was, after all, only four years old. But as I stood there waiting and staring, I thought, surely, they were supposed to say something.

"Who is it?" Mama asked, walking into the living room. Her face turned pale as she saw it was our old friends. Her eyes squinted through her glasses, which came to a point on each side. Mama was all of four-feet-eleven-inches tall and, as far as I knew, had always worn glasses. Her wavy medium-brown hair never grew far past her shoulders. Her belly protruded slightly, and I knew I would soon have another sister or perhaps a brother. "What do y'all want?" Her tone had zero anger but tinged with a touch of worry.

"Where's your husband?" one of the men asked, his tone completely indifferent.

By now, Neenah, who was six, and Julene, who was eight, stood on each side of Mama. Neenah had Daddy's features: black hair and dark brown eyes. Julene had blue eyes like Mama and me, but her hair was blond. Daddy made jokes often about the milkman, but I didn't get the joke. We never had a milkman.

"He's getting tomatoes from the garden. He'll be back any minute. If you don't want to wait, the garden is behind the house." With that, she guided Neenah and Julene back into the kitchen.

I just stood there holding the doorknob. I didn't know the proper protocol. Sweat trickled down my brow and dripped onto my bare chest. I never wore a shirt in the summer, and my bony knees protruded through holes in my hand-me-down jeans, the bell-bottom of each leg ending just above my flat feet. Getting hand-me-downs from two sisters was a nightmare, especially considering the clothes were purchased used to begin with. I learned about my feet earlier in the summer when walking behind my cousin who lived up the road. I noticed the weird prints his feet left in the sand: round spots formed from his heel and ball of his feet, connected with a thin strip on the outside, and five little round impressions at the top.

"How do you make prints like that?" I had asked.

When he turned and saw my full prints on the ground, he burst out laughing. "You got flat feet."

Of course, *I* was the weird one.

My sweating too was a genetic gift from Daddy. I rarely saw him not perspiring profusely.

"What the hell do y'all want?" I jumped again when I heard his voice . . . like always. Daddy was a little more direct than Mama.

The visitors didn't answer.

Daddy walked up to them so fast, they instinctively took a step backward. He handed me a small basket of tomatoes. "Give these to your mama," he snapped as he slammed the door shut.

I carried the basket to the kitchen, set it on the table, and then hurried back to stand at the door and listen.

"We know you know where he is," one of the men said. "Why don't you tell us and save yourself a lot of trouble?"

Daddy laughed. "What trouble? If you had anything on me, you'd have done something already."

"We're going to find him, and when he goes back to prison, you're going with him."

"Is that a threat?"

"You're damn right it is, and a promise."

"Well, here's a promise for you. If you don't have a warrant, get the hell off my property, or I will kick both your asses right here and right now."

I strained to listen, but there was only silence. Then, I heard the car start, so I quickly took my seat on the couch again.

When Daddy walked in and shut the door, his face was redder than normal, his buttoned-up shirt clung to his torso almost to his beltline with sweat. He removed that shirt and his undershirt, using it as a sweat towel, and sat in his chair.

Travis O'Neal Wooten, whom I was named after (but, in a breach of etiquette, I was appended with a "II" instead of a "Junior"), was an intimidating presence by all accounts. He was only five-feet-nine-inches tall but still had massive shoulders, chest, and arms. His fingers looked like Polish sausages, and his palms were two inches thick. What made him even more daunting was his incredible speed, strength, coordination, and unrivaled temper.

"You ready for a sandwich and some soup?" Mama called out from the kitchen.

"Bring me some ice water." Daddy was still steaming, and it wasn't just the heat. He was perhaps the only man in the South who hated sweet tea. Well, besides me. He looked at the television and quickly over to me.

I understood. He was not a fan of Saturday morning cartoons. I rushed over and grabbed the little pliers that we kept beside the television set and changed the channels until I found a baseball game. Daddy had warned me and my sisters not to change the channel too fast or we would break the plastic knob. He was right. Hence the pliers. Television—and electricity—was a new experience for us, so we had yet to figure out all the proper procedures.

Our television was a huge twenty-five-inch console set with speakers on each side of the screen. It had a dark walnut wood cabinet and was, by far, the fanciest thing in our home, much too fancy to serve solely as a stand. It had been given to us by relatives and had never worked since we had it. I'm not sure if Daddy actually expected to fix it some day or if it was intended for its current capacity, as a support for the working television, a thirteen-inch black-and-white model.

All of our furniture was passed down from relatives who had upgraded. The couch, chair, and coffee table were made of matching orange vinyl. The coffee table had a fake wood top and served as a storage unit as well. I used to wonder how it must have looked when it was new. It couldn't have been much more appealing. How did a salesman even manage to sell something like this?

Mama brought Daddy a large Mason jar filled with water and ice cubes. He preferred his water to be ice cold and made circular motions with his right hand, making the water slosh around in an attempt to make it colder faster. Daddy knew all the little tricks.

Ice was a luxury we didn't always have. We had one of those refrigerators that required electricity, and the company that provided the electricity preferred the payments to be made every single month. That obviously seemed excessive to Daddy. We only had it a few months in our rental house. This was the first time we had electricity in our new house, and I was hoping it would last, because it was pretty neat.

Looking around the living room, you could see the places where the kerosene lamps were positioned during our normal blackouts. Dark smoke stains decorated the light gray fake wood paneling walls like tornadoes rising to the ceiling, where the large, cloudlike black stains hovered.

Other than the stains, the only other thing on our walls was a huge framed print behind our couch. It was a painting by Paul Detlefsen of a blacksmith shop with two kids whose wheel had come off their wagon. I often stared at it for hours. The man seemed so happy to help those kids. We had no family pictures or other décor at all.

Mama's father, Harley Jackson, had given Mama and Daddy thirty acres of wooded land in Blake, Alabama, on Sand Mountain, and Daddy had built this house in a few days. Daddy was an expert carpenter, but patience was not one of his virtues. I'm not sure if he had any virtues at all. What did he need with patience when he knew a magic word he could conjure up like an incantation to speed up the process? If you know this word, you really never need a square, tape measure, or level. The word was "close-ter-nuff."

The living room and kitchen were the only rooms in the house that actually had wall panels on both the outside and inside. All the back rooms just had outside walls, and you could see the four-by-four framework. The studs were true four-by-fours, rough, unfinished, seconds bought directly from a sawmill.

We moved in while there were still a few tiny projects left to complete, like interior walls in the bedrooms, any interior doors, any type of flooring over the subflooring anywhere, and a room that most people had in their homes called a bathroom.

My bedroom didn't even have a ceiling, so I could see through the joists all the way to the inside of the roof, the knots and grain-lines in the flimsy plywood making monstrous faces that would scare me to sleep. But I finally made friends with them, named them even, once I learned that real-life monsters were far more dangerous and unpredictable.

"Neal, come eat," Mama said.

I didn't move. I was still worried about creating any ripples in the invisible tension in the room. I didn't understand who the men in the black suits were or why they bothered Daddy so much, but it seemed normal. When you're a kid, you never really know anything beyond your own little circle. I just assumed that every family in America dealt with them as well.

Daddy turned up the jar, downed half the water, and then went back to his sloshing as he watched the game. But it was clear the game was not smoothing things over. He drained the rest of the liquid in a second gulp and held the jar out toward me. "Get me some more water."

I obeyed. I always obeyed. I took the glass into the kitchen and set it on the table. I picked up a jug from the floor and began filling the jar. Even when we had electricity, we didn't have a well, so every day, my sisters and I walked through the woods down into the hollow where a spring surfaced with the cleanest water you can imagine. We filled our milk jugs there. That was how we got water into the house for drinking, cooking, and bathing. I was very small, even for my age, but could already carry two jugs in each hand while my sisters struggled to carry one.

7

I took back the full jar and handed it to my daddy. In my mind, I can clearly see it was his fault. He was not paying attention. I definitely saw his hand knock the glass from my hand. That point, however, was moot. The jar hit the particle-board floor with a crash, and ice, water, and pieces of broken glass went everywhere.

There was only one second of silence as my daddy stared at me. I wanted to apologize, but my fear kept the words from forming. It's like when you wake from a nightmare and want to scream, but nothing comes out. The difference is, in the nightmare scenario, you suddenly realize the worst is behind you. Here, the worst was yet to come.

Daddy stood quickly. My legs made me take a few steps backward involuntarily. He stepped over the bulk of the broken jar and grabbed for his belt buckle. Daddy was an artist when it came to punishment, his favorite medium being his belt, which he could remove with alarming speed and wield like a ninja handling nunchucks. Forget lions, bears, and even werewolves. There wasn't a scarier sound in the world than the noise from the friction of leather on denim as his belt came out so fast that I'm surprised it wasn't literally smoking.

"Travis, stop." Mama had hurried to the living room with a mop and broom.

But Daddy took orders from no one. "I'll teach you, you clumsy little son of a bitch."

Wait. That wasn't the right line. He always instructed me to bend over first. Not this time.

Daddy doubled over the belt and flung away. With the first lash, the belt went over my left shoulder, whipped around, and impacted my back so hard that it knocked me to my knees.

"Stop, Daddy!"

"Please, Daddy, don't!"

I don't know whose voice was which, but I knew it was both of my sisters pleading for me.

But Daddy's demons consumed him, and he swung away. I think he continued to yell profanities, but the only sounds I heard were from the impact of the leather serpent against my tender skin.

It was always the same surreal sensation. I wanted to believe it wasn't really happening. I tried to make my mind go somewhere else; I tried to think about cartoons or fishing or anything fun. But I could only manage to do that for a couple of seconds at a time, because each strike of that leather brought my thoughts quickly back to reality. I curled into a ball on the floor, knowing it would eventually be over. But not soon.

Once again, Daddy raised his trunklike arm nearly to the ceiling, clutching the belt in his massive paw, and brought it down with all his might. His eyes, which were normally dark brown, were now black and bloodshot.

I had watched him chop wood in a similar fashion. He could cut through a big log in a matter of seconds. He'd start with an inward cut; then, his next cut would be about a foot away, going inward as well. A huge chunk would fly away. Each following stroke always landed in exactly the same place on one side and then the other, creating a smooth *V* shape, which came to a point right at the bottom of the log, making it separate. He could do wonders with an ax, saying, "Let the ax do the work." I guess the same rule applied here.

Suddenly, one end of the belt slipped from his hand, and as my luck would have it, it was the buckle end. Daddy's rhythm never faltered. He continued chopping away as now the metal buckle tore into my flesh.

I tried to curl up tighter. It didn't help. The thoughts that went through my mind during these times were strange. I first wondered why I was a bad person. Then, I wondered why he was. Then, I wanted to kill myself. Then, I wanted to kill him. But mostly, I just wanted it to end.

Finally, he quit or simply became tired. He just stood there, breathing heavily, exhaling toxic fumes. "Go to your room." He pointed with one hand as he gripped the belt with the other.

I got up with effort and walked toward the hall. I stole a glance at my sisters as I passed. They clung to Mama as if she was the only safe place on earth, their arms wrapped tight around her waist, their faces drenched in tears. That hurt me worse than the belt and buckle ever could.

I lay on the bed and stared up at the plywood creatures under the roof. There was the giant spider that I swear I saw move a few times. There was the one that looked like an alien from another planet, or that was at least what I perceived them to look like. They didn't look scary today, only sad. My body hurt all over. Lying perfectly still was my only choice. Life didn't seem fair, but I knew it wasn't my fault. It was clear who was to blame: the men in the black suits.

❖

I drifted off to sleep and woke in exactly the same position. My body felt more stiff than sore now. I wasn't sure what time it was, but the sun was still very bright outside my window. I lay there still afraid to move.

I heard footsteps coming down the hall and could tell by the soft creaking noises in the floor that it wasn't Daddy.

Mama came into my room. "Let's go, sweetie. Supper's ready. Everything is okay now."

I believed her. For one thing, she never lied, and for another, this is how it always went. Daddy cooled off as fast as he became hotheaded. No matter how badly I screwed up and no matter how angry he got, he was always willing to forgive and forget. That's an admirable quality.

I walked into the kitchen and sat at my place to the left of Daddy, who sat at the head of the table. No one looked at me. I knew they were afraid to acknowledge the marks on my body.

He reached over and rubbed me on the head. "Boy, you're getting huge. Look at those arms. Show me your muscles."

I grinned and held out my right arm, bending it at the elbow.

Daddy squeezed my biceps. "Great day in the morning. You're strong."

He was right. I *was* strong.

After supper, Daddy ordered Julene and Neenah to do the dishes. He sat in his chair and watched television. He looked over and motioned for me to come to him. I walked over and he grabbed me up, put me on his knees, and started bouncing me up and down while singing. "Ride a little horsey down to town. Watch out, little boy, and don't fall down. Spill every drop of buttermilk you have got. A one, a two, a one two three . . ." At this point, Daddy spread his legs suddenly causing me to fall almost to the floor before he caught me.

I laughed so hard I could barely breathe. "Again."

Daddy repeated the performance.

There came another knock on the door. We were popular today.

Daddy sat me on the coffee table and opened the front door. He didn't even bother to put on a shirt. There stood a tall, large woman in a plain dress. Her long gray hair was pulled up in a huge ball, and she clutched a Bible in her arms. A small, short man stood beside her. He was almost bald and so spindly that it looked like a stiff breeze would blow him over.

"Who are you?" Daddy asked.

"Sister Johnson. I'm the new preacher at the Church of God of Prophecy by Cunningham Bridge. Just trying to get around to meeting all the neighbors. May we come in?"

"Sure," Daddy said. He motioned them in and had them sit on the couch, resuming his place in his chair.

Mama and my sisters walked in, introduced themselves, and stood around to hear.

"You have a lovely family," Sister Johnson said. "Do you attend our little church?"

Daddy shook his head. "No."

"Oh, I see. Where do y'all go to church?"

"We don't."

Sister Johnson looked troubled. "You don't go to church? Why not?"

Let me say here that this was perfect timing. Daddy was still upset from the visit earlier in the day from the men in the black suits, and he was weary from the beating. This was going to be the kind of moment he lived for, and it was fun to watch.

Daddy smiled. "Because churches are full of hypocrites."

Sister Johnson blinked three times, and her face became flustered. "Well . . . uh . . . I assure you that our church is not."

"Really?" Daddy asked. "Let me ask you a question. Do y'all pray in your church?"

"Of course."

"Out loud?"

"Yes."

Daddy went for the jugular. "Well, the Bible says that when you pray, you should go into a closet and pray in private. And those who pray for everyone to hear are hypocrites."

"No, no, you don't understand," Sister Johnson said. "Have you even read the Bible?"

"Of course." Daddy pointed to the coffee table where I sat. "We have a family Bible in there."

He was telling the truth. I had seen it. It was huge and had pictures in the back. Mama even used it to store important documents. I never knew it was for reading, though.

Sister Johnson tried to gain control. "If you don't go to church, you will suffer damnation. The wage of sin is death. You'll find that in the Bible too."

Daddy nodded. "So, you're saying I'm a sinner?"

"Of course."

"What about you? Doesn't the Bible say that we all fall short of the glory of God? So, aren't you a sinner too?"

Sister Johnson was becoming more flustered. "Yes, I am. But Jesus died for my sins."

"Oh," Daddy intoned, "but he didn't die for mine?"

"Yes, of course. But you need to go to church."

Daddy laughed. "So, I need to go to church and be a hypocrite or it doesn't apply to me. Is that what you're saying?"

"You're twisting the scripture!" Sister Johnson yelled. She looked over at her husband. "Come on!" They got up and walked out the front door.

I suddenly realized her husband had never uttered a word. I felt kind of sorry for them. It seemed they came with good intentions, but it had backfired terribly.

Daddy sat back and chuckled. He loved doing this. I could see the clever smirk etched across his face. He was truly the king of his castle. Well, our little brand-new shack was as drafty as a castle, but that's where the similarities ended. Daddy really only knew enough about the Bible to make this one argument. If it's true that a little knowledge is a dangerous thing, then when it came to Christianity, Daddy was the most dangerous person in the world.

CHAPTER TWO
PETE MEETS ELSIE
1926

I got a quarter says you can't do it."

Pete Wooten grinned as he stared at the shiny coin between the guy's callused fingers. "You're on." Pete didn't have a quarter, but he was confident and he wanted that money. And it was easy money because he had already successfully accomplished, on many occasions, what this idiot was betting couldn't be done.

The sounds of merriment echoed across the area as men threw horseshoes and chewed tobacco, kids played Red Rover and stickball, and the women shooed flies off the food placed neatly on two long wooden tables. Dozens of families were in attendance, and people were scattered out across the grounds, standing in small groups or sitting in circles on worn patches of earth. A slight breeze danced across the clearing, and clouds raced across the sky at a turtle's pace, as if floating upside down on a deep sea of blue. Tall evergreen sentinels stood guard around the clearing.

The stock market had rebounded somewhat from the depression of 1921, but that meant little to the farmers on Sand Mountain. It was a hard life before the collapse, and things were still hard. A decline in agriculture resulted in fewer clothes and even less money. Education had lost importance as parents and children worked together to keep families, farms, and homes intact.

Community get-togethers were still common though, and Pete *loved* them. He enjoyed the attention. He was seventeen, a charmer through and through, and was always the life of the party. He stood six feet tall, slender, with crystal blue eyes. His dark brown hair was cropped short and neat. He wore no shirt under his overalls, and his bare shoulders and arms showed off tan, lean muscles.

"Let's do this," another young fellow said.

The first guy tucked the quarter back in his pocket and walked up to Pete, staring him in the eyes for several seconds, turning around, and then standing up as straight as he could.

Pete smiled, glancing left and right to ensure enough people were standing around and that they were all paying attention. Planting his shoeless flat feet firmly in the dirt behind his challenger, he squatted down and jumped as hard as he could. His feet sailed completely over the guy's head, and he landed in front of him.

Everyone watching cheered.

"Pay up," Pete said holding out his hand.

The guy shook his head. "Your feet touched my head. I felt it."

No one moved. Those who knew Pete couldn't look away.

"My feet did not."

"You're a liar," the guy said.

Pete hated being called a liar more than anything in the world. When he really was lying, it bothered him even more. His outstretched hand formed into a fist as his eyes turned a darker shade. "You're gonna feel it if you don't pay up." He stood there, waiting . . . hoping even that the guy would refuse to pay.

"C'mon, man," an onlooker shouted. "He cleared you by a foot."

Pete's jaw muscles clenched so tightly that it made the lines in his face look like scars.

"All right," the guy conceded, handing over the money. "Here."

Pete took the quarter and watched the guy walk away. He couldn't even feel the others patting him on the back as he debated whether or not to go after the guy to teach him a lesson.

"Let it go, man," a friend said. He knew Pete all too well. "Let's get some food."

They walked over to the tables, where Pete grabbed a chicken leg with his bare hands and began devouring it. He was a slim guy but could eat a ton.

"Pete, come over here."

He looked up and walked over to where his mama, Della, stood beside his little sister, Olive, and was talking to another woman. Olive clung to her mama's leg.

Della stood five-foot-seven, her coarse black hair parted in the middle and tied up in the back. It contrasted her alabaster skin, which stayed light even though she spent a lot of time outdoors. Her dark blue eyes glimmered, and her smile and laughter were contagious. Petite but callused hands rested in two pockets of her homemade floral dress. She always added two pockets to her dresses, one for personal items and one for her plug of tobacco. It was her only vice.

Pete's seven-year-old sister, Lorene, stood near their mama. Pete also had two teenage sisters, Rosa and Bertha, who were off playing somewhere, and one brother, Warnell, who was nine.

"Say hello to Mrs. Price. She's up visiting her sister."

"Hello, ma'am." Pete nodded respectfully as he noticed her store-bought dress, hat, and earrings. Her wedding ring, though small, had an actual diamond.

"Hello, Pete. It's nice to meet you." Mrs. Price's straight black hair, dark-toned skin, and high cheekbones belied her Cherokee heritage. She turned and scanned the area until she saw who she was looking for. She waved. "Elsie, come here, sweetie."

The young girl walked toward them. Pete was awestruck. He couldn't take his eyes off her. She was barely five feet two with eyes as dark as night and flowing black hair. Her round cheeks had a healthy, natural reddish glow. Her not-so-plain blue dress hung almost to her shoes and swayed as the mountain wind gently kissed it.

"This is my daughter, Elsie. Elsie, this is Pete."

"Ma'am," Pete said with a wry smile.

"How old are you?" Della asked Elsie.

"I'm fifteen."

"I'm seventeen," Pete blurted out, even though no one asked.

"Why don't you show her around?" Della asked.

He nodded. "Be glad to. C'mon."

Pete had a confident heel-toe spring in his step as the two of them walked, shoulder-to-shoulder, toward a group of men throwing horseshoes.

"Where y'all live?" Pete asked.

"Springville."

"Where's that?"

Elsie smiled. "Down close to Birmingham."

"Wow. Y'all came a long way." They stopped as they came upon the players. "We got the next game," Pete said.

Several men groaned.

"I can't," Elsie said. "I've never played. I don't even know how."

Pete laughed. "Don't worry. You don't need to."

Elsie watched as the men tossed the shoes toward the opposite side, making them flip backward in midair in the hopes of having them land near or around the stake in the ground. When the game ended, Pete positioned Elsie to one side and then walked to the opposite side where the opponent waited. To Elsie, the entire game seemed ridiculous and even meaningless.

Elsie picked up the horseshoes. Her arm hung loose under their weight as she said, "I don't know what I'm doing."

"Just hold it like this," her opponent said, raising his own arm. "Put your thumb right there so you can make it flip."

"Hey!" Pete yelled. "Back off."

"Just trying to be helpful."

"Well, she don't need your help."

Elsie flung the first horseshoe. It landed halfway with a thump and a spray of dirt.

Pete laughed. "Great day in the morning."

The others joined in the laughter.

She tried harder with her second toss, but it too fell short.

The man threw next, put on a ringer, and dropped the other close to the stake.

"Six to nothing," the man next to Pete said. He pitched next and landed both near the stake.

It was Pete's turn. He smiled as he took his position. Holding the horseshoe on the side instead of at the back, he took one step and released the shoe. It didn't flip like the others but stayed horizontal and made a complete clockwise rotation and hit the stake. The little spike inside the shoe grabbed the stake and clung on as the horseshoe spun around three times before settling on the ground. His second pitch was likewise a ringer. Smiling at his opponents, he said, "Ten to six."

Elsie never scored a point, but as Pete had mentioned, she didn't need to. It only took Pete three turns to win the match.

Pete stood proudly. "Next?"

No one stepped up.

"You fellows can have it," Pete said sarcastically and walked away. "Y'all need the practice anyways."

"Are they upset?" Elsie asked, taking double steps to catch up.

"Nah, just sore losers."

"Do you always win?"

Pete grinned. "Always." After a few seconds, he added apropos of nothing, "But I have big plans. I'm gonna be rich."

"Really?"

"Yep. I'm gonna buy a lot of land and have my own farm." Perhaps he wanted to show there was more to him than being good at sports. But it didn't last. "Let's go; they're about to start the foot races."

Pete loved to show off pitching horseshoes, playing checkers, or competing in just about anything, but racing was his passion. Even the old men on the mountain admitted they never saw anyone who ran as fast as Pete. When he entered a racing event, everyone knew they were now competing for who would come in second. Pete would often cross the finish line before the other runners were halfway there. His feet were perhaps the only thing quicker than his temper.

Every runner stepped up to the starting line as a thin section of twine was held on either end by twin boys with dirty blond hair and bare feet. Pete rolled up his britches' legs. The starter delivered the countdown. "On your mark . . . get set . . . go!"

Pete stood in place as the others bolted forward. He looked over, winked at Elsie, and then took off. His legs were longer and moved much faster than those of the other runners. In fact, his legs seemed to move faster than humanly possible. He passed the others at the halfway mark and went on to win.

At the end of the day, Pete walked Elsie to her father's old pickup. Her father sat behind the wheel, eyeing the couple the way fathers do.

"I had a great time. Will you write to me?" she asked.

"Sure." Pete had only attended school sporadically for a few years but picked things up well. He could read and write on a college level, and his sense of numbers and equations exceeded that. "Maybe I'll come and see you one day too."

Elsie's father cleared his throat.

"With your parents' permission, of course," he added.

He watched them drive away and decided to head home himself. He had to walk, but he didn't mind. He was in love, on cloud nine. Nothing could faze him.

"Hey, man, sorry about earlier."

Pete looked up to see the guy who had bet him a quarter he couldn't jump over him. Pete just smiled and nodded . . . and then decked him.

That night, Pete lay in bed unable to sleep. He was totally smitten. The next morning, he got up early and, as soon as his chores were finished, sat down to write Elsie. He was as charming on paper as he was in real life.

Thus began a six-month pen pal courtship, during which time Pete asked Elsie to be his girl and she wrote back with the answer he most wanted to hear: "Yes."

When planting season began in 1927, however, Pete worked from sunup to sundown helping his father, Van, plant over one hundred acres of corn and watermelons. So, his letters became fewer and fewer. He tried to convince Elsie that the long hours were leaving little time to write, but he sensed by her replies that she was either losing interest or thought *he* was and using farming as an excuse. It bothered Pete. It bothered him a lot.

The first crops came in, and Pete worked until dark loading twenty bushels of Silver Queen corn onto his daddy's old truck. It was a rusted and dented 1919 Ford Model T pickup with the fender missing on the passenger side front. The wood bed had been extended to haul more produce.

The next morning, his daddy woke him at four with "Pete, get up. Let's go."

Van was over six feet tall. Long dimples ran down both cheeks, making his leathery face appear forever young. His light-blue eyes were almost translucent. Long strands of dark brown hair curled around on top of his head in no particular order but was trimmed very short by his ears. It was how he had always worn it. How his father had always worn his. Van only knew the farming life: get up early, work hard all day, and make enough money to barely feed your large family.

Pete stumbled to the kitchen and sat at the table where his mama had eggs, sausage, biscuits, and gravy waiting. He didn't move. All of his siblings were still asleep, but Pete, as the oldest, didn't have a choice.

The old country house set a fair piece from the highway in Blake, not far from Cunningham Bridge, and was hidden among the pines and hardwoods. The gray weathered siding and rusted tin roof made it resemble a small barn more. The boys all slept in the same bedroom, as did the girls.

"Eat something, son," his daddy said. "Might be a long day at the market."

"I'm not hungry."

His mama looked worried. "You need to eat something."

"I said I'm not hungry!" Pete yelled so loud that the dogs outside started barking.

Neither Van nor Della said another word, only sat with their heads down and ate in silence. In a word, it was fear. They were familiar with this side of their son and knew when to let it go.

Van and Pete sat stoic in silence, Pete staring out the front windshield and watching the sky turn from dark to light as the sun made its way over the trees. When they got to town, Van pulled into an empty spot in front of the market. As he went to pay the one-dollar rental for the day, Pete set four bushels off the back and left the rest on the truck. He taped a sign to the back of the truck that read CORN $8 BUSHEL. The price of corn had just recently started to climb after falling for eight straight years.

The town was bustling with people. Pete watched shoppers drift around the stalls, looking for cheap necessities—produce, wheat, eggs, and even yarn. They looked worn, these folks. Their faces were tan and wrinkled by time, like antique leather. The men gathered in small groups, discussing crops and spitting tobacco, while the women, most of whom had a child on their hip or in their belly, lingered over items they could afford and items they couldn't. Bigger kids ran wild, throwing stones and rolling hoops.

By the time Van returned, Pete had already sold two bushels. He handed the money to his daddy.

Van took a gamble. "Maybe you should go see her after this market season ends."

Pete gave no answer, which was better than some possible responses.

A man approached, bought a bushel, and paid with eight one-dollar bills. After he walked away, Van handed a dollar to Pete. "Why don't you go find something to eat? You must be hungry by now."

Pete took the bill and laid it on the bushel of corn in front of him.

It was bad timing. A homeless kid of about fifteen years old had been casing the market trying to pocket some free food. The pangs in the kid's stomach made money too tempting to pass up. He snatched the dollar off the corn and took off running. Unfortunately, he had no idea from whom he was stealing.

Instinct and anger kicked in. Pete jumped up and made for him, the toughened soles of his bare feet shielding him from the small sharp gravel below. He caught up to the kid very quickly and rammed him in the back, causing him to fall face-first into the gravel and breaking his nose. Blood spurted in several directions. But Pete wasn't finished.

"You son of a bitch! Steal from me, will you?" Pete straddled him and wailed away, striking the kid on the back of the head. "I'll kill you!"

The kid kicked his legs, trying to get away, but all he managed to do was create a cloud of dust. The dirt under his face turned dark red from his blood.

Two policemen, who patrolled the market, rushed over and pulled Pete away.

Van just stayed with the truck waiting and watching.

One of the policemen eventually brought Pete back and shoved him into his chair. "I can understand being upset with someone stealing from you, but that kid didn't deserve that. What the hell's wrong with you?" He looked at Van. "The owner ain't gonna press charges, but he don't want this guy back here again . . . ever."

Pete stood, staring at the ground with his hands in his pocket. Finally, he found his words. "What was I supposed to do, just let the boy steal from us?"

Van didn't have an answer. He simply stooped down to pick up a bushel of corn.

"What are you doing?" Pete asked.

"The officer said we couldn't stay."

Pete shuffled his feet. "No, he said I can't. I'll go walk around outside the market a while and be back in a couple of hours." Pete knew this one day made up over half of his daddy's income for the entire year.

Van nodded. He stayed and, after selling out, picked up Pete outside the farmers market to head back to Sand Mountain. They were halfway home before either of them spoke.

"What I said about going to see her after market season . . . well, I guess you need to go sooner."

Pete looked at his daddy. "Who's going to help you?"

"I'll figure it out. Warnell can pitch in, and I can hire a fellow if I need to. But you need to get this out of your system."

❖

Pete got up the next morning, ate, and then headed south with twelve dollars in his pocket. He was able to hitch a ride a few times, then walked the rest of the way. He didn't mind. It gave him time to think about the life he was going to build for himself and Elsie. He remembered what he told her when they first met about buying a farm and becoming rich. He meant it. After all, what could stand in his way? He was young, strong, and healthy. Plus, he knew how to farm. He imagined more than corn. He would plant watermelon, sweet potatoes, and maybe even a few pecan trees. He worked hard. He deserved a good life, didn't he?

He found the tiny town of Springville and simply asked around until someone could tell him where the Price farm was.

When he found it, he was impressed . . . and he felt something else too, something he was unaccustomed to: he was intimidated or just daunted. The neatly painted house was surrounded by land, lots of it. The harvest being over, it was easy to see that the Price farm included acres and acres of lush soil. There was a barn. It was small, but the roof looked new. He saw hay stacked inside the door. Chickens pecked the ground in a coop off to the side.

He took a deep breath, opened the fence gate, and walked up the stone path. He knocked on the front door and waited.

Mr. Price opened the door.

"Mr. Price, I'm here to ask for Elsie's hand in marriage."

Mr. Price stood there a few minutes with his mouth open. He was a tall, thick man wearing brand-new overalls. He looked Pete up and down, paying particular attention to his ratty hand-me-down overalls and dingy shirt underneath. "Say again."

Pete swallowed hard, stood tall, and continued. "I know we're young, but I love her. I'm not talking right away—down the road a piece. And I'll always treat her right and make a great life for her."

Elsie heard Pete's voice and came to the door. She wore a gray dress almost identical to the blue one she wore the day she met Pete. "What are you doing here?"

"I came to find you."

Mr. Price turned to his daughter. "He asked me for your hand in marriage."

Elsie blushed. Then, she had a thought. "What did you tell him?"

"I haven't said anything yet. You're not sixteen yet."

Pete quickly reiterated one component of his plan. "Of course, we'll wait until after her birthday."

Her father still wasn't convinced. "Come on in and sit down, son." He led Pete to the kitchen, and they all sat at the table.

Elsie's mother came in and poured them all a glass of lemonade. Sitting at the table, she raised the lid on a tin of cookies. "Cookie, Pete?"

Pete smiled and shook his head.

"Where will y'all live?" she asked, getting to the subject at hand.

"At my mama and daddy's until we get our own place."

"And how will you support Elsie?" Mrs. Price asked.

Pete swallowed hard and stared around the quaint kitchen. It was a lot nicer than any kitchen he had ever seen. But it was beginning to feel very hot in the room, so he tugged at the collar of his shirt. "I help at my daddy's farm, but I will have my own farm soon."

Mrs. Price, like her husband, was skeptical. "I would rather her finish school first."

Pete felt his blood getting warmer, but he hid it. "When will that be?"

"She's got two more years," Mr. Price answered.

Pete sat there in silence. This had not gone as planned at all. He figured his best bet was to get Elsie alone. "Can we go for a walk?"

Elsie looked at her parents, who said nothing. "Sure."

As they walked around the farm, Pete turned on the charm and threw out promise after promise. "You can finish school up there, you know. That's fine with me. I just want us to be together."

"I want that too."

"Okay," Pete said. His broad smile expressed part joy and part relief. "We just need to convince your parents."

That was their plan, and they stuck to it. Pete made the trip once a week to spend every weekend with Elsie and her family.

Mr. Price was always cordial, but there was something about Pete that worried him, something he couldn't quite put his finger on.

Two months after Pete's first visit, not long after Elsie's sixteenth birthday, her parents drove her to Blake and she and Pete were married by a preacher at Van and Della's house in front of their families and a few friends. Marie, Elsie's older sister, stood by her, and Van stood by Pete. All six of Pete's younger siblings were dressed in their best clothes.

After the ceremony, everyone sat around and ate fried chicken and homemade desserts. It was a pleasant fall day with cool temps, the air filled with laughter and joy.

Van and Della were very happy and hoped this would be the event that would make Pete settle down and not be so angry most of the time. And they both really liked Elsie and knew she deserved a good man.

The entire day was like a dream to Elsie, and she hoped the dream would never end.

Pete was happy too. He loved Elsie with all his heart. "I'm going to make you the happiest woman in the world."

CHAPTER THREE

ROY AND HELEN HELMS

1970

I watched the bubbles as I held the milk jug under the water. When it was full, I handed it to Neenah, and she and Julene walked back toward the house carrying their two jugs. I started on my four.

The spring surfaced here. Years ago, someone had built a small block wall around three sides, which was now surrounded by beautiful green moss that was so lush our feet would sink into it. On the bottom was bluish-gray rock, smooth from the continuous flow of water that filtered across it over time, with a hole chiseled out in the center.

Daddy suspected someone at one time was going to build a meat-house since the water stayed cold year-round. He guessed that the hole was used to store milk. The spring only ran about two hundred feet through the woods before disappearing underground again. When the sun hit the pure, clear water, it sparkled like diamonds.

Because of the looming hardwoods and evergreens, this was one of the only places along the stream where the light poked through, making the entire area look like a rain forest.

After my four jugs were filled, I grabbed two in each hand and started back up the trail as well. The trail was a deep wide ditch right in the middle of the woods that marked our property line and stayed covered in leaves. It was about one hundred yards long and fairly steep. The spring was at the bottom of the hollow.

Halfway up the trail, I noticed movement and got excited when I saw what it was—two juvenile king snakes about eight inches long. I loved snakes of all kinds, but these red, white, and black twins were especially pretty, like painted children's toys that moved on their own.

I encountered the most beautiful snake I had ever seen just a few weeks earlier when I was walking through our cornfield. It was also the largest snake I had ever seen. It looked to be the size of a python I had seen on television.

I can't remember if it was during our brief brush with electricity, or if I saw it at my cousins', but it was on an episode of Mutual of Omaha's Wild Kingdom. Marlin Perkins and Jim Fowler—well, *mostly* Jim—well, Jim wrestled this monster in a swamp.

But in the cornfield, the shiny orange and yellow markings reflecting through the stalks told me right away it was a corn snake. I wanted to catch it, but it was curled around a full-grown rabbit and hissed loudly as I neared it. I decided not to interrupt its dinner. I never hurt the snakes, just played with them a while, only a few days, before setting them free.

I set the jugs down and caught these twins, but I wasn't sure what to do with them since Mama probably had dinner ready and I was expected. So, I did the only thing I could think of; I stuck them in my large shirt pocket and buttoned the top.

"There you are," Mama said as I walked in and set the jugs down on the kitchen floor in their designated area next to eight other full jugs. "Get you a sandwich."

Throughout the day, in between meals, we all would drink directly from these jugs instead of using a glass. We had a white metal dishpan for bathing. Our Ashley wood-burning heater had removable grates on top where you could heat water or even cook. During the colder months, everyone else in the family would heat water to bathe. Not me. I didn't care if it was hot or cold. I'd take a pan of cold water to my bedroom, hide behind the old quilt hanging on two nails that served as my door, and wash off with a cloth even in the dead of winter. I didn't hate the cold. What I hated was bathing at all, and that usually took an act of Congress. When I stank so bad that my pit bull Whitey wouldn't come near me, only that would convince me it was time to soap up.

On the table was a plate with several sandwiches: some tomato, some Spam, and some potted meat, which was my favorite. We were without electricity again, so we ate sandwiches a lot. It was a little past noon, and the house was well lit by the sunlight. I sat down and grabbed a potted meat sandwich and put it on a paper towel in front of me.

Mama poured a glassful of Pepsi and set it by my sandwich. It was room temperature, but still better than water. Suddenly, she screamed so loud that everyone at the table jumped, even Daddy. "Out. Out. Out!" she screamed.

Daddy started laughing as Julene and Neenah looked on in shock. I was confused myself until I looked down and saw those two snakes crawling out of my pocket.

"Take them outside," Daddy said as he tried to stop laughing.

I'm not sure if Mama was more upset with me for bringing them in the house or at Daddy for finding it funny.

I grabbed the two little fellows, who had gotten all the way to the tabletop, and let them go outside.

Mama was still shaken up when I returned. "Don't ever bring snakes or any critters into this house ever again. You hear me?"

"Yes, ma'am."

Julene and Neenah were laughing now too.

As we were eating, the front door opened and Uncle Doodle walked in. Mama had four brothers: Nuke, Bunt, Poss, and Doodle, all of whom were short and balding, and made homebrew in old butter churns. Doodle was almost an animated cartoon with short legs and a round face. Like Rudolph, his nose retained a reddish glow. One jaw usually protruded farther than the other as it enveloped a wad of Red Man chaw. If he wasn't chewing tobacco, there's a good bet he had an open can of Miller High Life in one hand.

"Hey," Daddy said. "You want a sandwich?"

He walked to the entrance of the kitchen. "No, I just came by to see if Neal wanted to help me get some worms."

"Yes." I jumped up.

"Finish your sandwich," Mama said.

I gulped it down. I loved fiddlin' worms, especially since watching television was out and there wasn't much else to do. I followed Uncle Doodle out of the house. He had a milk jug with a big hole cut in the top, which still left the handle on the side, and an old hand saw. We entered the woods directly beside the house and continued on about twenty feet.

I added some leaves to the jug while he cut down a sapling about two inches in diameter. Leaving a stump about knee high, he took the dull saw and began sawing across the top. As he pushed the blade forward, the teeth created a friction that made the leaves around the stump vibrate, and I knew it wouldn't be long.

Uncle Doodle loved to trotline on the Tennessee River for blue-channel catfish, and earthworms were his preferred bait. He'd set the lines out, each with about forty hooks, right as it was getting dark, leave them overnight, and go back the next morning. Each line would usually have a dozen or more catfish weighing anywhere from one to thirty pounds. He'd bring a few home to eat but sold most of them by the pound.

"There's one," I said and grabbed the foot-long worm and added it to the jug. Pretty soon the area was crawling with them. "Why do the worms come up when you do that?" I asked.

"Because it vibrates the ground."

I laughed. "I know that, but why?"

He shrugged. "I don't know, to be honest with you."

When we had the jug filled with huge earthworms, he thanked me and walked back home.

I always enjoyed spending time with Uncle Doodle. Six months earlier I had helped him load firewood. His trailer was the back half of an old pickup, which he pulled down into the woods with his Allis Chalmers tractor. It was a very heavy trailer, but loaded with firewood, there's no telling how much it weighed.

As he was driving a full load out of the woods, I was walking alongside. I tripped on a fallen limb and fell between the tractor and trailer, and the trailer wheels ran over both my legs.

Uncle Doodle jumped off the tractor and rushed back to me, fearing the worst, I'm sure. "Don't move," he commanded.

I stood up and asked, "Why?" I was fine.

He couldn't believe it. "Ride up here on the tractor with me."

He wasn't even angry with me and didn't even yell or whip me. He was a great guy, but he sure was weird.

❖

I spent most of the summer swimming and fishing at the creek, which made it pass too quickly.

One Sunday morning, Mama woke me early. "Get up and get dressed."

"Let's go!" Daddy hollered from the car. He stood by the driver's door wearing black slacks and a white short-sleeve button-up. He never wore jeans or pullover shirts and hardly ever wore a jacket or coat, even when the temperature plummeted. His one and only tattoo was partially visible on his left outer bicep. It was a heart with my mama's name inside. He got it when he was in the army well before asking my mama to marry him. I guess he was psychic.

Although the sun was barely peeking over the eastern pines, the house and yard were blanketed in bright light. It was October, and there was a nip in the air. We all walked outside and took our places in the station wagon. Julene and Neenah got in the back seat, and Mama handed them my little sister, Dinky, who was just a year old. Like Neenah, Dinky had Daddy's dark hair and eyes. Julene and I got our blue eyes from Mama, although Julene was the only blonde in the family.

I sat in the front seat between Mama and Daddy. I had to. I got sick as a dog on road trips when I rode in the back. That had always happened since I was little, and now, at the ripe old age of five, it showed no signs of stopping. Somehow seeing where we were going helped a little, even if I had no clue where we were going. I knew the church wasn't our destination.

"You feeling okay?" Mama asked as we headed out the dirt road.

I nodded. "Where are we going?"

Mama smiled. "We're going to see Uncle Roy. You remember him?"

"Yeah." I smiled. I did remember. We had only visited Uncle Roy once, but he was a nice older man. He was gentle and tall with a perpetual smile, albeit toothless. He was the kind of person you could sit with for hours just enjoying his company, his stories, and his laughter.

His wife, Helen, on the other hand, scared me to death. Her gray hair was always pulled up in a ball on the back of her head, and she wore an eternal frown. She was from what Daddy referred to as the old school, which meant she believed children should be seen and not heard. In contrast, Uncle Roy loved having kids around.

When Daddy got to the end of the dirt road, he stopped and just stayed there a while looking one way and then the other. "Is it clear?"

Mama looked around nervously. "I don't see anything."

I was confused. There wasn't a car in sight in either direction. I guessed it was always best to be safe.

Daddy pulled out and headed toward Fort Payne, the town in the valley. As he drove, he kept staring in the rearview mirror. It was a cool day, so the car windows were up. Daddy took out a Camel cigarette, the short ones with no filter, and lit it. Soon, the entire car was filled with thick smoke.

My eyes immediately began to water. I hated that smell. Thanks to Daddy, I hated cigarettes altogether.

About six months earlier, I picked up one of the butts he had tossed on the ground and ran behind the house. I thought I was hidden, but he caught me as I puffed out a small cloud of smoke. I thought for sure I was in for a whipping, but he didn't even seem angry.

"You don't have to hide if you want to smoke." He pulled a cigarette from his pack. "Here, have a full one."

I couldn't believe it. I grinned as he lit it for me, and I smoked away, mimicking how I saw him do it. Or so I thought.

"No, if you're going to smoke, do it right." Daddy lit one for himself, took a deep draw, and inhaled the smoke. I watched in awe as it disappeared down his throat. He blew it out and nodded to me.

I did it just like he did, but what came out was not just smoke, but everything I had eaten in the last twenty-four hours. I couldn't stop coughing. I thought I was going to die.

He just laughed. "You're a little green around the gills."

Gills? So, not only did smoking the right way make me sick, but it turned me into a green fish too? I decided right then and there smoking wasn't for me.

The smell of smoke in the car made it worse. I coughed.

"Don't get sick on me," Daddy instructed as he drove.

"You know he gets sick in a moving vehicle," Mama said.

"If you need me to pull over, you just tell me."

I nodded . . . and coughed again.

When we got off the mountain, Daddy took I-59 north. He drove exactly the speed limit and kept checking the mirrors. Mama also kept looking around. It kind of made me nervous, and soon I found myself searching out the windows. I wasn't sure what I was looking for but figured I'd know it if I saw it.

After we crossed the Georgia state line, Daddy exited to get gas. He always waited to get out of Fort Payne because the price of gas was so much higher there. He pulled in to the Georgia Game Park and parked at the pumps.

"How much you putting in?" Mama asked.

"Five."

"Okay, I'll go pay. You want anything?"

"Cigarettes."

"Can I come?" I asked.

Mama smiled. "Yes. You all can come."

Julene and Neenah hopped out too, Mama carried Dinky, and we all went inside. That was so much better than sitting in the car. Just the distance between the car and store with smoke-free air seemed so clean and refreshing.

My two older sisters and I explored as Mama went to the register. The Georgia Game Park was magical. There were dead animals everywhere, amazing examples of taxidermy, including a giant stuffed bear. It towered above us, its teeth bared, its paws ready to rip us to shreds. Julene had to pull me away to see the others. Most of the animals had deformities of some kind. It was like something out of a horror movie. In the back of the shop was a door with a sign. We stopped and stared.

Julene read aloud. "Game park entrance. See the two-headed sheep and other oddities."

All of our eyes lit up.

"Come on, kids, we need to go."

We turned to see Daddy standing behind us.

"Look, Daddy," I said. "Can we go back there?"

Daddy looked at me like I was crazy. "Didn't y'all read the sign?"

I nodded. "Yeah, a sheep with two heads."

Daddy pointed. "Read that part."

I looked back at the part of the sign Julene had failed to read. "A . . . Ad . . . Ad-mission two dollars."

"You have to pay to go back there," Daddy explained.

I knew what that meant.

We walked back out to the car and got in. Mama and Daddy, however, stood outside the car a little while, looking all around. Mama shielded the sun from her eyes as she scanned the panorama. Finally, they got in.

"All clear?" Daddy asked.

Mama kept looking around. "All clear."

As we drove away, I twisted my neck and stared through the back window at the tall wooden fence around the back of the game park. I couldn't help but wonder what strange beasts lived there. We continued on with the smoke so thick in the car I could barely see out the windshield. I coughed and the nausea coursed through me once again.

We exited the interstate at Rising Fawn and followed the path we had taken before. I had only been here once, but I recognized the small store in the curve when we passed. It was only a mile from where Uncle Roy and Helen lived. Helen walked there to buy food. We turned down the little dirt drive, and I began to get excited. This place was like Santa's workshop to me, and Uncle Roy was like Santa Claus.

The driveway melted into the yard, and Daddy parked in the front and got out. Uncle Roy didn't own a car, so ours was the only one there. Uncle Roy came out on the porch and waved. He always wore tan slacks with a white, long-sleeve button-up shirt, both of which seemed way too large. The shirt and pants were separated by a black belt, which was the only thing that seemed to fit. His hair was thick and white, cut neatly around the ears. Helen was his barber, of course. They were mostly self-sufficient.

Daddy walked up the steps and gave him a hug, but it seemed cold and mechanical. It was subtle but obvious, and it seemed less enthusiastic than what was the norm. Daddy was definitely a hugger, as were all my aunts and uncles on my daddy's side. Daddy was always hugging me and my sisters, in strictly a parental way, and he was very doting, loving, and caring. Well . . . except for when he instantly worked up a temper.

"Look how big you monkeys have gotten," Uncle Roy said, his gums on full display behind his grin.

We beamed with pride.

"Come on in."

We all walked in, and Mama and Daddy sat on the old couch. Mama held Dinky.

Helen came out of the kitchen and simply nodded, her face like stone.

"Dinner will be ready soon," Uncle Roy said.

"Can I help?" Mama asked.

Helen shook her head and disappeared again.

The small house had two rooms: the main room, which consisted of the living room and bedroom, and the kitchen. Like us, they had an outhouse. Around the walls of the main room stood a dozen beautiful antique grandfather clocks with swinging pendulums. When they chimed in unison, it was deafening. The walls themselves were adorned with gun racks, displaying beautiful rifles and shotguns.

That's how Uncle Roy made a living. He had taught himself how to repair clocks and watches at an early age. It was said he had a real knack. The same with guns it seemed.

"Can we go outside?" Julene asked.

"Sure," Mama said. "But don't go far."

Out we went and took off running. I knew exactly where we were going. In the wooded area beside Uncle Roy's place was a large rock enclosed structure. I was not sure what exactly it was, to be honest. It was constructed of large rocks mortared together like bricks and was about the same height as me, which, granted, wasn't saying a lot. It was almost two feet wide on the top, and we loved to walk around it. It was a large rectangular shape, a little bigger than Uncle Roy's house, but to me, it was akin to a castle and moat.

Julene and Neenah struggled a little to climb up, but it was easy for me, even though I was vertically challenged. Daddy often said I was part monkey.

The three of us were inseparable. Sure, we had sibling rivalries at times, but it could never dent the bond we shared. Even at family reunions, we three stuck together, secure in the knowledge that we had each other's backs. Plus, we thought all our relatives were kind of odd. Perhaps it was the belief that there was safety in numbers, although together, we were no match for our common enemy. But you rarely saw one of us without the other two.

"You know he's not really our uncle, right?" Julene asked regarding Uncle Roy as we followed her around the top of the walls.

"Really?" Neenah asked.

I was shocked too.

"No," Julene continued. "He's just a friend of the family. Mama said he just likes to be called 'Uncle.'"

It didn't matter to me if he was blood or not. He was the kindest and most fun person I knew.

When they called us for dinner, we jumped down and ran back to the house. Julene and Neenah went inside. I saw Helen by the well and went to join her.

The well had a circular rock wall that came to Helen's waist. There were wooden posts sticking out the top, which supported a small roof. Another wood post ran across and rods protruded through the upright posts; one side was bent in two places to create a crank. A long rope was wrapped around the cross-post and tied to a well bucket. It looked like the wishing wells I'd seen in paintings.

"Can I do it?"

Although it took all my strength, Uncle Roy always let me. Helen ignored me and lowered the well bucket down until we heard it fill with water. She spun the crank in reverse with amazing ease, her forearms flexing with lean muscles. The rope looped around the cross-post as the well bucket emerged dripping with water. Helen pulled it over a plastic five-gallon bucket and pulled the release. She grabbed the handle on the plastic bucket and walked toward the house.

I stood there a moment looking at this technological wonder. It seemed like most of my childhood was spent wishing we had things other people had. This well sure beat walking down to the spring to fill up old milk jugs.

Walking inside, I found Julene and Neenah on the couch, each with a plate of food. I walked into the kitchen. Mama held Dinky and sat at the small table with Daddy, Uncle Roy, and Helen. I took a plate and looked over the spread. There was some kind of meat. It was dark and in small pieces, but I wasn't sure what it was. There were mashed potatoes and peas. All had been cooked on a wood-burning stove.

I took a piece of meat, a scoop of potatoes, and turned to walk away.

"Get you some peas," Helen snapped, "and some tea."

I turned back around. Was she serious?

"Neal doesn't eat vegetables," Mama explained. "And he hates tea."

The look on Helen's face sent chills down my spine. She just kept staring at me like I had stolen money from her. I added a spoonful of peas to my plate, walked into the living room, and sat between Julene and Neenah.

There was no television set or even a radio. It wouldn't have mattered anyway, since they too had no electricity. Their walls were scarred with the same kerosene lamp tornado stains as ours. Julene took the plate from my lap and raked half the peas into her plate. Neenah took the rest.

I listened to the faint conversation coming from the kitchen. It was mostly Daddy asking how they were doing and if they needed anything.

Uncle Roy came into the living room and sat in a wooden chair across from the couch. He reached behind him and grabbed a little red contraption off a small shelf. I had watched him use it before and was always mesmerized. He placed a small square of paper on the gizmo, took a small pouch from his shirt pocket, loosened the string at the top, and carefully tapped until the right amount of tobacco sprinkled onto the paper. Then, he pushed a lever on the side forward and it rolled into a perfect cigarette.

When he was outside, he simply rolled the cigarette by hand and licked the paper to seal it. I loved watching him do it. It almost made me want to take up smoking . . . again, even though I was convinced it caused motion sickness.

Uncle Roy lit the cigarette, leaned forward with a smile, and said, "When y'all finish eating, I have some surprises for you."

Surprises? Plural? This was better than Santa's workshop. At Christmas, we usually only got one present each or at least one decent one. We quickly finished our food and took the plates and utensils to the sink, came back, and followed him outside and around to the side of the house.

He opened the small doors on a closet-type storage room he had built that was attached to the side of the house. Stored inside were his wooden toolbox and lots of old hand tools. He reached in and grabbed something and handed it to me. "This is for you."

It was awesome. It was a small wheelbarrow made of wood. The wooden wheel on the front actually rotated.

He handed Julene and Neenah each a doll also carved from wood. I assumed the dresses were made by Helen. The craftmanship was amazing.

"Ready for surprise number two?"

We all nodded eagerly.

He took out a spade, closed the doors, and pulled out a real wheelbarrow from beside the little closet. It was an exact replica of the one I was holding, or perhaps *mine* was the replica. In the wheelbarrow were three small plants with cloth wrapped around the roots. One was a holly tree, and the other two were cedar trees.

"Follow me," he said.

We all walked out in front of the house halfway between the road and porch. Uncle Roy got on his knees and dug a hole. The sun was almost directly overhead now, and we all cast tiny shadows. Uncle Roy whistled while he worked. He took the small holly tree, removed the cloth, and held it up. "This one we shall name 'Julene'." He planted it and then did the same with the two cedars, one on each side six feet from the holly. Those he named "Neenah" and "Neal," respectively.

When they were all planted, we stood there staring at our trees. I had never had a plant named after me, and it felt good. Actually, what I felt was something I rarely felt at home; I felt important.

As the sun was sinking below the evergreens, we said our goodbyes and piled into the car. Uncle Roy stood on the porch and waved as we drove away. It had been a great day.

Daddy lit up a Camel and took a draw. "Did you kids have a good time?"

"Yes," Julene said.

"We sure did," Neenah added.

I coughed.

CHAPTER FOUR

WEDDED BLISS

1930

The rooster crowed and woke Elsie. Sunlight flooded across the foot of the bed. She looked over at her husband. He slept peacefully. His eyelids were soft and pale, the muscles in his jaw relaxed. She still couldn't believe she was married. Pete doted on her like nobody's business. Everywhere they went, he showed her off with pride, making her feel like a movie star. She pressed her bare feet quietly to the floor as she eased out of bed, got dressed, and went to the kitchen.

Della was already there, standing at the counter, readying miscellaneous meats for the breakfast feast. Elsie and Pete were living with Pete's parents, but only until Pete saved enough money to buy their own place. It was, after all, crowded with all of Pete's siblings.

"Need some help?" Elsie asked.

Della smiled. "Sure. Been a long time since I had help in the kitchen. Biscuits need flipping."

Elsie walked over to the wood-burning stove and flipped the biscuits cooking in a worn-to-perfection cast-iron skillet. The old iron stove was now rust colored, and the small oven compartment had long since rusted out, so now everything had to be cooked on top.

When breakfast was ready, Van and Pete got up and came to the table before the rest of the brood soon filtered in. Pete wrapped his arms around Elsie and kissed her on the head.

"Good morning," Elsie said.

"Good morning, beautiful."

"We need to start turning the back field next week," Van said. "We did corn there the last three years, so this year, we need to switch it up."

"I won't be here," Pete said.

There was a brief pause charged with shock. Elsie laid her fork quietly on her plate and looked over at Della.

"What do you mean?" Van asked.

"I'm going to North Carolina. This fellow got me a job up there working in the tobacco fields. It pays a lot."

"What about Elsie?" Della asked.

Pete smiled. "She's coming too. This money is going toward our new home."

Elsie offered a smile too. This was the first she had heard of this plan, but she was glad to see Pete following his dream.

The next morning, they packed some clothes. A man came by in a pickup truck, and they sat in the back with other workers, all men. Some looked young and strong, like Pete, while others were more aged and work worn. Their faces showed the march of time, their knuckles raw and bulbous. As the truck carried them north and then east, Pete provided them entertainment. He told stories, jokes, and riddles. "What begins with T, ends with T, and has T in it?" He liked riddles, especially when he was the one telling them.

After a minute of everyone scratching their heads, he told them the answer. "Teapot."

Elsie forced a smile. She knew the real irony was that Pete hated tea, even sweet tea like everyone else drank.

By the time they arrived at the farm in North Carolina, Elsie was exhausted. The stale air in the back of the truck, the hot wind, and the constant banging against the wall of the flat bed had taken its toll. They were led to a small, dilapidated shed with a rusty, wire-framed, single-bed inside. Dust and dirt commingled on the floor underneath a wooden table and two chairs. A mirror on the wall had a single hole in it, as if someone looking had stabbed their reflection in the eye. There were several outhouses nearby.

"Is this where we're staying?" Elsie asked, moving closer to the mirror and putting her finger up to the gap.

Pete laughed. "Yeah. It's not so bad. We'll be working most of the time anyway."

The next morning, they were awoken by the sound of other workers shuffling around and talking outside.

"Come on," Pete said.

They followed everyone to the edge of a field where a huge jungle of tobacco grew as far as the eye could see. It was so tall and thick, it blotted out the sun between the rows. The man in charge showed them what to do. He extended his meaty hand and grabbed a stick about five feet long with another smaller stick tied on and running perpendicular on the bottom. There were dozens more like it lying on the ground. He set out a box of old knives with fixed blades and leather handles.

"Okay, for those of you who are new, here's what you do. Carry one of these sticks with you and a knife. Only take the ripe leaves. They look like this." He held out a huge leaf that was starting to wrinkle. "Cut the leaf off then cut a slit at the top. Slide it onto the stick. Once your stick is full, carry it to one of the trucks."

Pete smiled at Elsie and patted her on the shoulder. "Easy enough."

The picking itself was easy, but after a few hours, it was torture. Elsie had never worked in a field before. She had only handled a knife once, and that was when her father tried to teach her how to skin a squirrel. That lesson lasted a full second before her stomach turned and her dad laughed. Now, her hands ached. An angry blister had formed between her thumb and forefinger. Sweat dripped down her temples and her back. She was miserable and exhausted. Each trip she made to the truck took more out of her, but she endured it all for the sake of them having their own place someday. It would make them both so happy, especially Pete.

After a truck was finally full, it was driven to a large barn where workers ran a wire through the slits in the leaves and hung them up to cure.

They worked like that for six straight days, got paid, and were off on Sunday. Elsie just wanted to rest, but Pete had other plans.

"Let's go to town," he said. "I want to check it out."

They walked a mile or so into town. Like most small towns in rural North Carolina, there was a main street with several shops, a tavern, a restaurant, and a drugstore with a soda fountain and an ice cream counter. There were vendors set up everywhere along the street who came in just for the tobacco harvest, eager to cash in, because it increased the population of folks with money to spend. Pete and Elsie walked along with a group of other workers from the farm. They were from different towns and different backgrounds, but they were all just men and women who, like Pete and Elsie, were trying to earn a buck to make a better life. As Pete took in the scene, the money he had just earned began to burn a hole in his pocket.

"Look at that," Pete said pointing to a little toy horse. "I'm going to get that for you."

Elsie was shocked. What use did she have for a toy horse? "No, Pete. Let's save all the money."

Pete's face turned crimson red. His jaws tightened around his clenched teeth. He couldn't believe his wife would embarrass him in front of strangers when he was trying to do something nice for her. He bought the horse and pressed it firmly into Elsie's hand.

She grimaced as the toy left an impression in her palm, and although thoughts came to her mind, she said nothing and couldn't even bring herself to look up.

The rest of the harvest went the same way. Every week after they were paid, Pete wanted to go to town and spend the money as fast as they made it.

One Sunday morning, as Pete was sitting on the bed lacing up his boots, Elsie refused to go with him. She approached cautiously, stood next to him, and tried to explain that they weren't getting anywhere.

"If we keep spending money each time we get paid, it's going to take that much longer for us to save enough to buy our own place."

At this, Pete stood up and slapped her so hard across the face she had to grab the bedpost for balance.

Elsie wanted to scream. She wanted to cry out in pain. She wanted to vent her frustration. She wanted to confront this betrayal. She wanted to, but she did nothing. The force of the blow stuck with her all day. She felt dizzy and nauseated. The next day, she couldn't go to work.

❖

When they returned to Blake after the harvest job was finished, they had nothing to show for it. Had it not been for Van and Della, they would have had no place to live or money to live with. They continued to work at the farm, Pete helping Van in the fields and Elsie keeping house and cooking meals with Della. Pete's aggressive behavior continued. Little things, like a chair in his way or a lukewarm cup of coffee, could send him into a vicious rage. Elsie, Della, and Van managed around him, existing in a pall of fear and anxiety. They had learned not to challenge and to do their best to keep their distance.

A year passed like this, until the time came when Pete was ready to head back to the tobacco fields. This time, however, he went alone. Elsie, relieved to have an excuse and to have some time away from him, stayed behind on the farm.

❖

One day, shortly after Pete left, they received an unexpected visitor.

"Hello, Mr. and Mrs. Wooten," the woman said through the screen door.

"Why, Marie!" Della said. "Come on in, sweetie."

Van walked up with his arm in a sling and greeted her gingerly. "Hello, Marie. You're looking good."

Like her sister Elsie, Marie had the same Native American features, which were beautiful. "Thank you, Mr. Wooten. What in the world happened to you?"

Van hesitated before answering. "Oh, I'm gettin' too old for farming, I reckon. Fell off the back of my dang truck."

"Tsk, tsk, you better be careful now." Marie pulled out a gift and handed it to Van. "I think this is your brand, right?"

Van looked at the small plastic bag with a plug of chewing tobacco inside and smiled. "Right brand, wrong person." He handed the gift to Della.

"Thank you," Della said as she stuck the tobacco in her dress pocket.

Marie chuckled. "Well, is that little ole sis of mine around?"

"She's in the backyard," Della answered. "She'll be so happy to see you."

Marie walked around to the backyard and found Elsie leaning against the large pecan tree. "Hey, lazy bug. What are you doing out here?"

Elsie smiled when she saw her sister. "Just enjoying the shade. I didn't know you were coming."

Marie gave her a hug. "Well, I heard you were finally staying home for a spell. Why didn't you go—What happened to your eye?"

Elsie tried to hide the dark area. "Oh, I hit it on the door."

The thoughts in Marie's mind bounced back and forth like the needles of a polygraph, and it reflected on her face. "That dog won't hunt, little girl. Is he hitting you? Is that why you didn't go with him to North Carolina this time?"

Elsie didn't answer.

Marie looked back at the house. "His parents just let him treat you like that?"

"Don't blame them. They're scared to death of him. Can't nobody do nothing when he gets mad."

"Van didn't fall off no truck, did he?"

Again, no answer.

"Well, you did right not going with him then. You need to come back home with me."

"That's not the reason." Elsie put both hands on her belly.

"Oh my God. You're gonna have a baby?"

Elsie nodded.

"Then, you really need to come back home with me."

"I can't. He'd kill me. I just know it."

Marie leaned up against the tree beside Elsie. "What do we do then?"

Again, Elsie didn't answer, but this time, she really didn't know the answer.

They went into the house and visited over lunch and coffee. Marie, feeling the tension and sadness in the room, did most of the talking. She caught her sister up on how their parents were doing—just fine—and on the gossip in Springville. The doc's daughter ran off with an elephant trainer after the circus came to town. It was a pleasant afternoon. They all enjoyed having a conversation that wasn't in danger of boiling over into a fury.

After her sister left, and for the next month, Elsie busied herself with chores waiting for Pete to come home. That day came too quickly for her.

"Where's my baby?" Pete asked as he came in the door of his parents' house. He rushed over and picked her up off the floor to hug her.

"Put me down, dang it. I'm getting too fat to lift."

Pete set her feet back on the floor and patted her belly. "How's my son today?"

"You don't know it's going to be a boy."

"'Course I do. You're gonna give me a son." Pete's eyes lit up. "Hey, I got something to show you." He slid his hand in his pocket.

Elsie took a deep breath. Pete had always promised her a ring one day since he couldn't afford one when they got married.

Pete held out his closed hand and slowly opened it.

Elsie stared in disbelief. "A knife?"

"Yeah, I got this from one of the fellers. Ain't it great?" he said, running his tobacco-stained fingers along the blade. "It's an Old Timer, and it's really sharp. The handle is made of bone."

Elsie looked up slowly. "Did you bring home any money this time?"

Pete swallowed hard and jammed the knife back in his pocket.

"You said you were working up there instead of here with your daddy so you could save up money. Are we still planning on buying our own land?"

Elsie immediately regretted saying that. She didn't see his hand at all, not even a blur. She only felt the impact on the side of her face, tasted the blood running into her mouth from the corner of her lips. She turned and walked into her bedroom and sat down on the edge of the bed. She grabbed the quilt at her sides with both fists and began to sob.

Pete followed. "Why do you make me—" He threw up his hands and spun around. "I'm going to town."

Thankfully, he was gone most of the day. When he came back around late in the afternoon, his parents and Elsie were sitting on the porch shelling peas. "Why didn't y'all tell me there was a dance tonight?"

"No one feels like dancing," Elsie said, focusing on her hands.

"I don't feel like dancing either, but it will be fun to see folks. C'mon, y'all, let's go."

The mood was somber, but nobody dared argue. So, everyone got ready to go to the dance. Rosa and Bertha, Pete's sisters, were left in charge of the younger ones. The four of them walked the four miles in silence to where the dance was being held beside Blake Elementary School. A canopy was set up to cover the dance area where a live band played. Around forty people were there, all adults and mostly farmers.

Many of them greeted the Wootens with a tip of the hat as they walked up. Several came over to speak. Pete loved the attention.

"Hey, Pete," a younger man said, "R.C. was telling me about your knife. You have it on you?"

"You bet." Pete took out the knife and handed it to him.

The man took it with both hands, pulled it close to his eyes and looked it over like a jeweler before opening each blade, testing the sharpness, and handing it back. "That's a nice knife."

Another man who was standing nearby overheard and asked to see it too. Pete obliged.

A third man walked up. "Hey, Pete, how did it go in North Carolina. How was the crop?"

Pete nodded. "It was great. Tobacco was so thick you could barely walk through it."

Pete's attention was on the third man, so the guy holding the knife handed it to Elsie. As she stood there holding it, another man walked up and asked to see it, so Elsie let him.

Pete turned his attention back just in time to see the exchange. He became noticeably upset. He held out his hand, and the man handed the knife to him. Pete opened his clenched fist, grabbed the knife, stuck it in the pocket of his overalls, and walked away.

Elsie went off to the side of the bandstand and found a seat.

Just an hour later, Pete was ready to go, so he, Elsie, Van, and Della began walking back home. When they were about a half a mile down the road, out of sight of the others and under the cover of dusk, Pete grabbed Elsie by the wrist.

"Where's my knife?" he shouted.

Elsie tried to pull away. She was confused. "You have it."

"No, I don't." Pete was fuming. "I saw you give it to that man. Is that your boyfriend? Are you messing around on me?"

"I saw him give it to you," Elsie pleaded, yanking her arm away.

Pete stepped forward and hit her with his fist so hard on the back of the head it almost made her fall down. She stumbled forward in the dirt, off balance, but managed to catch her footing.

"You calling me a goddamn liar?" Pete slapped her again, this time across the face.

Van and Della were walking in front, paralyzed with fear. Each one wanted to reach for the hand of the other, but instead, they kept their eyes straight ahead. They knew from experience that trying to intervene would only make the situation worse.

Pete shouted obscenities and accusations all the way home, his arms flailing this way and that, landing blow after blow on Elsie's head, face, arms, and back. She shuffled alongside him, crouching instinctively each time a fist appeared in her periphery. The episode did not stop until they got home.

Van and Della went straight to their bedroom.

"I'm going to bed," Pete announced to no one in particular. He pounded across the kitchen and slammed the bedroom door behind him.

Elsie stood there a moment and took a deep breath. She looked around the room in disbelief. Dishes wiped clean sat next to the sink. A folded towel hung over the rack. The chairs were even pushed in at the table. In the center, a bowl of fresh pecans waited to be cracked. All of it was so neat and tidy, suggesting order and control. It was totally out of sync with the chaos she was feeling.

She pressed her hand against her forehead and followed Pete into the bedroom. When she entered, she saw him throw his overalls on the floor by his boots. She had had enough. She walked over, grabbed the overalls in her fist, rifled through his pockets, found the knife, pulled it out, and handed it to him. She knew there would be trouble to follow, but she figured it couldn't be any worse than what she'd already endured. "I told you that you had it."

Pete's bloodshot eyes grew wide and shone red like a demon. Before she could move an inch, he grabbed the knife, flipped it open, and plunged the blade into her side.

Elsie stood there a moment as it dawned on her what happened. Then, she pressed her hand against the wound and sat on the edge of the bed. Dark warm blood poured over her fingers and onto the quilt.

Pete looked at his wife on the bed as blood rushed through her fingers, then down at the knife in his hand. Blood dripped from the blade. His hand shook as he dropped it to the floor. "Daddy, Mama, come here." He scrambled to throw his overalls and boots back on.

"Oh, God," Della said as she walked into the room. "Van, get me some rags. Pete, get Doc Morgan."

Wide-eyed and panicked, Pete bolted out the front door and kept on running. He didn't bother trying to crank his dad's old truck. Doc Morgan only lived a mile away, and he could get there faster running. The dirt road underfoot was lit by a half-moon. Pete ran faster than he ever had before. He had to. His wife had hurt herself.

He ran up onto the porch gasping for breath and banged on the door. "Doc? Doc, open up."

The door swung open revealing a stocky elderly man in a shirt and vest, his salt-and-pepper hair standing straight up. He took in the worry on Pete's face. "What is it, Pete? What's wrong?"

"Elsie hurt herself."

Without question, Doc Morgan reached for the bag that he kept ready on the wooden bench next to the door and rushed to his car as fast as his spindly legs would carry him. Pete scrambled into the driver's seat.

Doc Morgan was not a real doctor. There weren't any in this area. But, because he had studied modern medicine with the aid of a mail-order book, he was the closest thing to it. And he knew all the mountain remedies passed down through the generations. "What happened to her?" he asked as Pete started the car.

Pete didn't answer.

They pulled onto the dirt road, kicking stones in their wake. Doc Morgan repeated the question. "What happened?"

Pete ran his free hand through his hair agitatedly and searched for an answer. "Uh . . . there was a nail sticking out of a post on the porch," he lied, "and when she walked up the steps, she tripped and fell against it."

Arriving at the house, they quickly went inside and rushed into the bedroom. Della was kneeling next to the bed applying pressure to Elsie's wound. Rags soaked with blood were piled on the floor. She made room so Doc could get to her.

He immediately took a small pair of scissors and cut a section out of Elsie's dress at the injury. "This is going to sting a little," he said, soaking a fresh rag with alcohol. He began cleaning the wound.

Elsie didn't seem to notice. Her eyes lacked expression, her face pale.

When he got it cleaned, he leaned in for a closer look. "This doesn't look like a nail puncture. Are you sure you fell into a nail?"

Elsie stared up at the ceiling. "Yes."

Van and Della shot each other a look but said nothing.

Doc took notice of the looks and the tension in the room. He knew better than to make it worse. "I hope you removed the nail."

"I did," Pete answered. "Is she going to be okay? What about my son?"

Doc Morgan shook his head. "Got to stop the bleeding." He continued to work.

Pete couldn't watch. He walked outside to pace in the dirt.

Thirty minutes later, Doc Morgan had successfully stopped the blood flow. "I'm going to put in a few sutures to keep it from bleeding and help it heal," he announced to the room.

Elsie nodded.

After stitching, he cleaned the wound again and dressed it. "I think you and the baby are going to be just fine, but I'm going to need to look at this every day for a couple of weeks. We have to keep it clean and get the bandage changed daily to ward off infection. At any sign of infection, I'll pick up Fleming's penicillin. Meanwhile, I want you to stay in bed as much as possible, young lady. No lifting or working. Understood?"

"Yes," Elsie answered. "Thanks, Doc."

He looked at Van and Della. "If she starts running a fever or getting sick, come get me. If she starts showing any signs of labor, come get me. Understand?"

They nodded.

After he drove away, Pete went back inside. "Is she going to be okay?"

Della nodded and picked up the stained rags. She followed Van out the door and closed it behind them.

Pete walked over to his wife. "You gave me a scare, but they say you're going to be fine. I don't know what I would do without you. I love you, you know?"

Elsie looked through him with a blank stare. Her eyes matched her blank mind and blank heart. "I know."

CHAPTER FIVE

THE FAMILY

1971

Mama sat in the living room with Dinky while the rest of us sat at the kitchen table with Daddy. The kerosene lamp in the middle of the table cast eerie shadows around the walls, mocking us, mimicking our every move. It had been two years since we had power, but we were used to it. In fact, we had only had it once since moving into our house, and that time only lasted just over a month because the stingy people at the power company wanted a second payment. But having no electricity was no excuse to forgo our lessons, and Daddy believed in making sure his kids at least knew and understood the basics.

"Okay, seven card stud, deuces wild." Daddy's hand glided effortlessly as he flicked one card first to me on his left, then to Julene and Neenah on his right, and finally to himself, each card spinning and sliding across our old Formica table and stopping right in front of us. "Two down," he continued and spun another.

"Okay, four up. King to Neal, nine to Julene, jack to Neenah, and a pathetic three to me. King bets."

I grinned and pushed a penny from my stack. Everyone called.

"Next card. Six to Neal with no help, seven to Julene with a straight possible, deuce to Neenah, and a ten spot to me with no help. Two jacks are high."

"One penny," Neenah said and added to the pot.

Daddy loved playing cards, especially poker games. Seven card stud and blackjack were his favorites. I assumed most poor families sat around playing cards, because it was cheap entertainment. I mean, how expensive could a used deck of cards be? We played often, and Julene, who was just ten years old, could handle a deck like a Vegas dealer.

After a couple of hours, Daddy got tired of winning and went to the living room and sat in his chair. The three of us stayed put, switching back to crazy eights. We played and goofed off and joked around until we were giggling out of control.

Here was a paradox of unparalleled proportions, a Catch-22. Daddy loved to laugh and make others laugh, so we either inherited this from him or just picked it up over the years. We were still learning, however, that Daddy only liked laughter if he was the cause of it. Random laughter that he had nothing to do with was apparently like a dagger twisting in his brain.

"Shut up in there," he bellowed. "I have a headache."

We bit our lips. I always thought Daddy should have contacted the *Guinness Book of World Records* folks, because anyone who could have a headache every day of their life was astonishing to say the least. And it didn't end with headaches. If Daddy read about an ailment or heard someone talking about one, he suddenly developed the symptoms.

We played on, being as silent as possible, as the conversation in the living room between he and Mama grew louder and louder. I finally made out the words when Daddy yelled as loud as he could. "I'll burn this goddamn house down."

We had heard this particular threat so many times it had lost validity. We looked at each other, shrugged, and kept playing.

As the hour got late, Mama walked into the kitchen. "Time for bed."

Julene stood up. "I have to go to the outhouse."

"Okay," Mama said. "But straight to bed after."

Julene nodded and looked at me. I understood and followed her out of the house. When it was dark, I always went and stood guard for her, and she did the same for me. Neenah, for some reason, never needed anyone. She wasn't afraid of the dark or of anything that could likely be lurking therein.

There was no moon to be seen, and it was almost pitch black as we walked down the familiar trail through the woods, our eyes struggling to adjust to the darkness that smothered us. Objects slowly began to take shape as we arrived at our destination. Julene went in, and I took my post, scanning the perimeter, trees and bushes finally taking shape in my mind. Of course, they were the shape of beasts and monsters, but I stood my ground. My eyes lifted for a more calming view. The night sky seen from the mountain was a phenomenal sight with no lights from the moon, towns or cities, or streetlights to diminish the twinkle of a gazillion stars.

When Julene was finished, she came out. "Okay, let's go."

I could hear it in her voice and was feeling the same anxiety. Now, the real challenge—making it back to the house alive. I'm sure that for most kids the fear is very real, the belief that a monster lurks in the dark, in the woods, under the bed, or in the closet. With us, however, it wasn't just the belief that an ambush awaited us; it was *the probability*. We just didn't know if it would be a wolf, a werewolf, a bear, a deranged killer, or what.

Suddenly, a scream pierced the stillness. Great, it was a black panther.

Julene and I took off running.

"Don't scream," I commanded. "Don't scream."

She screamed, making me scream too. We ran as fast as we could, scrambled into the house, and slammed the door shut. We doubled over trying to catch our breaths and still our hearts.

"Sorry," Mama whispered.

Daddy came in laughing his butt off. "You should have seen your faces."

At least it was good to see his headache was gone. How could this never get old? How much honing did our fight-or-flight reflexes need?

We all headed off to bed. My bedroom was first on the left and Mama and Daddy's was the last on the left. Julene and Neenah had the long bedroom on the right. My bedroom was the only one that had no ceiling at all, just the bare joists acting as bars keeping the plywood monsters at bay. The other two bedrooms had partial ceilings made from the blackboard insulation sheets.

As I lay there in bed staring upward still trying to get my pulse back to normal, it was too dark to see my friends in the plywood above. So, I fantasized a while. I could never fall fast asleep, and my mind raced. I daydreamed of winning first place with a 4-H entry. Of course, I was never allowed to join 4-H. I dreamed of winning a merit badge in Boy Scouts. Of course, I was never allowed to join that either. I grew tired and lay there in the twilight zone between sleep and consciousness.

Suddenly, a sound shattered the quiet. I sat straight up, my blood again pumping like a raging river. It was Julene screaming at the top of her lungs or screaming bloody murder or shrieking like a banshee. Take your pick. My first thought was that it was a killer trying to get into her bedroom window. Of course, this was Blake, Alabama, and not New York City, so how many killers would ever make their way all the way out here? I vaulted out of bed and ran to the blanket that served as the door to my bedroom to peek out.

Mama and Daddy were rushing to her room.

"What is it?" Daddy yelled.

I couldn't make out Julene's hysterics, but it passed quickly. I saw Daddy storm back to his bedroom, muttering under his breath.

Mama caught my eye as she passed by. "Go back to bed."

"What was it?"

Mama hesitated as if wondering if she should tell me. "A rat fell out of the ceiling and landed on her face."

Oh, was that all? I lay back down. I had been worried for nothing. We always shared our house with plenty of rats. Some even got huge. Of course, they tried to steer clear of us. This was the first time one had reached out.

Poker, panthers, and rats. It was a typical day.

The next morning, Julene and I got an early start on the day. She figured it was time to teach me how to ride her bicycle. And I wanted to learn. I'm not sure where she got it, but I'm guessing from one of several nearby dump sites. It was a rusty bike with long handlebars and a banana seat that was once yellow, but now was the color of that stuff that oozes out of a blister when it pops.

"Pedal," Julene said as she ran beside me trying to keep me from falling over.

If it's true that timing is everything, why was my timing always off? Why did Daddy have to rise and shine so early? He walked out and saw what was going on, and realizing this was a parental responsibility, he quickly took over. "Let me show him," he said.

Julene looked at me like she knew the fun was now over. She knew this, because she had taken Daddy's bicycle crash course before. Pun intended.

Daddy grabbed the back of the seat as Julene backed away. "Okay, get ready and remember to pedal."

I nodded. I don't know why I was expecting him to run alongside.

He shoved me with all his might. The bike took off at what I imagined to be the speed of sound. My cheeks pushed back to my ears, water streamed from my eyes, and I felt I finally understood astronaut G-force training a lot better. The sheer momentum kept the bike upright for thirty feet until I fell over. I lay on the ground with the bicycle flopped on top of me, paralyzed from the shock.

"I told you to remember to pedal," Daddy yelled.

Remember to pedal? I was trying to remember to breathe. Each time I had to push the bike back and let him do it again . . . and again . . . and again. I eventually caught on. I had to. I couldn't have survived training much longer.

Daddy was a firm believer in the sink-or-swim methodology. In fact, that's also how I learned to swim.

My siblings and I faced similar trauma whenever we had a loose baby tooth. At the slightest hint of movement, Daddy decided it was time for the tooth to come out. He'd sit us down and tie a string around the tooth, the anticipation of what came next being somewhat akin to awaiting electroshock therapy. Then he'd hit us on the top of the head with a semi-cupped palm, a massive skull-crushing palm, so hard it made *all* our teeth rattle. As we were rubbing our heads from the pain, he'd hold the string in front of us to display the dangling tooth. We would be so happy it was over; we didn't mind the blood gushing from our gums.

I quickly got to where I could take off on my own and keep the bike upright, but there was no time to celebrate.

"Enough fun and games," Daddy said. "Grab a hoe."

Daddy had cleared a patch of land behind our house for a garden, and it was coming in well. He used an old tiller, a monstrosity from a bygone era, to turn the land, but everything else was done by hand, like keeping the weeds at bay, which was a never-ending task.

I gripped the splintered gray handle and carried the old rusty hoe toward the garden, the only shiny part being the strip across the edge of the blade, while Daddy left in the car. Sweat dripped and poured as I worked. Occasionally, I would stand, not an easy feat as my back would get used to being slumped over, and stare at the remaining area left to be completed, knowing it was hours of work still ahead.

I heard a ringing in my ears. I searched around and found the source. Honeybees had made a huge nest in a towering black walnut tree that dwarfed the surrounding trees. Time or lightning had hollowed out the inside, and a living cloud of bees hovered around an entrance in a large knothole.

Bees were those things parents taught, or *warned*, us about in the South, along with spiders, scorpions, fire ants, and snakes. But I hardly ever heeded those lessons. I loved the magnificent gray fortresses the hornets built in the trees while still giving them a wide berth. I liked wasps and bumblebees too. Yellow jackets, however, with their underground bunkers just waiting for you to accidentally walk over them so they could mobilize their vengeful army, were spawns of hell.

I walked over and tiptoed to try to see inside the knot as bees swarmed around me, landing in my hair and on my face. The entrance was too high for me to see in, but I was able to slide my hand in slowly and feel around. When my fingers felt the cool mushy substance, I gently broke off a piece and brought it out. Brushing the clinging bees away from the oozing chunk, I walked back toward the garden and savored the fresh honey, even devouring the honeycomb.

The mountain was a veritable Candyland filled with natural sweet-tooth appeasements. Blackberries, redberries, dewberries, and muscadines grew in abundance. I knew the location of every walnut, pecan, plum, and pear tree. Or if you wanted to come over to the tart side, persimmons and crabapples were handy too. You could bite the tips off honeysuckles and suck out the nectar or chew on the bark from birch trees. But fresh honey was definitely my favorite.

Okay, break was over. Back to work.

A few days later, we loaded up the car to go to Aunt Esther's house. I always assumed Aunt Esther was rich. Her house wasn't much larger than ours, but it was filled with wonders, and I'm not just talking about flooring, walls, and ceilings. Besides water that came right out of a faucet, there was a bathroom actually inside the house. I'm not making this up. She had a large console television like ours, and it *worked . . . in color*! They got many more channels than we did, and there wasn't even an antenna outside. Not once was I sent outside to turn the antenna to maximize reception. But the contraption in her window must have been sent to earth from the gods. It made me never want to leave her house. It was a huge metal box that actually blew cold air. Her living room felt like the inside of a refrigerator.

Since she lived in Fort Payne, which was right off the mountain from where we lived and only ten minutes away, we visited her several times a year. But it was every couple of years that everyone came together at her house for a family reunion. Today was such a day, and all of my daddy's siblings and their families were there.

Two years in age separated each of the first five of my paternal grandparents' kids: Talmadge, who lived in Clinton, North Carolina; Ilene, who lived in Loxley, Alabama, down by the coast; Travis, my daddy who was in the middle; Boots, whose real name was Zelma and who also lived in Fort Payne; and Esther. Then, there was Jerry, the little brother who came much later. Uncle Jerry and his family moved around a lot. Like my sisters and me, some of Daddy's group had similar dark hair and eyes, and some had lighter hair and blue eyes. Only Ilene retained the slender figure from her youth.

We were the only ones who lived on the mountain, which made us the only bumpkins. My cousins all seemed very worldly and knowledgeable about everything. They had been around the block, so to speak. We didn't even have blocks on the farm, except those under the house and those used for steps. So, I spent most of my time inside listening to the adults and enjoying the cold air.

And, at every reunion, Daddy would spend a couple of hours regaling them with the same army stories over and over. Even at age six, I had heard his stories so often I had them memorized. Some of his stories, like the one he was telling now, seemed a tad farfetched.

"There was one guy in my company who was scared to death of snakes. One day, we were having live-fire exercises. Gunners were firing bullets just a few inches over our heads, and we had to crawl all the way to the end. Well, this guy is crawling and this snake slithers up to him. It was just a harmless black snake, but it scared him so bad that he jumped up, and the bullets cut him in half."

I used to wonder if bullets could literally cut you in half, but it had to be true because I had heard other men from other branches of the military, and from different timeframes, tell the exact same story with exactly the same wording: "cut him in half."

Daddy continued with stories that seemed more realistic, because they had no point of interest or really a point at all. I looked at all the people in the room. They would occasionally glance at Daddy with a slight nod and go back to staring into oblivion, with sad and painful expressions on their faces.

There always seemed to be a tension between Daddy and his siblings. I wondered why that was. I thought it was because of the boring stories or because Daddy was the only farmer. No matter what caused it, it was always clearly there. Maybe that's why they never came to visit us.

A few times, we had learned that Ilene and her family had come to visit from lower Alabama, or that Talmadge and his brood had come all the way from North Carolina. They had visited with Aunt Boots and Aunt Esther only, without even letting Daddy know they were in town. Daddy never let on, but I knew that hurt him.

Everyone just seemed to tolerate Daddy because he was family. Daddy was a charming person to everyone outside the family and people were drawn to him. He was like a people magnet. I truly believed he retained every joke and every riddle he ever heard.

For the most part, Daddy was always laughing and was a very caring person. He doted on me and my sisters like we were sent from heaven. But it only took one little word or one little action, and Daddy would transform into a monster. His temper ruled over him with absolute authority, and the transformation was more Dr. Jekyll and Mr. Hyde than, well, Dr. Jekyll and Mr. Hyde. Within our close family circle, we walked on eggshells because no one knew what might set him off. If only there had been eggshell-walking classes we could have taken, that might have helped, because Daddy's demons made several appearances daily.

Daddy's brothers and sisters knew this side of him well, but not so well as Mama, my sisters, and me. Maybe that's why they seemed uneasy and distant when Daddy was around.

Uncle Jerry was the exception. For some reason, Uncle Jerry not only patiently listened to Daddy's stories but encouraged them too. Even when Daddy got angry, Uncle Jerry hung in there with words of encouragement. Everything my daddy did that made others in the family cringe, Uncle Jerry always supported. I never understood that.

"That's a good one, Travis," Uncle Jerry said. "You have great stories." He looked like my daddy, only taller. He had the same dark hair and dark eyes, but his hair was long. They both had the Native American features passed down from their mama's side of the family.

When Daddy finally took a break from army stories, Paul, Aunt Esther's husband, seized the moment. "Hey, Jerry, did you bring your guitar?"

That was a silly question. It was like asking me if I brought my left arm.

"Of course." Uncle Jerry didn't need prodding. He went out to his car and came back with his guitar, sat down, and started strumming. He was a brilliant musician who had taught himself to play by ear. He could play any tune after listening to it a few times, and his deep mellow voice could make some famous singers jealous. "What do you want to hear?"

People offered up their favorites, and Uncle Jerry played and sang every one of them effortlessly. This was it. This was the catalyst that brought the brothers and sisters together. All faces smiled and nodded when their younger brother, the one who grew up well after they did, played his guitar and sang.

Uncle Jerry finished a song and looked at me. "What do you want to hear, Neal?"

I grinned. That was another great thing about Uncle Jerry: He loved to include the kids. I could only think of one song, and I wasn't even sure if it was a song or something I heard from a movie. "'Thunder Road'?"

"You got it." Uncle Jerry played and sang that song so well. It was better than I remember hearing in my head and way better than it sounded coming out of my mouth. There were a lot of talented musicians in my family, but that particular gene leapt over me like a gazelle.

As it cooled off in the afternoon, I finally ventured outside with my cousins to join in on whatever games they were playing. Everyone was in the backyard, and when I walked back, I saw something frightening. Two of my male cousins were driving stakes into the ground where two areas of missing grass marked the spot of previous games.

Oh no, I thought. *Not horseshoes.*

Too late. They formed into two-person teams and began a match. As horseshoes began to clang the stakes, I knew it wouldn't be long. And it wasn't.

"Hey, y'all pitching shoes?" My daddy walked out the back door with a big smile. That pinging sound was like the call of the wild.

"I want Uncle Travis on my team," one of my cousins quickly yelled.

Of course, I mean, who wouldn't?

After the first game ended, Daddy and my cousin, his partner, took their places and demolished the defending winners. Seldom did Daddy's pitch *not* end in a ringer. And he threw them in an odd way, not like how everyone else made the shoes flip backward. No, Daddy held his on the side and made it fly through the air in a clockwise spin. All it had to do was touch the stake or land anywhere in front of it, beside it, and I think possibly behind it, and it ended up a ringer.

"Come on, Neal," another cousin said. "We'll take them on." Unfortunately, he also walked to the opposite side of my daddy. I knew what that meant.

"Well, come on, son," Daddy said. "I'll let you go first."

I already knew what was going to happen from this point, but I was powerless to stop it. Had I refused to play, that would have angered Daddy more. I slowly walked up beside him and picked up the blue set of horseshoes.

"Go ahead," Daddy said.

I took my stance and held the shoe the only way I knew how, at the back like everyone else in the normal world did.

"No, hold it like this, the way I taught you." Daddy showed me the proper way . . . again. "Then, just release it and it will turn perfectly."

I had been here before. It was kind of like the world's strongest man explaining to a two-year-old that if they just grabbed the weight bar, which held one thousand pounds of weights on it, and simply stood up, the weights would come right up with them. Then, when the toddler couldn't get the bar to budge, the world's strongest man couldn't understand why and became enraged, thinking the little kid was faking.

I held the horseshoe as instructed and pitched it. It wobbled through the air, landed on its side, and rolled ten feet past the stake.

One of my cousins laughed. "That one still had the horse on it."

Everyone laughed.

Well, not everyone. "What the hell was that? Do it right," Daddy bellowed.

I tried again with the same disastrous result.

"Damn it. Watch me." Daddy pitched his first shoe and then the other. Each time, they stayed perfectly level with the ground, rotated once in midair, and ended up on the stake. "You got it?"

I nodded. I lied.

After the cousins on the other side pitched them back this way, Daddy went again and put on two more ringers and stared at me.

At this point, I figured I was safer throwing them at Daddy's head than I would be trying again. But with my luck, I'd miss. I tried to do it just like he did but failed miserably.

"Goddammit. I oughta beat your ass. Get the hell back in the house."

Daddy did this often. It didn't matter if we were working in the garden, working on a car, or whatever—he'd become very frustrated and extremely angry. Uttering one of his favorite passages— "You're about as useful as tits on a bull"—he'd make me stop helping him and send me to the house, tail tucked between my legs, shamed by the stinging realization that I was inept and had ruined his project. In his eyes, it was the ultimate punishment. In reality, it was like a judge sentencing a bank robber to a two-week vacation in Hawaii. He never knew how relieved I was or how hard I was laughing on the inside.

But all laughing had ceased in the backyard. I felt guilty for spoiling the mood for everyone. The weird thing was that everywhere else in my little world, I was quite athletic and coordinated. Whether it was to play flies and skinners with my cousins or dodgeball at school, I was always chosen early. I had just finished first grade at Sylvania and had ruled the playground. Around Daddy, however, it was like I became physically and mentally handicapped. He wasn't shy about making it known that I embarrassed him.

"What are you doing back inside?" Uncle Jerry asked.

I could see in Mama's eyes that she knew. As always, she covered for me. "He prefers the air conditioning."

Uncle Jerry grabbed me around the neck and rubbed the top of my head with his fist. "Smart boy."

"Hey, fellows!" Aunt Boots called out from the kitchen. "Y'all want to play some cards?"

"C'mon," Uncle Jerry said. "Neal's my partner."

I grinned. It was quite a contrast to feel important and needed. We joined them in the kitchen, taking seats across from each other.

"What are we playing?" Uncle Jerry asked.

Aunt Esther, who sat across from Aunt Boots, shuffled the cards. "Setback."

Uncle Jerry looked at me. "You know how to play, right?"

I nodded. You couldn't live in the same house as my daddy and not know how to play pretty much every game invented. Heck, I learned to play setback and a dozen other games before I turned three.

Thirty minutes later, Uncle Jerry and I had won three straight games.

Daddy came in. He either got tired of winning at horseshoes or everyone else got tired of losing. Cards excited him almost as much. Well, pretty much anything competitive did. "What are y'all playing?"

"Setback," Uncle Jerry said. "Neal and I are kicking butt. This boy is a card shark." He gave me a quick wink.

"He sure is," Aunt Esther added.

"I could have warned you," Daddy said. "He's sharp as a tack." He put his arm around my shoulder and beamed with pride.

When we were saying our goodbyes, Daddy and all his siblings stood in a circle. I walked closer to hear what was said, but I could make out only a few words in the conversation. "When are you going up?" And "Be sure to take some . . ."

We all got into the station wagon, and Daddy backed out of the little driveway. He stopped and sat there a few seconds staring in the rearview mirror. "Son of a bitch."

I looked out the back window, as did Julene and Neenah. There, on the little hill a block away, was the black car.

"Don't look at them!" Daddy shouted.

I had heard this command before when a police car was behind us. I was too young to realize that to look at a police car following you was a sure sign of guilt. And now, I knew it also applied to the men in the black suits.

I wondered why they hadn't joined in at the reunion. They were practically family, after all.

Daddy lit up a cigarette and took a couple of draws. He stuck his arm out the open window, held up his middle finger, put it in drive, and went on.

I coughed. Motion sickness.

CHAPTER SIX

LIKE FATHER, LIKE SON

1941

C ome on. I wanna get home."

Elsie looked behind her and smiled at Marie. "I still have two minutes. I can't sneak out early like you."

Both Elsie and her sister worked at W. B. Davis & Son Hosiery Mill in Fort Payne. It was a three-story building built in 1889 as a hardware store during the boom years. In 1907, the building was bought by W. B. Davis, who began making socks there.

It was a thriving industry. Using the same machines patented in the mid-1800s, yarn fed through eyeholes and a spinning cylinder of needles made the sock. Knitters took the newly formed socks, turned them inside out, and stacked them on a tray. You could always spot knitters, because they had no hair on one of their arms from about halfway down the forearm to the wrists. The repetitive rubbing of the socks had rubbed it all away. Fixers kept the machines maintained and working. From the knitting area, they went to seamers who sewed in the toe and then on to trimmers, who removed the extra threads. From there, they went to the dye house to be colored or bleached and then to the boarders to be pressed on metal boards shaped like feet. The finishing department packaged and shipped the socks all around the country and even to other countries.

After they got off work each day, Marie and Elsie walked across town to Marie's house, retracing the same steps they had taken to get to work. It was busy both ways. The town had come alive over the years, as more and more families made their way off the farms and into towns like this one to find steady work. Fort Payne had a bustle, a heartbeat in the morning and afternoon, as people made their way up and down the sidewalks of downtown and inside the parks.

Little River Canyon on Lookout Mountain, Sequoyah Caverns, and several other natural wonders brought tourists and money to the area from all around the country.

Marie was married with her own kids at this point. Elsie and her three girls, Ilene, who was eight, Zelma, who was four, and Esther, who was two, stayed with Marie during the week so Elsie could get to work. On the weekends, Elsie and the girls went back to stay with Van and Della.

Pete wasn't around much anymore. He spent more and more time in North Carolina with family there instead of coming home after tobacco season. He had also started going to Florida before tobacco season to work in the orchards. Ostensibly, all of this was so he could continue to build their nest egg, which never seemed to materialize. But Elsie didn't mind not having Pete around all the time. She knew not to hold her breath anymore in the money department, and Pete's absence let her shoulders relax a bit.

"When I get enough money saved, I can start paying you a little," Elsie said as they walked. The afternoon sun cast their shadows out in front of them that seemed to almost wait on them and then quickly jump ahead.

"Don't worry about it," Marie said, waving her hand as if she was swatting a fly. "Ilene babysits for me all the time. Y'all stay with me as long as you need to. Plus, you'll have school clothes to buy in a couple of months, so you need to be saving anyhow."

"Thanks."

"How's Talmadge doing?" Marie asked.

Talmadge was Pete and Elsie's oldest at ten years old.

"He's good. Going to school up there." Elsie decided to let Talmadge stay in North Carolina to go to school. He spent so much time working the tobacco fields with Pete anyway that she sensed he felt more at home there than he did here. A part of her believed that he had a better opportunity for an education in a larger town. Part of her cried a little every day for being so far away from her firstborn. And all of her wanted to avoid a confrontation with her husband by insisting that Talmadge stay in Alabama and live with her.

Marie smiled. "You know, Travis can come stay with us during the week too. We'll make room for him."

Elsie shook her head. "He prefers to stay with Van and Della. Plus, they're the only ones who can handle him. He might only be six, but he's just like his dad."

"He looks just like you, though," Marie said.

Elsie chuckled. "Yes, he does." She knew Marie was right. Travis was a walking miniature of his mama: jet-black hair, the darkest of eyes, high cheekbones, and a darker complexion. But the physical was where the similarities ended. She had already seen Pete come from somewhere inside her younger son too many times in the form of an uncontrollable temper, and it worried her.

As they walked past a thrift store window, Elsie stopped and pressed her hand against the glass, making a circle of fog appear on it. "Oh my, look at those adorable little boots. Zelma's birthday is coming up, and that's what she wants. I wonder how much they are."

"They look too big for her."

"Yes," Elsie said, "but she'll grow into them."

She couldn't help herself. A bell over the door rang as she pushed it open and walked toward the boots. They were too big, but they had bright yellow and green wildflowers embroidered around the heel, up the sides, and on the toe. Zelma loved gathering fistfuls of flowers and handing them off to her mother, grandmother, and even her brothers and sisters. The boots were perfect for Zelma. Elsie scooped them up and made her way to the counter to pay.

When they got home, she couldn't wait. "Zelma, come see what I got."

Zelma came running in from the bedroom, her blond curls dancing. "What is it, Mama?" If Travis looked like Elsie, Zelma—with her white skin, light hair, and eyes the color of a clear sky—was a more feminine version of Pete. There was no tomboy hidden inside of her; she was straight up a *girlie* girl all the way and already a charmer.

Elsie showed her the boots, and she squealed with delight. She put them on her chubby little feet, laced them up, and began clomping around the kitchen floor like she was parading down a runway in a fashion show.

Marie burst out laughing. So did Elsie. The boots were beautiful, but clearly years ahead of little Zelma.

"So," Elsie said, with a hand to her mouth, hiding a big smile, "they are a little big."

Zelma pranced to and fro like a princess. She didn't care.

"Oh, Elsie," Marie said, "they have a photographer today at the hardware store in the middle of town. You should take her and the others."

"No, I can't afford that."

"I'll pay for it."

Elsie thought about it and smiled. She didn't like taking charity from anyone, even family, but she really wanted a picture. "Okay. Thank you."

They gathered Ilene, Zelma, and Esther and headed to the hardware store. They followed the sign to the area set up for pictures. There was no one currently having their picture taken and no one standing in line.

"Hey, ladies," an older gentleman said, grinning at the three little girls. "Y'all need a picture?" He was very slender and had a kind face. His thick silver mustache curled upward when he smiled.

Elsie nodded. "I was wanting to get pictures of all three of my daughters."

"The special is for up to two people," the gentleman said. "It'll be a little extra for three."

"That's okay, Mama," Ilene said. "Just get one with Zelma and Esther."

"Are you sure?"

Ilene smiled and nodded.

The photographer grabbed a small table and slid it over. It had a blanket draped over it. He lifted Zelma and Esther up onto it and then positioned himself behind the camera. "Look at me, girls."

Esther was only two but seemed to understand. She smiled really big and stared straight ahead. With her dark hair, she looked like a tiny Elizabeth Taylor with brown eyes. Zelma, on the other hand, was too in awe of all the items in the store, and her blue eyes looked everywhere but forward.

"Hey, over here," the photographer called out while snapping his fingers above the camera. "Hey, Boots."

That got her attention. She looked at the camera and smiled.

"That's it, Boots. Keep looking this way."

Elsie and Marie were giggling so hard, they were doubled over.

"Oh, that's going to be a good one," the gentleman said. "We should have these in about two weeks. Just fill out this form, and we'll contact you."

Elsie set them off the table and took Esther by the hand. She looked back at Zelma. "Come along, Boots." From that day, the name was stuck for good.

❖

When Elsie and Marie got home from work that Friday, Marie's husband drove Elsie and the girls to Van and Della's. They spent the weekends helping the Wootens with the gardening and other chores.

"Oh, my goodness. Where'd you get them boots?" Della asked as they entered the house.

Zelma and Esther ran to give her a hug.

Elsie told her the whole story.

"We've been calling her Boots since," Ilene said.

Boots smiled and nodded, looking down and admiring her new shoes, turning this way and that.

"Where's Van?" Elsie asked.

"In the garden with Travis and Cotton."

Cotton, whose real name was Alton, was Van and Della's youngest, much younger than Pete. He was only a few years older than Travis, his nephew, so they were more like brothers. They called him Cotton because his hair was solid white when he was a small boy.

"Girls, put your stuff in your rooms," Elsie instructed.

Van, Cotton, and Travis swung the front door open and walked in. Travis ran and hugged his mother.

"Thought we heard a car," Van said.

"Hey, little man. You been helping Pawpaw in the garden?" Elsie asked, while running her fingers through his messy black mop and leaning his head back so she could get a good look at him. Even though it had only been a few days, he looked older to her somehow. His face was starting to thin around his cheekbones and jaw.

Travis gave a quick nod, like a little man. "Haven't I, Pawpaw?"

"You sure have," Van agreed. "He's a hard worker."

As the girls came back into the living room, they all heard another car pull up. Van looked out the screen door and then back at Elsie with a somber expression.

Elsie knew what that meant before she heard the footsteps on the porch. She felt her back stiffen and her throat go tight.

"Hey, honey," Pete said as he bounded in and made a beeline for Elsie. "I was hoping to catch you when you got home." He threw his arms around her and hugged her tight. "Boy, have I missed you."

"Hey, Daddy," Boots said.

"Hey, sweetie," he said, letting go of Elsie and squatting to hug Boots. He looked at his youngest. "Come here, Esther."

Esther had only seen her daddy a few times and was hesitant. She took a small step back and hid behind her mother's skirt.

"Come here," Pete said louder.

"You're scaring her," Elsie said. "She barely knows you." She bent down, put her hand on Esther's back, and gently rubbed in small circles. "It's okay, honey, this is your daddy."

Pete walked over and lifted her over his head and swung her around. She giggled hysterically, three parts excitement, one part fear. "That's my fault. I've been working too much." He set her down and hugged Ilene next.

"Hi, Daddy," Ilene said.

"Where's Talmadge?" Elsie asked.

"He wanted to stay up there. He has a lot of friends from school." He looked around and located his youngest son. "There's my little man. Come here, Travis."

Travis stood there by his grandmother, an angry look on his face. He folded his arms across his chest and didn't move a muscle. He was old enough to know Pete was his daddy and kind of understood what that meant. But he had seen Pete talk down to his mama and even hit her too many times. And that, in Travis's mind, could not be forgotten . . . or forgiven.

Pete took a deeper tone. "Boy, I said come here."

Travis didn't budge. He wasn't afraid of this person, which meant he was the only one in the room who wasn't.

Della leaned down and whispered. "Go say hi to your daddy."

Travis had no desire to do that, but he obeyed his Mawmaw. He stuffed his hands in his pockets, walked over slowly, and stood in front of Pete. Without tilting his head, his dark eyes stared upward.

Pete patted him on the head. "You're growing like a weed. You been a good boy for your Mawmaw and Pawpaw?"

Silence.

Pete laughed. "Well, that's okay. I'm glad to see you. All of you. It's sure good to see my family. Honey, I have big news. Let's take a ride."

Elsie sighed. "I just got off work. I'm pretty tired."

Pete walked over and kissed her on the forehead. "I know, but it won't take long. I just need to show you something."

Elsie looked at Della. This behavior was odd, a little too jovial.

Della nodded. "We'll watch the girls. They can help me make supper."

"That's great," Pete said. "I'm starved."

Elsie followed Pete out to the car. A man she didn't know sat behind the wheel. Pete opened the passenger door, and Elsie got in and slid into the middle. Pete got in behind her.

"Honey, this is Bud."

Elsie nodded.

"Ready?" Bud asked. He was about Pete's age but dressed nicer with a paid haircut.

"Let's go," Pete said.

Bud stepped on the gas, and they made their way down the long dirt drive. A cloud of white chickens parted around the car.

"Where are we going?"

Pete smiled. "It's a surprise."

No one talked for a while, so Bud turned on the car radio. It was news about the war in Europe. Elsie stared straight ahead, her shoulders tucked behind Pete's and Bud's, her hands tucked under her legs. The war in Europe seemed like it was a million miles and a million problems away. Through the clear spot in the middle of the dirty windshield, she saw the horizon begin to turn pink. She wondered where they were going but couldn't hazard a guess. *Pete,* she thought, *what in heaven's name are you up to now?*

After they had driven about ten miles, Bud pulled the car over and stopped atop a small hill.

"What do you think?" Pete asked Elsie.

"What?"

"Look out there." He pointed. "What do you see?"

Elsie looked. Rows and rows of sugarcane stalks ran away from edge of road as far as she could see. It was young, still purple and green at the bottom, and not fully flowered, but it was maturing. "Sugarcane?"

"Exactly. Fifty acres of it. It will be ready in a couple of months." He motioned to Bud, who drove on.

Elsie was confused but sat in silence.

Ten minutes later, Bud turned down an overgrown dirt road and came to a stop in front of an old, run-down shell of a building. It was about one hundred feet long and fifty feet across. There were no outer walls, but the weeds and young trees made it hard to see inside. Metal posts supported a roof and rusty corrugated tin covered the top.

"Where are we?"

"This is a syrup mill," Pete explained. "This belonged to Bud's dad. Bud, tell her how much money y'all used to make with this?"

"We made a lot."

That was specific.

"I don't understand," Elsie said.

Pete smiled. "I'm going into the syrup business. Me and Bud's gonna be partners. Right, Bud?"

"That's right."

"Do you know how many cans of sorghum we can make with fifty acres of cane?" Pete asked.

Elsie knew it was a rhetorical question and was certain that neither of them knew either.

"This is the break we've been looking for, baby," Pete explained. "We'll make enough to buy our own place."

Elsie had heard that line from Pete more times than she could count, but she had long given up trying to talk sense to him when he was excited about the prospect of making money. It never changed his mind, and it always made him angry.

"That sounds great," she said, nodding her head and feigning excitement to equal Pete's.

Pete was very happy. "The mill grinds the cane, and we boil the juice from it. Tell her how y'all used to do it."

"With a mule," Bud said flatly.

"But we'll have a tractor," Pete explained. "And we can use that to cut the cane and haul it here too. And the good news is, I'll be able to work right here instead of going back and forth to North Carolina."

Her throat went dry. She put her hand up and massaged her neck.

"What do you think?"

"Will Talmadge be coming back?"

"I mean, what do you think about the deal?"

Elsie lied. "That sounds great." Then, she had a thought. "This is your mill now, Bud?"

"It's still my dad's, but he's letting us use it."

The cogs in Elsie's mind kept turning. "And who paid for and planted the sugarcane?"

Pete pointed to Bud.

"It's his mill and his sugarcane?" she asked.

Pete nodded.

"And you're going to be partners?"

"Yep," Pete said enthusiastically. "All I have to do is provide the tractor and do half the work. This is going to be a goldmine."

Elsie knew when to stop asking questions. She knew Pete didn't have a tractor, which meant he would need to buy one.

Bud drove them back to Van and Della's house, dropped them off, and drove away.

Elsie started toward the porch.

"Wait."

She stopped and turned around. The sky was purple now, the sun almost down.

Pete walked up beside her. "This is a great opportunity. This is the one we've been waiting for."

Elsie didn't say anything but knew the next part was inevitable.

"So, how much money you got saved?"

She looked Pete in the eye. "I have enough to buy Travis and Ilene clothes and shoes to start school in the fall, and I'm trying to save a little for Christmas for all the kids."

"That's the great thing," Pete said. "We'll already be making money when fall starts, and we have enough cane to last until the next harvest. This is a year-long money maker. We'll probably have to buy trucks to start shipping syrup all over the country." Pete always planned big. He had never had a "normal" job and apparently didn't realize they generated paychecks all year.

She finally put the pieces together from that afternoon and fully understood why Pete was being so civil. He always got this way when he wanted something, but it never lasted. She also knew that if she refused, he would beat her and take the money anyway. "Okay, how much do you need?"

He needed every penny she had, of course. So, just like that, Pete got into the syrup industry.

When fall came around, Travis and Ilene started school in their old clothes and shoes with holes in them. Boots and Esther also went without new clothes, but at least Boots had her boots.

Elsie kept staying at Marie's during the week and working at the hosiery mill, trying to save a little money before Christmas came around. Travis stayed full time with Van and Della and went back to school at Blake Elementary.

The school at Blake only went to the eight grade and consisted of an old building that was a lot longer than it was wide with six classrooms, three opposite one another. A small log building outside served as the lunchroom, serving meals for one nickel. Behind the main building was where the student smoking section was located. Yes, the elementary school had a student smoking section.

In the beginning, things seemed to be going well. Pete appeared to be putting in a lot of time getting the mill going. He came home late each day and was happy at night. But after a few short weeks, he began staying out for a day at a time and then two, saying that things got busy and he slept at the mill. Finally, Elsie hadn't seen him for over a week. She knew it was time to start cutting the sugarcane and hoped he would actually put in the effort to make this idea work. Maybe that's why he had been gone for so long. Maybe he was working very hard to get the syrup mill up and running. She could always hope.

One Saturday in late September, she was sitting on the porch with Van, Della, and the kids when a familiar car drove up the driveway. She shaded the sun with her hand and saw Bud hop out. He walked up to them, looking rather disquieted.

"Have you seen Pete?"

Van, Della, and Elsie all looked confused. Elsie asked the obvious. "When's the last time you saw him?"

The guy looked more confused. "That day the three of us rode to the mill."

CHAPTER SEVEN
LIFE'S A GAS
1972

I can't believe my tree is taller than I am."

Uncle Roy looked down at me and smiled. "That's not saying a lot, little man."

He was right.

I enjoyed spending time with Uncle Roy, but I was a little surprised we came to see him today. For the first time since, well, *ever*, Julene, Neenah, and I had found the perfect Father's Day gift for Daddy. He was notoriously hard to shop for. He never wore ties, didn't follow a specific sports team, and only enjoyed playing cards and checkers.

We had collected bottles all summer and took them to stores to get the ten cents. I had mowed lawns, and Julene and Neenah had even had a few babysitting jobs. But we saved enough to get a gift we knew would be perfect and couldn't wait to give it to him.

Of course, we would have to wait since we set out at daybreak to come here to Rising Fawn.

"So, how are things at home?"

I looked up and squinted through the sunlight rimming around Uncle Roy, making him look like a ghost. It seemed an odd question. Did he know something? We weren't allowed to talk about our home life, so I didn't know what to say. "Fine. How are you?"

He laughed. "Fair to middlin'."

I had heard that before but didn't understand it. "What does that mean?"

"What?"

"Fair to middlin'."

"Well, now," Uncle Roy said, "those are two grades of cotton. There are four total: poor, fair, middlin', and top grade. So, when someone says they're doing fair to middlin', it means they're doing pretty good but not great. Kind of in the middle."

"Oh." I nodded with a grin. "You know a lot, don't you?"

He smiled. "I sure do. In fact, I know everything. Anything else you need to know?"

I thought for a second. "Yeah, why do earthworms come up when you fiddle?"

"That's easy. Because it jars the ground."

I laughed. "I know that. But why does jarring the ground make them come up?"

Uncle Roy thought for several seconds. "You know, I don't really know."

"So, you don't know everything?"

He laughed loudly. "No, I don't. I just like pretending I do."

That sounded like Daddy.

I took the opportunity to ask Uncle Roy a question that had been burning in my mind. "Are you a witch?"

He laughed. "I've been a called a lot of things but not that. Why do you ask?"

"Daddy said you can find water."

He laughed again. "Oh, yes, I'm a water witch. You might be one too."

"Really?" I grinned at the possibility. "How does it work?"

"Come on, I'll show you."

I followed Uncle Roy to the edge of the woods as he searched the area where smaller trees tiptoed to peek into the dense darkness of the adults.

"A sassafras tree works best," he said. He found one, took out his pocketknife, and cut off a forked limb. He trimmed until all three sides were about a foot in length and formed a Y. Grabbing the two extensions that were closest together, he held them in each fist in front of his chest with the third side pointing straight forward and began walking toward the well.

I watched closely, skeptical yet intrigued. I had never seen it done in person.

He was still a good fifty feet from the well when the end of the fork started bending downward. "You see that?"

I nodded. His forearms stayed perpendicular to the ground, and his fists never tilted at all. But the forked stick was clearly bending in the middle. I could even hear the outer bark cracking as the end of the branch twisted toward the earth. I couldn't believe what I was witnessing.

"Here," he said, "you try it." He handed me the stick.

I held it just like he did, but nothing happened.

"Walk closer to the well," he said.

I did, and there was still nothing.

"I guess you don't have it. Maybe you will when you're older."

Figures. I guess it was like horseshoes and checkers; you either have it or you don't.

There was something about spending time with Uncle Roy that was best described as peaceful. I never saw him angry and never heard him raise his voice. We were always on edge at our house, because we never knew what would upset Daddy. But I could do or say anything around Uncle Roy without fear.

"Can I have this forked stick?" I ask.

"Sure. What for?"

"I want to make a flip."

Uncle Roy smiled. "A slingshot? I think we can do better than that. Come with me."

I followed him to his tool closet on the side of the house and watched as he took his hand tools and a thick plank of wood. He cut out a perfect flip stock, whittled it down, sanded it, and added a notch a half inch down from the uprights. He cut two strips of rubber from an old inner tube, folded them over the top of the uprights, and tied them on with string. Next, he cut out a small piece of leather that would fit in your palm, poked holes in the sides, threaded each rubber strip through the holes, folded over the ends, and tied those with string. When he was finished, he handed it to me.

I was in awe. It looked like something you'd buy from a store.

"Let's give it a try," he said. He took a tin can and set it on the ground. Backing up about thirty feet away, he nodded to me.

I found a small rock and placed it in the leather patch, pulled it back, and released. The rock arched through the air and fell close to the can—well, if you consider landing in the same county close.

"What are y'all up to?"

I turned to see Daddy walking up.

"Travis," Uncle Roy said, "show Neal how to use a flip."

A sinister smile crept across Daddy's face. He inspected the flip carefully. "That's a fine flip." He picked up two small rocks and loaded one in the pouch, holding the other in his right hand. He clutched the flip in his left, rotated clockwise a little, pulled it back very far with the hand where he held the extra rock, aimed, and released. The rock fired out of the pouch like a bullet in a straight line and connected square with the can, making it jump off the ground a foot high and roll. Daddy quickly switched the flip to his right hand, loaded the second rock, and fired again. This one hit the can while it was still moving and knocked it farther away. He handed it back to me. "They don't call me Old Eagle Eye for nothing."

Daddy was just as coordinated with both hands. He could switch midstream while throwing, chopping wood, writing, or wielding a belt.

I was still in shock. "Do you think I can get as good as you?"

"You mean if you practice a lot?" Daddy asked.

I nodded.

Daddy laughed. "No."

Uncle Roy laughed too.

I didn't mind. This was still the nicest thing I had ever owned.

"We have to be going, so say goodbye to Uncle Roy."

We said our goodbyes and drove back home.

Once home, we all got out and went inside. Normally, I would have stayed outside, but I knew what was coming. Finally. Daddy sat in his chair with a glass of Pepsi, which was his favorite brand of coke. My favorite brand of coke was Sprite.

"Travis," Mama said, "the kids have something for you."

Julene went to her bedroom and brought back the large wrapped gift.

Daddy's eyes lit up.

"Happy Father's Day!" we all chimed.

Daddy unwrapped it and stared at the picture on the box. "Great day in the morning."

We had outdone ourselves for sure. It was a fishing chair that folded out. It had blue canvas material in the seat and back, a blue tacklebox was mounted under the seat, and it had a rod holder on one arm and a drink holder on the other.

"Do you like it?" Julene asked.

"I sure do. Come here, kids." Daddy hugged all three of us.

It was a great moment. Daddy took it out and set it up right there in the living room and sat in it.

We all looked on quite proud of ourselves.

The following Saturday, he was ready to try it out. He woke us early for breakfast.

I walked into the kitchen, wiping the sleep from my eyes. The table was crowded with cheese omelets, homemade biscuits, gravy, grits, bacon, Daddy's famous hash browns, and sliced tomatoes. Daddy made breakfast every weekend, but on the rare occasions we had electricity and he could use the stove, his breakfasts were amazing. He could do wonders on the Ashley heater as well, but we couldn't keep meats and cheese without the fridge.

Mama and my three sisters came to the table as well, and we all told him how great it looked. That was kind of mandatory. And it wasn't fake praise. Daddy's cooking was truly incredible, each bite a fabulous chorus in your mouth.

Daddy soaked in the praise. "I outdid myself this morning."

He also said that every Saturday morning.

After I finished off my plate, which included three biscuits already, I grabbed the can of sorghum syrup. I always saved one biscuit just for that. I was an artist when it came to mixing butter in syrup.

"You sure you want to do that?" Daddy asked.

I froze. "Why?"

"Well, I thought after we eat, we'll go to Sylvania Lake and we're gonna need bait."

I grinned, put the can down, and ran outside to find a hoe. Where our water drained out behind the kitchen was where we found the red wigglers. I quickly filled a tin can.

By then, everyone was in the car ready to go. Daddy drove to the lake and around the scenic road that winds around like a snake to the end. He went around one curve a little fast, making the tires squeal.

"Careful, Travis," Mama said.

Why did she go and say that? The loose particles of air inside the car suddenly stiffened with tension.

Daddy kept driving, but you could tell by his demeanor that he was no longer in a cheerful mood as his jaw muscles clenched. He found a spot with a concrete picnic table and pulled into the chert area off the side of the road. Daddy set all the rods out, and Julene and Neenah waited for Mama or Daddy to bait their hook.

I didn't need help. I grabbed my pole and a worm and walked off a little ways. I didn't want their talking to run off my fish, and that talking was getting very loud. I knew Daddy was upset at Mama chiding him in front of us, but I was hoping that once we started catching fish, he would calm down and enjoy the day.

I slid the hook into the worm and cast my line out as far as I could. Then, I watched as the line slowly began to disappear beneath the surface. I never used a floater. I wasn't after bluegill. I wanted one of those blue catfish that lay on the bottom, the ones that weighed over one hundred pounds.

Suddenly, Daddy called Mama a few choice words so loudly that I'm sure it echoed across that huge lake to everyone fishing on every bank and in every boat on the water. I turned to look just in time to see a blue UFO spinning across the lighter blue sky. Then, it dawned on me what it was.

When we bought that chair for Father's Day, it had advertised so many excellent qualities, but being aerodynamic was not one I had even considered. But there it flew, thirty feet out into the lake, making a big splash as it hit the surface. It was an impressive feat, but hey, they didn't call him Old Eagle Eye for nothing.

I picked up my rod and began to reel it back in, my shoulders slumped in defeat. Another day, giant catfish. Another day. I knew this fishing trip was officially over.

Daddy vented and cussed all the way back home. Once, and only once, we witnessed his massive right arm sail right over Dinky's head, as he held the steering wheel with his left and delivered a backhand to the side of Mama's face. She never even reacted.

When we got home, we all moved toward the house like you might walk by a casket at a funeral. The mood was as dark as the bottom of a lake. Only then did we notice that Mama was no longer wearing her glasses, but instead holding the two pieces in her hands. Blood ran down from a small gash beside her left eye. No one dared say a thing. No condolences. Nothing.

We left the fishing gear in the trunk, sans one brand-new fishing chair, and went inside. Once we got into the house, Daddy went after Mama before she could even sit, his anger still emanating from every pore. Suddenly, something came over me. I did something I've never done before. I stepped between them. Mama had, after all, done this for me many times.

I learned a valuable lesson that day. When Daddy's demons took control, it was never really directed at a specific person.

He just needed to get it out of his system, and the target was irrelevant.

Then, as quickly as it began, it was all over. Everything was back to normal. Well, normal for us. We played cards and had dinner. For all practical purposes, you would never have been able to tell that anything had happened out of the ordinary at all. No one spoke of the chair again.

❖

Life continued on the mountain, as life has a way of doing. People drove up and down the mountain every day to work in the mills. Churches outnumbered the bootleggers . . . barely. I went with Mama to Decoration, a holiday where you put fresh flowers on the graves of your relatives. Tent revivals popped up everywhere, and even from the road, I could hear the sacred harp singing and preachers screaming fire and damnation.

A few months after the flying fishing chair episode, I was helping Daddy work on the car. And by "the car," I mean the one that was running. The rest were just "collector" cars. At least that's what we called them. Our front yard, which was just packed dirt, normally always consisted of about five or six cars, but only one at a time worked.

Daddy bought cars like they were a disposable commodity. They were always used and not in the best shape to begin with. He'd drive a car until it quit, never doing any maintenance, not even checking the oil. If it wasn't an easy fix when it finally quit working, he'd park it in the yard and buy another. When we had collected so many that there wasn't a place left to park, he'd sell them to a junkyard for fifty dollars each, and they'd come haul them away.

The sun was directly overhead, but the air had cooled off a little. We always looked forward to the fall and even winter, because the humidity in the South is a living entity that envelops you, suffocates you, and makes you feel like you're breathing in motor oil. That's why we don't have psychics who read your spectrum. In the South, in the summer, everyone's aura is bright red.

"Get me a nine-sixteenths."

I rushed over to the little toolbox and started searching. That was basically my job, to get things for my daddy or hold the flashlight if it was dark.

There were shade-tree mechanics all over Sand Mountain, folks who could yank a motor from a car using a low tree limb and a come-along in the morning, completely rebuild it, and have it back in just in time to run to the bootlegger and be back by suppertime. They might not understand Shakespeare or calculus, but they knew every bolt, wire, hose, and cog of an internal combustion engine. When it came to cars and tractors, these people were amazing.

Daddy was not one of those people.

I handed him the right wrench. I had learned not to ever hand him the wrong one or to hand it to him by the wrong end, for that matter.

"Get me some gas."

This was a little trickier. I found an empty milk jug and the short piece of garden hose we used for siphoning, went to the back of the car, flipped down the tag, and removed the gas cap. I pushed the hose into the hole, blowing on the other end as it descended, just like I'd been taught. When I heard the bubbles, I knew I was there. I took a deep breath, the anticipation of what came next clouding my thoughts. I hated it. I sucked on the hose twice and put the end down in the jug.

Nothing.

I blew everything back into the tank and tried again. This time I sucked three times.

Nothing.

I prepared for the inevitable. I sucked four times and gas filled my mouth. I spit it out, stuck the end into the jug, and it began to fill. Gas has such an odd flavor. It's hard to explain, but it ignites every taste bud and burns worse than a jalapeño pepper. Luckily, it evaporates quickly. If you've never had gas inside your mouth and over your tongue, I highly recommend you not try it.

I collected about three inches of gasoline and took the jug to Daddy.

He poured a little into the carburetor. "Try it."

I sat in the driver's seat and turned the ignition. The car backfired loudly. I stopped.

"I didn't say stop! Try it again."

This time, the car sputtered a few times and started. Daddy closed the hood and gave me the hand-across-the-neck gesture.

I turned it off.

"Try it again to be sure."

I turned the key, and it started right up. Whew.

Daddy took the jug inside to the kitchen sink to wash off the grease. I sat in the living room with everyone else. After Daddy finished cleaning his hands, he set the jug, which still had two inches of fuel, on the floor right beside the water jugs. He walked into the living room and took his seat.

"I fixed it," he said waiting for us to acknowledge and congratulate him on his mechanical prowess. In reality, all he had done was remove the breather and pour gas down the carburetor, but in his mind, it was a feat to be recognized. Everything Daddy did commanded praise, from cooking breakfast to major auto repair jobs like this one. Some he really did outdo himself on; others, not so much. "Is there a game on?"

I walked to the television and grabbed the little pliers. For the third time in four years, we had electricity again, and each short period felt like winning the lottery.

And no one noticed little Dinky, who was about to turn three, barefoot and wearing a small shirt and droopy shorts, wander into the kitchen. She was thirsty and did what we all did; she took a jug and turned it up. It was the God-awful coughing that got everyone's attention. Mama and Daddy rushed to the kitchen to see her gagging and holding the jug of gasoline. Her eyes made her look unconscious, but she stood like a mannequin . . . coughing . . . gagging.

Daddy yanked the jug from her hand and yanked her off the floor.

"Oh God," Mama said. "How much did she drink?"

Dinky continued to cough.

"I don't know," Daddy said, "but I can smell it on her breath."

"What do we do?"

"Goddammit," Daddy screamed. "Get everyone to the car!" Daddy rushed out the front door, and we followed.

Mama got in the front passenger seat and held Dinky as she continued to barf like I did when I tried to eat vegetables. I felt so sorry for her. I knew how bad it was to get gas in your mouth, but I never swallowed.

Daddy drove. The rest of us were in the back seat trying to hold on to anything as we sped recklessly away, tossed around like stowaways on a ship in a storm. After we reached the end of our long private driveway and topped the little hill by our cousins' house, the dirt road became darker. That meant the road grader had recently come. I hated the fact that I missed it. One of my few pleasures in life was watching that giant yellow skeleton with tractor tires taller than I am and a long-angled blade under the midsection scrape the top level of dirt away from our road, erasing the ruts and grooves caused by a month of torrential downpours.

I don't know if the loose dirt accounted for what happened next, but the left tires of the car slid into the deep ditch on the side of the road. Daddy never let up as we continued at a slanted angle, my sisters and I sliding into a pile of confused youngsters. The front tire finally struck a huge rock in the ditch and that bounced us back onto the dirt road. Daddy blew past the stop sign at the end of our road as the tires spun into clouds of smoke on the asphalt. How we got off the mountain in one piece is still a mystery.

We pulled into the emergency room entrance at DeKalb General, and Daddy rushed in to tell them what happened. Folks came running out and took Dinky from Mama's arms and carried her inside.

"Come on," Mama said to us, bright lines zigzagging down her face from where the tears had run and dried.

We got out and followed her inside. Julene, Neenah, and I took seats in the waiting room as Mama and Daddy followed the hospital workers into the back.

"What happened?" Neenah asked.

It had happened so fast that my older sisters were still in the dark.

"Dinky drank gasoline," I explained.

"Is she going to die?" Neenah asked and started crying. Neenah was always the most sensitive of us.

I shrugged. I didn't have an answer. But my mind instinctively played out the worst-case scenarios over and over. I wondered how life would be if she didn't make it. We were all kind of fond of her, but she was not entirely one of us, at least not yet. The bond between me and my two older sisters was akin to that of the brotherly commitment of soldiers in a war. We had also been through hell and had survived—so far at least—but I wasn't sure how. I didn't know how we made it to the ages of seven, nine, and eleven, or even if we'd see the next year.

It seemed like we waited for hours. Maybe we did. I went to the bathroom six times.

Finally, Mama came out to talk to us. "She's going to be fine."

We all breathed a sigh of relief.

"They had to pump her stomach," Mama continued. "She'll have to stay here a little while so they can keep an eye on her."

I have never experienced the euphoria that comes with news like this.

A few minutes later, Daddy came out of the back. He seemed amazingly calm or perhaps just emotionally drained. "Go on back and sit with her, and I'll take the kids home."

We walked out to the car, and we all got in the back seat, even though Mama and Dinky weren't in the front now. Daddy drove in complete silence. I felt sorry for him. I knew the guilt of setting the jug with the gas right beside the water jugs had to be weighing on his conscience. I thought of offering words of encouragement to lift his spirits, but I decided against it.

We assumed Daddy would simply drop us off and go back to the hospital. The three of us had been staying home alone for years when Mama went with Daddy to put on dinners to sell stainless-steel cookware. But Daddy followed us in.

"Sit down," he said pointing to the couch.

We obeyed. I wasn't sure what was coming, but I assumed it was going to be a soul-searching speech on the importance of safety or perhaps of the bonds of family. I was wrong.

"Y'all almost killed your sister tonight."

We all three looked at each other in confusion.

"Y'all know you're supposed to keep an eye on her, because she's too young to look out for herself." Daddy began unfastening his belt buckle.

It was a familiar scene, and what followed next was all too familiar also. Neenah started crying right away. She did this at the mere possibility of a whipping, and Daddy could never bring himself to whip her with tears running down from those big brown eyes. That old softie.

One thing was clear—Neenah was a heck of a lot smarter than Julene and me.

"Neenah, go to your room."

She didn't have to be told twice. It's not that she wanted to abandon us; she just didn't have the strength to disobey. Neenah was devoted to our three-person band, and I have no doubt she would have taken a bullet for us. But a belt? Daddy's belt? No way in Hades. We didn't blame her at all.

Julene and I were defiant, especially when we thought Daddy was in the wrong, which he was most of the time. And this time, we had zero doubt. Our goal was to show him he couldn't hurt us. Our goal was to show him we were stronger than he was. Our goal was not to cry, no matter what until he realized his attempts were futile. Our goal was pure idiocy.

Daddy doubled over the belt, snatched Julene up by the left arm, and swung away. Julene gritted her teeth, pure hatred flowing from her young face. Her eyes stayed locked on mine.

My war face was on full display as well. It was my way of offering support.

Daddy continued to swing as hard as he could. The sounds of the belt connecting with my sister were louder than you can imagine, and each blow chipped away at her hate and slowly replaced it with pain.

As I said, Neenah was much smarter. Mine and Julene's plan had one serious flaw: Daddy did not consider the punishment successful until he saw tears.

Julene held out for an amazing amount of time, but it was not possible to go on forever. As she began to cry from the pain, Daddy tossed her back onto the couch. She stared at me, and I could read her mind. She was so sorry. She wasn't sorry for what happened to Dinky, because we both knew that wasn't our fault. She was sorry, because she couldn't last forever. She was sorry that she couldn't protect me, because we knew it was now my turn.

Daddy yanked me off the couch so hard, my feet left the floor. I kept my eyes on Julene. I wanted to make her proud. I wanted to break her record. I wanted to do everything I could to not give that son of a you-know-what the satisfaction. I'm not sure how long I held out, but it was a personal best. When Daddy left to drive back to town, his right arm had to be hurting. We showed that bastard.

CHAPTER EIGHT

A BROTHER'S LOVE

1956

M arie walked right into Pete and Elsie's house, the one they were renting in Rainsville, without knocking. Van, Della, and Cotton followed. Van carried a loaded double-barrel 12-gauge shotgun tucked under his reedy arm and pointed at the unfinished hardwood floor.

The room was dark except for a current of light reaching through the gauzy curtains. It smelled of stale air and sweat. Pete stood in the entrance to the kitchen, leaning against the battered doorjamb, casting a shadow, and staring at them.

Elsie sat on the couch, her face bloodied and bruised.

Jerry, who had come along much later than the rest of Pete and Elsie's kids, sat beside her, his small hand on her thigh, sadness and confusion on his face. He was seven years old and, like Travis, had the dark complexion, black hair, and very dark eyes like Elsie. All the rest had moved away. Talmadge, Ilene,

Boots, and Esther were all married, and Travis, who was still single, was in the army.

"Let's get their stuff," Marie said.

Della followed her into the bedroom, where it looked like the latest fight had started. A bedside lamp lay broken in the corner; shards of blue and white porcelain had scattered among the dust under the bureau. On the wall next to the nightstand, a spray of dark dried blood. Della and Marie began throwing Elsie's clothes onto the bed.

"Jerry," Van said, "take Cotton to your room and get your stuff."

Cotton was now in his early twenties, tall and very lean like his father and with the same haunting almost-clear blue eyes. He and Jerry squeezed by Pete as he continued staring at Van. They gathered Jerry's clothes and took them to Elsie's room.

"Just toss them on there," Marie said, pointing to the center of the bed.

Pulling the four corners of the threadbare quilt into a makeshift bag, Marie swung it over her shoulder and carried it out to the car. Then, she came back in and sat beside Elsie. "Come on, sweetie. Come with us," she said, stroking the back of her sister's hand. Her skin was still smooth and soft. Time, though, had lifted veins and swollen joints.

Elsie stood up, her face void of expression, almost like she was in a trance, and let Marie lead her out to the car.

"You keep away," Van said, slowly backing over the threshold and out the door. He was old and feeble, his body had kicked its youthfulness to the curb long ago, but his shotgun was in pristine shape.

Pete stood stock still but for a slight twitch in his jaw. He demeanor was somehow indifferent, yet at the ready.

❖

Elsie moved back in with Van and Della. She and Jerry slept in the bedroom at the back of the house where Della kept her knitting tools. Needles poked out of balls of yarn sitting in a wicker basket under the window. A nearly finished sweater—disconnected arms, a front and a back—covered the seat of an old rocking chair. Elsie looked at the two twin beds, their crisp pillow covers, and matching wool blankets, feeling a sense of calm for the first time in a long time.

It was far from over, though, as Pete showed up every day.

The first day he brought denial. "Elsie, sweetie, I know you're not really leaving me."

The second, anger. "I'll kill you. I'll burn this damn house down if you don't come out."

And on the third day, bargaining. "If you come back, I'll change. I swear."

Then, depression. "I will kill myself if you don't come back."

This went on for weeks. Some days, he went through all four stages in one day. His sky-blue eyes changing shades and mimicking each emotion like a chameleon.

One day, a car rolled up on the hard-packed dirt outside Pete's house, and his oldest son got out.

"Talmadge? What are you doing here? Did someone call you?"

"No. I came to get you. We have a huge tobacco crop this year, and we need you."

Pete shook his head. "I'm too old." He was actually still in great shape, but he didn't want to leave, because deep down, he believed he could get Elsie to come home.

"I know," Talmadge said. "I figure with your experience, I can get you a job as a foreman."

Pete, having nothing left to lose, gathered up an old leather sack of clothes and rode back to North Carolina with his son. He stayed with Talmadge and his wife, Macy. After a few weeks of working in the tobacco fields, at supper one night, the real reason why Talmadge brought Pete back came to light when they had a guest.

"Pete, this is my Aunt Etta," Macy said.

Etta had never been married. Her straight black hair was teased with gray lines and mostly tied up on top of her head with several strands settled softly down her back. Her dress was plain, simple, and navy, with a modest neckline and long sleeves. She wore no makeup or jewelry. She was from a strict Holiness family.

After they ate, Pete and Etta talked about the weather, the crops, and the men now working under Pete. He shared how the work was difficult at his age, but it felt good to come home every night to a home-cooked meal, quiet conversation, and a soft bed.

She laughed when he told a story about how his two youngest pickers had to grab hold of the harvester seat to balance out the weight of "Big Lou" and keep the whole works from tipping over. When she smiled, her cheeks gathered up around her almond-colored eyes. She and Pete hit it off right away.

Elsie was shocked when she received word from her attorney that Pete had signed the divorce papers. She tried to settle back into a normal life, working and doing chores around the house. Several months after her divorce was final, Marie came to see her.

"Come on, it'll be fun. You need to get out."

Elsie shook her head. "I don't know. I mean, a church social?"

"Van and Della can watch Jerry." Marie looked at them. "Right?"

Della nodded. "Absolutely. Go out and have some fun, sweetie. You deserve it, you know."

Elsie reluctantly agreed.

That same evening, Marie drove them both to Henagar just up the road from Blake, where a huge tent had been erected.

Elsie took one look at the tent and said, "You sure this isn't a revival?"

Marie laughed. "I'm sure, but I think this is the same tent they use for that."

Cars lined up in rows on a large swath of crushed ryegrass surrounded by poles fixed with barbed wire. Marie parked next to a stack of hay bales, and they went under the cover of the large tent. A dozen tables in the center area were filled with all kinds of food—platters of cold fried chicken and biscuits, bowls of boiled peanuts and pimento cheese, pulled pork, peaches, and, of course, sweet tea. Folding chairs lined the exterior, although most people stood around talking. An empty stage took up space in one corner, even though there was no sign of a band or any type of music.

"Grab a seat, and I'll get us some tea." Marie walked toward one of the tables.

Elsie looked around and picked out the chair farthest away from everyone and sat down. When she saw Marie walking back with a man, the hair on the back of her neck stood up. She debated about running back to the car but decided that would just look silly, so she stayed.

Marie walked up wearing an impish smile. "Elsie, this is Herschel Killian. He owns a farm just down the road from here."

Elsie pulled her eyes up, nodded, and offered her hand. His handshake was firm and polite. He looked like a nice enough fellow, with trimmed hair and a clean shirt, a quaint smile gracing his clean-shaven face. You didn't have to tell folks Herschel was a farmer; his tanned skin and rough hands betrayed him. He had a calm, gentle way about him, but still, Elsie couldn't believe her sister was pulling this.

"Oh look, there's someone I know. I'll be back." Marie hurried off.

Several seconds of awkward silence passed. Herschel cleared his throat and fiddled with the buttons on his flannel shirt. Marie looked over at the stage and tapped her foot to a rhythm she wished was present.

"I'm sorry about this," Herschel said. "Your sister's not very tactful."

"No, she's not. Do you come to these things a lot?"

Herschel shook his head. "No, I hate them."

Elsie laughed, and he did too. At once, they both felt themselves relax. His shoulders softened. She sighed and smoothed out her skirt.

"Can I get you some tea?"

"I thought my sister was going to do that."

Herschel smiled. "I'll be right back."

They sat and talked for a long time, enjoying their own little private space among the crowd. Elsie learned that he was widowed, and she explained to him that she was divorced. It was pretty frowned upon, but she wanted to be honest. He didn't seem to mind. He knew what it was like to be alone in the world, and he wasn't one to judge how a person got there.

Much to Marie's delight, a courtship began and continued through the summer and into the fall. Elsie saw a kindness in Herschel she knew existed but always seemed beyond her grasp. The way he touched the small of her back when he opened a door for her, and how he laughed when she pointed out the milk on his upper lip—these things made her feel wanted, enjoyed, and at ease.

After learning the details of her relationship with Pete, Herschel savored her straightforwardness, her strength, and her ability to forgive. It amazed him how, despite everything, her light remained in her eyes and in her smile.

❖

Three months after they met, Elsie and Herschel married at the tiny courthouse in Trenton, Georgia. It was a short ceremony, with just Jerry, Van, Della, Elsie's parents, and Marie in attendance. Herschel's kids were grown and had moved away. He treated her like a queen, and she was happy.

Herschel owned forty acres, a patchwork of soybeans, sweet potatoes, and corn, making a living by farming. His house was a small but comfortable wood-frame cottage with a front porch surrounded by black walnut trees. Inside, the kitchen had an electric stove, a cherry wood table with four chairs, and a brand-new refrigerator. There was a small bedroom in the back for Jerry, while theirs was larger and through the kitchen.

Herschel and Elsie spent a lot of time sitting at the table, whether eating meals or just sitting, drinking tea, and talking. He was a hard worker and liked to do things the old-fashioned way, like running a plow with a mule.

Elsie continued to work in Fort Payne at the big mill. She worked Monday through Friday and caught a ride with a coworker. They had settled into a nice routine, and life seemed like it was finally working out.

One Saturday around noon, Herschel came in from plowing. He looked at the homemade vegetable soup and ham sandwiches on the table. "Oh, honey, that looks so good. Let me wash up." He washed his hands at the kitchen sink and took a seat at the table.

Jerry came in and sat at the table too.

"Wash your hands, sweetie."

"Aw, Mama, they're not dirty."

Herschel leaned over and smacked Jerry across the face so hard his chair scooted back nearly a foot. "Don't backtalk your mother."

Jerry jumped up, holding his hand to his cheek, and ran to the sink.

Elsie sat there with her spoon hallway to her mouth. Herschel had not taken to Jerry at all and yelled at him all the time. She knew it was tough for a man to accept a son that was not his own, but this was the first time he had struck him. She said nothing.

❖

Time passed, and things only got worse.

One day, Boots and Esther stopped by for a visit.

"Hey, Mama," Boots said as they came in. She gave her a hug.

Esther did the same. "Good to see you, Mama."

"What on earth are y'all doing here?"

"We wanted to come see you," Esther explained.

Jerry heard the voices and came running. He threw his arms around Boots and then Esther.

"Hey, little man," Boots said. "How are you doing?"

"I'm good," Jerry said with a toothy grin.

"We want to take y'all for ice cream," Esther said.

"Oh, I can't. I have to start getting dinner ready for Herschel."

Boots nodded. "Well, let us take our little brother."

"Can I, Mama?"

Elsie thought for several seconds. "Okay," she relented. "But don't stay gone long."

Jerry jumped up and down as they walked out the door and toward the car.

"Don't spend too much on him," Elsie added as she watched from behind the screen door.

Jerry was on cloud nine sitting between his two sisters. Boots drove off the mountain and into Fort Payne. They arrived at the Dairy Queen and walked up to the sliding glass window.

"What flavor you want?" Esther asked.

"Chocolate."

"Of course." Esther ordered three chocolate cones, which started to melt almost immediately in the warm weather.

"Jerry," Boots said, "you're dripping it all over your shirt."

Jerry licked as fast as he could and then laughed.

"It's an improvement," Esther added, noticing a tattered collar and holes in the sleeves. "When's the last time you had some new clothes?"

Jerry shrugged.

"Well, I guess we know where we're headed next," Boots said.

"We better go to a thrift store," Esther added. "Mama will kill us if we spend money on a brand-new shirt."

Boots agreed, so after they finished the ice cream cones, they went to the only thrift store in the middle of town. It was a long slip of a redbrick building between a laundromat and a hardware store. A family of mannequins in the window sported used clothing. The woman's hand lingered just above the head of the little boy.

The three of them wandered in and out of the racks, Jerry tailing Esther and Boots as they thumbed through button downs, T-shirts, jackets, and pants.

"Oh, look at this one," Esther said, taking a blue-and-white-striped shirt from the racks. "You like this one, Jerry?"

"Yeah."

"That doesn't even look like it's been worn," Boots said. "Try it on."

Esther led Jerry to the dressing room, which was basically a small closet with a flowered pink curtain for a door, and beckoned Jerry to step inside. "Here, let's take off your ice cream-flavored shirt."

Jerry followed orders.

Boots heard Esther gasp.

Esther stuck her head out through the curtain and looked alarmed. "Boots, come here."

Boots looked in and gasped as well. "Jerry, turn around."

There were angry red welt marks up and down his back.

"Has Herschel been beating you?" Boots asked.

Jerry shrugged.

They bought the shirt, drove Jerry home, dropped him off, and headed back to town. Neither of the sisters wanted to confront their mother or her new husband.

"What do we do?" Esther asked, looking out the window with her hand on her forehead.

"I don't know, but we have to do something."

"Should we call the police?"

"What can they do?" Boots asked. "Besides, do you really want to put Mama through that? It will probably make things worse for both of them."

Esther knew her sister was right. Then, she had an idea. "Let's write to Travis and ask him what to do."

"Do you even know where he is?"

"Yes, he's at Fort Benning. I have his address."

Boots wasn't sure. "I don't know. That's like asking the devil for help to deal with a demon."

Esther nodded. "That's true, but I'm sure he can tell us the best way to handle it."

Boots agreed, so that afternoon, they penned a letter to their older brother, explaining their dilemma, and dropped it in the mailbox.

It took almost a week for Corporal Wooten to receive the letter. He sat alone in the barracks early on a Saturday morning and read it over and over, feeling the blood build behind his cheeks.

He went to see his commanding officer. He was a fair enough man, old for a lieutenant, but stiff about the rules. Travis was not hopeful about getting a positive response, but it didn't really matter. He would leave regardless. He couldn't bear the thought of his little brother under the thumb and fist of any man, much less one he had never even met.

"Sir, I have a family issue and need to go home this weekend."

His CO looked up from his desk, thumbed his army regulation mustache from left to right, and asked, "Did someone die?"

"No, sir."

"If you don't have furlough scheduled, you'll just have to wait."

"Yes, sir."

Travis returned to his barrack, packed a few items in his army-issue duffle, and walked down the steps, hearing the door slam against the jamb behind him, and out the front gate. On the road, shuffling backward with his thumb out, he thought about his mother, sisters, and younger brother. He knew the army was right for him, but he couldn't help but feel a twinge of guilt over leaving them.

A car pulled over within minutes, which was typical. It was not uncommon to see soldiers hitching a ride near the base or really anywhere in the country at that time. There were a few times he had to walk a while, but mostly, he was able to catch a ride pretty quickly. After a long and quite ride with a young couple, who happened to be heading straight to Nashville, he arrived on Sand Mountain.

As the sun rose high above the pines, Jerry, who was now eight, sat on the front porch playing with a little red truck. His mama had left a few minutes earlier to go to town. Jerry could see his stepdad about a hundred yards away in the field plowing behind his mule. He had often thought of asking if he could go live with one of his sisters or of running away, but even at his age, he couldn't imagine leaving his mother or being out in the world without her.

He looked up and something caught his eye. It was the outline of a man far away walking down the road toward the farm. The image got bigger as Jerry watched. He seemed to be dressed in light tan clothing.

As the man reached the side of the field, he cut across the newly plowed dirt and walked toward Herschel.

Jerry, curious, kept watching.

When Herschel saw the man, he stopped plowing, removed the straps from around his back, and awkwardly stepped toward him. Suddenly, he threw up both hands, palms facing toward the stranger, as if signaling him to stop.

There was no conversation at all. The stranger walked right up and hit Herschel square in the face. Herschel went down hard. The impact made the mule jump, and it took a full second for the loud pop to reach Jerry's ears. The man stood over him and swung again and again as Jerry's stepdad lay in the loose dirt. Jerry could hear the delayed sounds of the punches echoing across the span.

The stranger finally stopped and walked away the same way he came. Jerry watched as he disappeared back down the road.

He looked at his stepdad, who wasn't moving at all. Was he dead?

Finally, his stepdad sat up and struggled to his feet. He staggered toward the house, walked right past Jerry, went to the kitchen, soaked a rag, and wiped the blood from his face. After several minutes, he exited the house, walked right past Jerry again, and went back to plowing.

Travis walked back to the main road, caught a local bus to Fort Payne, where he'd find more travelers to catch a ride, and took a seat. A few miles down the road, a woman flagged the bus down. Travis smiled.

"Thanks," the woman said as she paid the fare. The bus was loaded, so she walked back halfway and stood holding the bar running a foot below the ceiling.

Travis reached over and grabbed her leg. "Hey, good looking."

The woman jumped. "Leave me alone."

Travis laughed. "You don't recognize your own son?"

Elsie couldn't believe it. Sadly, she really didn't recognize him. She saw so little of him when he was growing up, and three years in the military had hardened his outside to match his inside. "Travis? Oh my God." She hugged him. "What are you doing here?"

"Just in town on some business. Headed back to base."

Travis gave her his seat, and they talked all the way to Fort Payne. He never mentioned the real reason he had come home.

Elsie went on with her shopping, and Travis headed back. He hitched all the way back to base. He walked to the gate and turned himself in. MPs came in a jeep and picked him up. He was arrested for going AWOL, given a week in the brig, assigned to KP for four weeks, and busted down to private first class.

It was worth it, at least to Travis.

Elsie got home around noon and started making dinner. Jerry came in to help.

"I saw your brother, Travis, this morning."

Jerry looked surprised. "What was he doing here?"

"I don't know. Just said he had some business to take care of."

Jerry smiled. Suddenly, the missing pieces of the puzzle connected.

When Herschel came in for dinner, Elsie gasped. "What happened to your face?"

He looked at Jerry and then back to Elsie. "Oh, the damn harness broke and that mule drug me right into the plow."

"That's what happened," Jerry said. "I saw it."

Herschel looked at Jerry and nodded. After that day, things were much better. In fact, Herschel never so much as raised his voice to Jerry again.

CHAPTER NINE
DINNER AND A MOVIE
1973

Daddy was the ultimate salesman. He taught me that in life, everyone's a salesman, especially when it comes to the one thing you have to sell every day—yourself. He had been selling heavy-duty stainless-steel cookware for a company called Townecraft since before I was born. It offered everything he liked in a job: no set hours, no boss looking over his shoulder, and he could work whenever he was in the mood, which wasn't very often.

I was about to turn eight, so he figured it was time for me to pull my weight in this family outside the farm. So, I went with him and Mama as Julene stayed home to watch Neenah and Dinky. Mostly, I was just there for physical labor as I carried in all the food and cookware from our car into the person's house who was hosting the dinner.

Four couples—mostly farmers, I assumed—sat around the kitchen table. The men, all wearing old jeans and flannel shirts, sat with their arms folded across their chests and had the look of folks ready to hear a con man. Even the wives' faces were chiseled with the prominent frowns of skepticism.

"Thank you all for coming," Daddy began. "Just relax and enjoy the evening. If nothing else, you'll get a free meal. And believe me, getting something free from me is something to be proud of."

They all laughed. And just like that, it went from a sales pitch to a neighborhood social. Daddy went through his presentation, throwing out more one-liners than anything else. He had it down pat. He could read people and know exactly what to tell them and how to make them laugh, think, and enjoy themselves. He not only dazzled them with information and a great meal but also made them laugh, and then, he scared the crap out of them.

"Let's make some string potatoes," Daddy said as he took already peeled white potatoes and turned the handle of the cutter. The cup-shaped cutter blade spit out perfectly cut pieces. "This is the King Cutter, and Mrs. Wilks will be receiving one as a free gift for hosting this dinner. Any of you want one, just host a dinner at your house and have four qualified couples there."

"Qualified" meant couples who didn't already own a set of cookware like this.

I could see the eyes of the women glaze over as Daddy made that cutter sing. It's like watching a commercial on television, ordering the item, getting it home, and then realizing you can't do with it what the guy on television could.

"Now, I'm gonna put these potatoes right on top of the meatloaf I have in the Dutch oven. You'll see that the flavors will not transfer."

The Dutch oven was the largest of the pots in the set and came with both a regular lid and a high-domed lid with a flat surface for stacking other pots and pans. Daddy dumped the potatoes on top of the raw meatloaf, which Mama had made up at home.

"Now, I'll take this piece and put it on top." He held up the round flat disk with six holes in it. "You can use the little stainless-steel cups in this to make poached eggs. Now, on top of that, I'm going to put this pineapple upside-down cake and cover it with the high-domed lid. On top of this, we're going to put this pan full of cabbage, and I'm going to add a whole onion right on top of the cabbage, again to show you the flavors will not transfer. On top of that goes this pan with peas, carrots, and corn. Now, we'll set the eye on low and let it cook. That's an entire meal on one eye on low heat."

It was impressive and often made me wonder why we didn't do that at home. Usually, Mama or Daddy just made chili, pintos, or spaghetti in the Dutch oven and placed it on the table, and we all dug in.

Daddy always paused here to soak in the stares of doubt. Then, he took out a bowl of chicken thighs, from which he had already removed the veins, and removed the lid of the electric skillet, which had already been heated. This item wasn't part of the large set of cookware, which came with a lifetime warranty, but could belong to customers for an additional $149. Financing was available.

Daddy took off the plastic lid from a large can of Crisco and looked at one of the women. "If you were going to cook this much chicken, how much lard would you use?"

The woman laughed. "A lot."

Daddy scooped up half a tablespoonful. "This much?"

"More."

Daddy scooped up a huge amount. "This much?"

The woman nodded. "At least."

Daddy smiled and held the spoon in front of her face. "Will you take a big bite of this for me?"

Everyone laughed as the woman shook her head and held up her hands to block the advancing spoon.

"You wouldn't eat this?" Daddy asked.

"No."

"What do you think you're doing when you cook with it?"

It was a rhetorical question, but everyone got the point.

Daddy continued. "Do you know the number one killer in America is heart disease? And what causes that? Your arteries becoming blocked." He held the spoon up higher. "And this is a perfect source of blockage. We're going to cook all this chicken with no lard at all." He threw the first thigh into the skillet, and it hissed so loudly it made several of them jump. It was like a fire alarm going off that told everyone that the chicken was about to burn. He continued until it was completely filled with chicken thighs. He laughed at their expressions. "Y'all think it's going to burn, right?"

They all nodded.

Daddy put the lid on the skillet. "We're going to let that cook, and I'm not even going to turn them."

Daddy added two more pans with other food to two of the other eyes, leaving one available for demonstrations. He asked the hostess for one of her aluminum pots. "This pot is clean, correct?"

"Yes."

This is where Daddy, with sweat already making his face shine, went for the kill. "Sir," he said pointing to one of the men, "if you dropped a piece of food on the floor, would you eat it?"

"No."

"What if you dropped it on the floor and stepped on it? Would you eat it then?"

The man laughed. "Still no."

Daddy smiled. "Okay, let's see then." He dropped a napkin on the floor in front of the guy's shoe. "Step on that and really rub it in."

The guy obliged.

Daddy picked up the napkin and showed everyone the faint stains on both sides of the napkin. "This is the dirt from your shoe and from the floor. I don't blame you; I wouldn't eat it either. But you'll eat food cooked in that pot?" He pointed to the aluminum pot on the stove as the guy nodded. Taking a clean napkin, he rubbed the inside of the pot and showed it to the group.

They gasped. The napkin had filthy dark stains much worse than the napkin the man had stepped on.

"You see," Daddy explained, "aluminum is a dirty metal. It has huge pores that cannot be cleaned. Every time you eat food cooked in an aluminum pot, this is what you're putting in your stomachs." Daddy wasn't finished. He took a stainless-steel pot and brought water to a boil and added salt and pulled out a tarnished silver fork. He actually had a little jar of some chemical that made it tarnish quickly instead of it taking years. He didn't share that information. He held it up for all to see. "Have any of you ever tried to clean tarnish from silverware?"

All of the women nodded. "It takes forever," one of them added.

"I'm going to show you a trick." Daddy put the fork in the stainless-steel pot with the boiling water, and nothing happened. "No reaction at all." He then replaced the stainless-steel pot with the aluminum pot provided by the hostess, brought water to a boil, and added the salt. He placed the fork in the water with the handle propped up against the side. It instantly began foaming and putting off a toxic odor.

"Oh, that smells terrible," one woman said.

Daddy removed the fork and showed it to them. The lower half of the fork that was in the water was now sparkling clean. "You all know how hard it is to remove tarnish from a silver fork, but look at this: if it will do this to tarnish, imagine what it's doing to the linings of your stomachs."

By now, he had them all terrified to go home and eat in their own kitchens. He then pulled out some old literature on the dangers of cooking with aluminum and read them aloud. I was never a believer in conspiracy theories, but Daddy had shown me all these old magazine articles, which used to be printed often. Then, one year in the 1960s, they simply stopped.

Daddy emptied the water from the aluminum pot and held the pot up for all to see. "People have suffered for years with ulcers, stomachaches, indigestion, heartburn, and even headaches, and this could very well be the culprit. As soon as they start eating out of healthy cookware, it all goes away." By the time he was finished with his demonstrations and horror-filled articles, the food was ready. All the folks there were amazed that not only was everything cooked perfectly with nothing burnt, but it was all absolutely delicious.

After everyone ate, the proper procedure was to have everyone fill out contact cards and call them the next day in the privacy of their homes. But Daddy believed that would give them time to doubt or forget everything they had learned and were feeling right now. He struck while the iron was hot. He laid it all out right there, the different sets available, the extras, and the low monthly payment options, emphasizing how much they would save over a lifetime of replacing the much more inferior, much more deadly cookware.

As I helped Mama clean the kitchen, a scary feeling hit me. I had to use the bathroom, and I don't mean number one. I always wondered where that ridiculous numbering system originated, but now was not the time. I knew I'd never make it home, so I walked over to where Daddy talked with all the prospective customers.

"Excuse me."

Daddy stopped in the middle of his pitch and turned around, his expression more of shock than anything else.

I looked at the lady of the house. "Can I use your bathroom?"

Daddy laughed.

"Sure, sweetie," she said. "Just go down that hall. It's the first door on the right."

"Thank you, ma'am." I walked with urgency.

"He's very well mannered," I heard someone say just before I walked in and flipped on the light switch.

I had used the bathroom at the home of several relatives and was always in awe. But it was always just to relieve my tiny bladder. I yanked down my pants and sat on the commode. Oh my, it was wonderful. So, this is how the other half lives. I could only hope that when I grew up, I would have a home with a bathroom. Hey, a boy can dream.

I scanned the neat little room. There were magazines on a little stand. There was one towel draped over a shower curtain rod sporting a plastic curtain with colorful circles, and one hanging in a circular handle by the sink. A bar of soap and a cup of toothbrushes also set on the sink.

Then, I saw something that worried and confused me. Right by the commode was a small trash can only about a foot in diameter and a foot and a half high. And it was almost full of used tissue. I didn't know what that meant.

I was finished and looked at the convenient roll of toilet tissue hanging on the wall. I knew what that was for, of course, but I was now confused about what to do with it after I used it to clean. What if I try to flush it and it backs up and floods the entire house? They'll come running in screaming, "What are you doing? You can't flush paper."

They'd know I was a dumb country bumpkin. I mean, sure, I was, but that didn't mean I wanted everyone to know.

Was this small trashcan where the used paper was supposed to go? I truly didn't know. I tried moving some of the top pieces around, but I couldn't see any with dark stains.

I had to do something. So, I emptied half the paper out of the can onto the floor, wiped myself, folded the tissues up so you couldn't see what was on them, and placed my pieces down deep in the can. Then, I took the pile I had dumped out on the floor and placed it over mine.

I flushed and the commode drained successfully. Whew. I washed my hands and went back to helping Mama.

Daddy was concluding his sales pitch. All four couples bought the large set, and two of them paid cash on the spot. At least one of the women asked about scheduling a dinner of her own. As I carried everything back to our car, I wondered how many of them would go home and throw away their current cookware.

For many years, Daddy was a top-producing salesman for this company, and he had several huge trophies and plaques to testify to this. He was proud of those. They were displayed prominently on the floor of Mama and Daddy's half-completed closet, covered in cobwebs, dust, and old never-worn-again clothes, right beside a broken bowling trophy. The odd thing was that Daddy was not that committed to sales. He would follow up with a few of the ladies wanting to host dinners of their own, but he always lost interest and went back to farming. I never knew why, but I always wondered how much money he could make if he really put himself into it.

On the drive home, Daddy sang. He loved Tennessee Ernie Ford and Johnny Horton and could sing all their songs. His voice was smooth and mellow, and he sang a lot. He had tried many times to teach me how to sing, only to get frustrated when I sang way off-key. He told me once, "You can't carry a tune in a bucket." I hardly thought that was fair since he had never provided me with a tune bucket in the first place.

Mama sat quietly and enjoyed the singing . . . and peace. Mama had prepared most of the huge meal for the dinner, and her work was far from over. It would be late at night by the time we got home, but the next morning would be for cleaning all the cookware and accessories. And, as much as Daddy talked up how easy the cookware was to clean, it wasn't. Especially after using almost every piece and letting it sit overnight.

I wasn't sure how Mama did it. She worked full time at the sock mill, cooked most meals at home except for weekend breakfasts, did all the laundry in the valley, and did many other chores, and still did most of the behind-the-scenes work on these dinners.

And I never could understand why they called them "dinners," since it was always suppertime when they did them. I think it was a company thing. I had begun to realize already that people outside Sand Mountain didn't always use the correct words or pronunciations.

The next morning, I unloaded all the stuff from the car while Daddy cooked breakfast. After we ate, Julene and Neenah helped Mama wash breakfast dishes and the cookware from last night.

After a successful sales dinner, Daddy was always in a good mood for a while. He looked over at me sitting on the couch and pulled up the back of his T-shirt. "Come scratch my back."

I was always in the wrong place at the wrong time. My sisters, Mama, and I were often called upon to undertake this menial and most disgusting task. Daddy never specified a particular area, so

I knew it wasn't about an actual itch, but more along the lines of a free massage.

As my fingers dug into the square yardage of flesh that made up his enormous back, the tips of my fingernails clogged with dirt, dried sweat, and dead skin. I wondered if I would be able to use this on a job resume later in life. Skills: back-scratcher, dishwasher, channel-changer, worm-fiddler.

Ten minutes later, he was satisfied. He put on his button-up. "Come on, let's go get some ice cream."

"Okay." That sounded a lot more fun.

Daddy loved ice cream . . . and ice cream shakes, and ice cream sundaes, and ice cream sandwiches, and ice cream cones, and ice cream bars, and whatever else they made out of ice cream. Since we didn't usually have use of a refrigerator, we had to eat it as soon as we got it. But a half gallon of ice cream stood little chance against me, my daddy, and my sisters. And we had many times watched Daddy devour an entire six-pack of ice cream sandwiches like a snack.

As we drove out the little dirt road, we slowed down as we neared Granny's house.

"What are we doing?"

Daddy smiled. "I thought I would see if your grandmother needed anything from the store."

Something wasn't right. Daddy loathed Granny. Granny loathed Daddy. I'm not sure how long she had detested him, but I'm guessing ever since the day my mama brought him home.

We walked in without knocking.

"What the hell do you want?" Granny snapped from her padded rocking chair.

She was a tiny woman with a huge personality, gray, frail, and vicious. If you looked up "political correctness" in the dictionary, it would read "not her." I guess "feisty" would describe her best. From a bygone mountain era, she was tough as nails and ornery as a rattlesnake. She would break off a stalk from her aloe vera plant and ooze the sap onto cuts and scrapes, cook a mess of wild poke salad when she had a tummy ache, and smoke rabbit tobacco when she had a cold. She only liked to eat what she could grow, catch, or kill, or what any of her relatives could grow, catch, or kill.

Granny hated piss ants. I never understood exactly what breed that was, but I think they were kin to fire ants. They seemed to be the only ants that got into her house. To be clear, Granny hated any animal she couldn't fry in a cast-iron skillet with a huge scoop of lard. She hated snakes. She hated rats. She hated dogs. She hated cats. But it was the piss ants that really got her goat. That's just an expression, because she also hated goats.

A couple of months earlier, she had grown tired of the bull from the huge pasture across the road from her house jumping the fence and munching away in her young garden. "I put a stop to that," she told us. "I took my shotgun and fired both barrels in the air, and he jumped his ass back over that fence and ain't been back."

Technically, she was correct. What she failed to mention was that the air she fired into was the air directly between her and the bull. It jumped back over the fence all right, with a butt full of buckshot. And it never came back because the owner had to have it put down. Neither he nor the local police pressed charges, perhaps worried of suffering the same fate.

Daddy smiled a fake smile. "Just wanted to see if you needed anything from the store."

"Not if you're going, I don't."

"It's no problem," Daddy said and pulled out the wad of cash from his pocket and waved it in front of her. "I can afford it."

"You probably stole it," Granny said. "I hope somebody hits you in the head and steals all that from you."

"I'd like to see them try."

"Hell, I might do it my own damn self."

Daddy put the cash back in his pocket. "Try it, you old fool, and I'll go upside your head."

Granny wasn't finished. "I'll get my shotgun and blow your ass off."

"You couldn't hit the broad side of a barn, you blind old bat."

"Get the hell out of here, you sumbitch!"

Daddy turned and walked out.

I stood there like a child lost in the wild. I finally snapped to attention. "Uh . . . bye, Granny."

"Bye, sweetie."

I ran to the car and got in. Daddy had this strange look of satisfaction on his face. He looked at me, smiled really big, and drove on. I guess it's true what they say: you have to enjoy the little things.

All day long, Daddy seemed happy and barely flew into fits of rage at all. That afternoon, he surprised us. "Y'all want to go to the drive-in movie tonight?"

We couldn't believe it. We had never been to a movie . . . ever. Needless to say, we were all in agreement. "Yes!"

I was very excited. Besides when visiting Aunt Esther, I only got to go to the valley a few times a year, usually to accompany Mama to the laundromat. There were no laundromats on the mountain, at least not our end of the mountain. But Fort Payne was a huge city. I had heard they had over ten thousand people living there. Amazing. And the downtown strip had huge tall buildings on each side, several with two stories.

On one visit to town back during the summer, Mama dropped me off at the city park, called Union Park, while she and Julene washed and dried clothes. I found several kids my age to play with.

Across the street from the park was a seedy gas station—the Red Ace. In the men's room, which you entered from the outside, were the most magical contraptions on one wall that sold the most incredible items: deluxe water balloons. I never figured out why half-naked ladies adorned the fronts of these machines, but assumed it was just to grab your attention. It worked.

They only cost a quarter and would hold ten times as much water as a regular balloon. We'd fill them up and chase each other as the adults stared with eyes wide open and jaws dropped. I knew they were wondering where we got such awesome water balloons.

As my sisters and I were getting dressed to go to the movies, Mama took our own Dutch oven and popped popcorn. She always saved empty bread bags and the ties. She filled four of these with popcorn and tied them.

Daddy took a small Styrofoam cooler and added canned drinks and ice. It was one thing to pay the three-dollar entrance fee for one car, but he wasn't going to splurge on items from the concession building.

We piled into the car and headed out the dirt road. Halfway out, we met another car coming in. Not just any car, but *the* car. I was very worried that our first movie adventure was going to be over before it started. But Daddy stopped our car right beside the black car and rolled down the window. The men in the black suits were confused.

"We're going to the drive-in to see a movie," Daddy said with a grin. "Y'all want to ride with us?" At that, he laughed, rolled up the window, and drove on.

I had only been by the Hamilton Drive-In on those rare trips to town. The name was on the back of the huge screen that towered above the trees. It was like the Roman Coliseum as far as I was concerned.

Daddy navigated down the long dirt path to enter and stopped at the little booth.

"Three dollars," the young guy said and handed Daddy a sheet of paper.

Daddy paid, and we went where we had never gone before. I always wondered what the other side looked like and drank in the glorious sights as we rounded the entrance. There were long rows, each on a rise higher than the one in front, which made semicircles across in front of the giant screen. Hundreds of gray poles stuck three feet out of the ground, each with a gray box speaker on each side attached by a wire. It was like another planet.

Daddy pulled into a spot in the middle and rolled his window halfway down. He took the speaker and hung it on the partially open window and rolled it back up. I was always amazed at how he already knew how to do everything.

"What movie are we seeing?" Neenah asked.

Mama looked at the paper the guy at the booth had given us. "It's a Disney movie. Thank goodness. It's called *Superdad*."

That sounded great. And it was a fitting title since that is what we had—a super dad.

"Can I have some popcorn?" I asked.

Mama laughed. "I'm surprised you held out this long." She untied one of the bags and passed it back to us.

The big screen came to life, and I was in awe of the technology. I was in for another great surprise when they played a cartoon first. But staring around three heads in the front seat to see the screen was a little frustrating. And when Daddy lit up a Camel, that was about all the family time I could take.

I noticed several rows of benches right in front of the concession building. "I'm going to go sit up there."

"Okay," Mama said. "But don't wander off."

"I won't." I hopped out and walked to the benches. The night air was a little chilly, but the view of the screen was phenomenal. There were speakers behind the benches, so people could hear as well. I looked up and noticed the beam of light flickering above me coming from a small hole in the building. I knew that's where the projector must be. I could almost make out the scenes in the flashing colors. It was like science-fiction come to life, and it truly dazzled me.

After the movie began, I didn't move the entire time. Well, except to run to the bathroom twice. It was the most awesome experience ever. With ten minutes left to go in the movie, I had to go again, but I didn't want to miss the ending, so I held it. When the credits rolled up, I rushed to the bathroom, but there was a long line. Figures. I gritted my teeth until I finally got to a urinal partitioned on each side by plywood boards attached to the cinderblock walls.

When I came out, I was turned around. I couldn't remember where we parked, and all the cars were leaving. I panicked. I walked one way, stopped, and walked the other.

Suddenly, I winced in pain as I felt what I thought was a metal claw around my neck. I looked around and saw Daddy. He was not a happy camper. He pushed me all the way to the car.

The drive home was a little more solemn.

After we got home, Mama, Julene, Neenah, and Dinky all brushed their teeth and went to bed. I got to stay up a little later.

I stood there replaying scenes from the movie in my mind. I was still amazed at the splendor of it all. I knew I would forever be a movie buff from now on.

The loud popping noises ceased, and I turned around to see Daddy putting back on his belt.

"You don't ever wander off like that again. You hear me?"

"Yes, sir."

"Now, go to bed."

I brushed my teeth, got into bed, and stared straight up into the darkness. What a great night.

CHAPTER TEN

POTATO PACT

1962

S o, what do you think?"

"Explain it to me again," Pete said.

Etta nodded. She wanted to hear it again as well. She didn't know all of Pete's family well, and she was by nature a cautious woman. But the man currently in her living room had "snake oil salesman" written all over him.

Etta and Pete were now married. He met her while visiting his oldest son in North Carolina. In fact, she was the aunt of Talmadge's wife, Macy. She was about five-foot-five and stout with a strong jawline, and being Holiness, she only wore plain ankle-length dresses and kept her dark hair in a tight bun, which was slowly being colored gray by Father Time.

The couple lived in a rental house in Blake not far from where Pete was born. It was a small, two-bedroom homestead with a pignut hickory tree out front and a chunk of workable land out back. Pete would plant corn and tomatoes every year and haul them in his old beat-up truck to Fort Payne and park alongside Main Street and sell out in a day, like he had done all those years ago with his father at the market in Chattanooga.

Pete and Etta sat in wooden chairs brought into the living room from the kitchen table, and Ilene, his second oldest, and her husband, Raymond Styron, sat on the couch.

Ilene was now thirty, a grown woman of course, but she still had the face of a young girl. Her skin was flawless and pale, her eyes a light brown, like tea-colored diamonds looking out at the world with indifference. She wore a tan skirt and a pink blouse. Next to Raymond, she looked like a doll.

He was older, thirty-five, and a bit rougher around the edges. His hands and face were brown and corrugated from years of farm work. A scar across his forehead told the story of a meeting with an angry mule in the cotton fields when he was twenty. The two had been married for twelve years and had three children: ages eleven, three, and one.

"Okay," Raymond said, moving forward to the edge of the couch and rubbing his hands on his pants. "All you have to do is rent the land. I already have a hundred acres picked out, and you have ten here behind your house. That's all you have to do. I'll do the rest. I have my dad's tractor and equipment, so it won't be a problem."

"Potatoes?" Pete clarified.

Raymond nodded. "Prices are through the roof. Do you have any idea how much money one-hundred-and-ten acres will make us? We'll split it right down the middle, so we'll make the same amount."

Pete's mathematical mind was always turned on without effort. "Well, I'll still be out the cost of renting the land."

"Right. Right. No, I'll pay you back for half of that."

Etta, who normally stayed very quiet, finally spoke. "How are you going to do this if you live down in Foley? That's almost six hours away." She worked doing laundry for several families, babysitting, cleaning homes, and whatever she could find within walking distance. And she knew that this would involve money she had worked hard to save.

"We're staying at his family's house over in Pea Ridge right now," Ilene said. "The field won't have to be tended every day."

Raymond nodded in agreement. "Right." He looked back at Pete. "I'll be right here close by. I've got it all worked out in my head. Hey, this is easy money."

Raymond knew his father-in-law. And he certainly knew the words to include in a sentence to get Pete's attention: "easy" and "money."

Pete was now fifty-four years old and still looking for that pot of gold, the big score so he could finally buy a farm like he always wanted to. Every attempt over the years had seemed to fall just beyond his grasp. How many more opportunities would he get like this?

Etta could sense what he was thinking. "Maybe we should talk it over with Travis first."

But Pete was too stubborn. Plus, the prospect of making money with no work was too appealing. He agreed and shook Raymond's hand.

After Raymond and Ilene drove away, Pete still struggled with his decision. But he definitely thought it best to keep it under wraps. "Let's not tell anyone about this."

Etta nodded in agreement.

Travis was currently living in Rainsville with his wife, Hazel, and one-year-old daughter, Julene, anyway, so Pete figured he wouldn't find out. He was wrong. Rural Alabama back then had a way of communicating that required nothing but the ether. Stories, true and false, seemed to blow in the breeze. Just two miles away and just two days later, this story landed with Travis. He had been busy clearing land given to them by Hazel's father, Harley, as a wedding present. His goal was to build a house and move back to Blake. When he heard the news of Pete's deal with Raymond, he drove straight to his daddy's house.

"What the hell's wrong with you?" he said, staring Pete straight in the eyes. "Why would you go into business with that cheatin' son of a bitch?"

"I'm a grown man," Pete said. "I can make my own decisions."

"Then, act like it." Travis was fuming. "Boots and Esther tell me he's been beating Ilene. Did you know about that? There are some lines you just don't cross."

Pete shook his head. Time had forgiven him his brutality. Age had helped him forget. Plus, things were different when it came to his daughter. Neither he nor Travis could understand why a man would treat a woman that way.

"You wait and see; he's gonna stick it to you. You just keep that bastard away from me, or potatoes won't be the only thing planted in that field." Travis, disgusted, stormed out of the house and drove away.

Pete just could not understand why his son had such an awful temper, but it scared him.

❖

Pete went through with the plan and rented the land. It took all their money.

When the time came to plant, Pete hadn't heard anything from Raymond. He drove over to the rented field. Hundreds of wooden crates of cut-up seed potatoes had been delivered and set out along-side the field, but it had not been plowed. Pete couldn't believe it. He took his hat off and slapped it against his thigh. Butterweed had sprouted up as far as he could see. He saw rocks too, here and there near where he stood, which meant there were many more hidden in the middle. This was going to require real work. He went back home and walked to a neighbor's house to borrow the phone.

"Where the hell is Raymond?" he asked when Ilene answered.

"He's very sick, Daddy."

"I don't care. We had a deal. He needs to get over there and plant those potatoes before they rot."

But, of course, Raymond never showed. Pete had to borrow a tractor to plow the fields and plant the potatoes. He carried enough over to his house to plant the ten acres there. It was very hard work. And when it came to hilling the potatoes—no Raymond. Time to weed—no Raymond. Time to dust—no Raymond.

As the days grew hotter and the work continued, Pete grew more and more angry, especially with Travis's words echoing in his head. The time came to harvest the potatoes, and Pete sat having breakfast with Etta. "Well, the good news is we don't have to split it. We should make enough to get our own place."

Etta smiled and touched his hand. She had been worried about Pete working so hard. He had lost weight. His face looked thin. She knew he was still strong, but where there used to be muscles around his neck and shoulders, she now only saw bones poking underneath his shirt. His overalls even clung to his narrow frame like a tent.

Pete drove the tractor over to the field. Already looking ahead, he knew that he could get all the potatoes plowed up, but he would have to hire several men to help load them for the market. But the money he would make would easily cover the salaries. He pulled up to the field and what he saw made his blood boil. The entire field had been harvested, and the potatoes were gone. He jumped off the tractor and kicked his boot in the dirt. The sour taste of fury rose from his stomach to his throat. But he didn't know what to do. He drove to his neighbors to use the phone again, but he couldn't get an answer.

He walked back home and explained the situation to Etta. All day long, he went back and forth to the neighbor's house to use the phone for always the same results. He thought of driving to Pea Ridge a few times, but he didn't know where they were staying. Mostly, he just sat and got madder and madder.

"What are you going to do?" Etta asked that night.

"I don't know. I'd like to kill that son of a bitch."

Pete was so angry he couldn't sleep, tossing and turning all night long and pouring cold sweat into the sheets. The next morning, he went to the neighbor's again. This time, Raymond answered. Pete tried to control his words since he wasn't in his own house. He was not successful.

"What's the problem?" Raymond asked as if he had done nothing wrong.

Pete saw a smug smile on Raymond's face. "You stole my potatoes. You didn't honor our agreement, and I did all the work. Those potatoes belonged to me."

"I paid for the seed, remember?" Raymond said. "Look, I left those behind your house. You can have those."

"You listen to me—"

Raymond hung up.

As much as Pete hated what he had to do next, he did it. "Can I make another call?"

"Sure," the neighbor said. "Do whatever you need to."

Pete reached in his wallet, unfolded a worn piece of paper, and dialed Travis's house.

After several minutes of Travis cussing and saying, "I told you so," he offered some sound advice. "Go see the sheriff in the morning."

Pete did just that. He got up early and drove to see the DeKalb County sheriff, W. L. Edwards, whom everyone called Buck.

Buck was a kind man who had been the sheriff in DeKalb County for several terms. He was a small man in his early sixties, and his soft voice and quick smile made him appear like a much younger man. Almost everyone around thought him to be fair, and they looked on him as a friend. He had a nose for police work but would rather be on the river in his boat tempting largemouth bass.

"Do you have a written contract?" Buck asked.

Pete looked shocked. He had never done that. "I thought a man's word was his bond."

Buck shook his head and moved some papers around on his desk. "It should be, but times have changed, I reckon, and not every man adheres to that."

"What can I do?"

Buck shrugged. "Make better decisions next time is all I can offer. At least you still have the ten acres behind your house, so it won't be a total loss."

Pete was seeing red when he drove home. His heart seemed to race along with the speed of the truck. His hands shook. He took heavy deep breaths, not to gain any sense of calm but to keep from veering off the road. When he pulled into his driveway, Etta rushed out the front door with a distressed look.

"What is it?" he asked as he slammed the truck door.

Etta couldn't get the words out, so she pointed to the back of the house.

Pete walked around back and couldn't believe what he was seeing. There was Raymond on a tractor harvesting the field. *His* field. Ilene was standing beside a truck watching.

"That son of a bitch." Pete went into the house, grabbed his double-barrel 16-gauge shotgun from where it stood behind the kitchen door, slipped shells into both barrels, and walked out the back door.

"Pete, no," Etta called out, running toward him and grabbing his shirtsleeves.

Pete shrugged her off and kept moving. He walked right up to within ten feet of the tractor and pointed the gun at Raymond's chest.

"Whoa. Put that gun away."

Ilene was scared to death. "Daddy, don't."

Pete didn't budge. "Get off that tractor, you goddamn thief."

Dust from the tractor hung in the air, mingling with the smell of gasoline. Thick white clouds stood motionless against a pale blue sky. A barn swallow landed on a fencepost and watched.

Raymond jumped off the tractor. "You crazy bastard." He reached back on the harvester, grabbed a three-feet-long steel rod, and started toward Pete. "Now, let's just—"

BOOM!

Pete fired one shot right into his chest.

Raymond's knees buckled, and he crumbled to the ground.

Ilene screamed and rushed to her husband, who lay completely motionless in the dirt. Blood pooled underneath him, turning black as it seeped into the ground. "Raymond? Raymond? Get up!"

Pete backed away. His ears rung. The world went silent. It didn't seem real. He looked around and saw Etta running toward him. What had he done? He looked at Raymond lying there in the dirt and Ilene crying by his side. He looked at the sky. It seemed too beautiful a day to have things go so horribly wrong. His entire life flashed before him, not just the past but an undeniably gloomy future. He could see Travis's anger. He could see the expressions of all his children. He could see his daughter being a widow. He could see handcuffs, bars, and gray walls. He never had much in life, but he always had freedom. Finally, he looked down at the shotgun. He knew there was one more loaded barrel and that suddenly seemed like the only answer. Pete pointed the gun at himself and fired.

Etta stopped in her tracks and put her hands over her mouth. She tried to scream, but nothing came out. She slowly walked two more steps forward, stopped, then turned, and ran to the neighbor's house to call for help. After dialing the sheriff's office and blurting out what happened, she ran out. The neighbor followed her as she rushed back to Pete.

Pete lay on the ground alone, his shirt covered in his own blood. His eyes wide open, blinking slowly. He had shot himself in the chest, but his chest was still moving, albeit slowly.

"Put pressure on his wound," the neighbor said.

Etta knelt down and pressed both hands on the wound to stop the bleeding, but the area was bigger than her hands could cover. The blood was flowing like a river of lava and impossible to stop.

Sheriff Edwards and Chief Deputy Roland Weldon were the first to arrive, and they went first to where Ilene knelt by her husband. Raymond had no pulse. Weldon moved over and asked Etta to let him work on Pete while Buck questioned Ilene.

Ilene stood like a statue and recounted exactly what happened as if she was describing a movie she had seen, her eyes focused on the distance.

Buck took down notes. He lifted his fedora, the one he preferred to his official hat, and wiped the sweat from his brow. He looked over at Weldon, whose county-issued cowboy-style hat with his badge on it lay in the dirt beside him. "Is he alive?"

"Barely."

Buck looked toward the road. "Where the hell is that ambulance?"

Crucial minutes passed. Finally, the ambulance arrived and drove past the house and into the freshly harvested field. Two men got out and first checked on Raymond. Gray and growing cold, he was pronounced dead at the scene. They moved over to Pete and packed the wound with layers of bandages before lifting him onto a stretcher and placing him in the back of the ambulance.

As the ambulance sped away, Buck walked over to Etta. "Did you see what happened?"

"I just heard the shots." That wasn't true, but Etta was afraid to say anything. "Can someone give me a ride to the hospital?"

Buck nodded. "I'll find someone who can." He went to his car and radioed another deputy to come get Etta. He looked at the neighbor. "Did you see anything?"

"No." He shook his head. "I came over after they used my phone to call for help."

The other deputy came and took Etta to DeKalb General. Etta stared silently out the side window as they drove, the bushes and trees blurring by mocked her mindset. She couldn't focus. She couldn't think. The only coherent and recurring thought was that her world as she knew it was over.

The deputy let her out at the emergency room entrance. She walked in slow motion, her head hung low, her eyes scanning the pavement.

She could hardly get the words out when she approached the information counter, her hands and dress were both caked with dirt and blood. The petite woman behind the desk said they didn't have any information yet, so Etta found the nearby waiting room and sat down in a stiff chair with wrought-iron arms. She could smell the metal. She looked around at the drab peanut-colored walls and felt a chill run through her.

Within an hour, Boots and Esther came bursting into the waiting room.

"We just heard," Boots said. "Any word yet?"

Etta shook her head. "How did—"

Esther took her by the hand. "Ilene called us."

The three of them sat there in silence for what seemed an eternity. Finally, a doctor came into the room. "Etta Wooten?"

All three of them stood up.

The doctor walked over. His thick black hair was matted with perspiration. A white cotton surgical mask hung around his neck, and a stethoscope dangled in front of his chest.

"How is he?" Etta asked.

"He's in a critical condition."

"Can we see him?" Boots asked.

The doctor shook his head. "He's being airlifted to Erlanger."

"Oh Lord," Esther said, grabbing her stepmother's hand again.

Boots looked around. "Where's the pay phone?"

The doctor pointed to the front entrance.

"Who are you calling?" Esther asked.

"I better call Travis."

Esther took a deep breathe. "What are you going to tell him?"

Boots shrugged. "What we know, I guess." She went to the phone and punched the number zero.

"Operator."

"I'd like to make a collect call from Boots Hulgan." She gave her the number.

Travis answered and accepted the charges.

"You may go ahead," the operator said.

"Travis, it's Boots." She paused for a second, not knowing how to put it, and then decided straightforward was best. "Daddy shot Raymond and killed him."

"Goddammit. Where's Daddy now?"

"He was shot too. Etta said he shot himself. They're flying him to Erlanger. We're gonna drive up, but I wanted to let you know."

Travis hung up the phone and looked at Hazel, who was holding Julene against her shoulder. He told her what Boots said. "I'm going to the hospital."

"Want us to go with you?"

Travis shook his head and ran his fingers through his hair, as if that might clear his thoughts. "I don't think he's there yet. I'll call you when I know something." He threw on his shoes and a button-up shirt, went out to his car, and drove to Chattanooga, all the while cursing his father *and* Raymond. He shook his hands against the steering wheel as if he was shaking each of them by the neck. He knew. He *knew* when they went into business together, it would end badly. But he just couldn't believe it ended in *bloodshed*.

When he finally arrived at the hospital, he went in and let the staff know why he was there, so they could inform him of when they knew something. He found a waiting area, took a seat, and worried and fumed, his mind playing what-ifs and questioning everything. He kept thinking back to when his daddy told him about the business deal and wondered why he hadn't done more to stop it.

About thirty minutes later, Boots, Esther, and Etta came in. Travis greeted them with hugs.

"Have you heard anything yet?" Boots asked.

Travis shook his head. Then, he turned to Etta and took her by the shoulders. "Tell me exactly what happened."

Etta recounted everything from going to the sheriff's office to when they gave her a ride to the hospital.

"Where's Ilene?" Travis asked.

No one knew.

"I told him not to get involved with that guy. Are you sure he was killed?"

Etta nodded.

Two hours passed before another doctor came out to speak to them. "We operated and removed the pellets from the shotgun shell, but he has lost a lot of blood and is still in a critical condition. He's in the ICU and still unconscious. We're giving him blood and antibiotics. The first twenty-four hours will be the most crucial. If he survives that, he's got a fair chance of pulling through. You won't be able to see him for a while, so there's really nothing you can do here. You should all go home and get some rest. We'll call if there's any change."

Boots thanked the doctor and then looked at Travis. "What'll we do?"

"Etta can come stay with us," Travis said.

"What do you want us to do?" Esther asked.

Travis's cogs were turning. "Get a hold of Ilene and find out if she's planning to come here."

Boots was confused. "I'm sure she's going to be busy the next few days burying her husband."

"I understand," Travis said. "But Daddy will more than likely be here a while, so I assume she plans to come check on him sometime."

Boots and Esther exchanged a look. They had their doubts.

"We need her here with all of us," Travis explained.

"Why?" Esther asked.

Travis's answer shocked them all. "So we can get our stories straight."

CHAPTER ELEVEN

WHEN IN ROME

1974

The house looked like a mansion to me. It wasn't very big, but it was partially brick and had a paved driveway, a carport, and, most importantly, it had a bathroom with running water. Just like Aunt Esther's house. I assumed we had won the lottery.

The folks that owned the cookware company Daddy sold for convinced him that Rome, Georgia, was a wide-open market. I guess they also convinced him that he had already sold cookware to every person on Sand Mountain, which might have been true. That was why we moved from our thirty-acre farm to the big city of Rome—all for the prospect of the big score. Daddy was always looking for that pot of gold.

"This is Neenah and Neal's room," Mama said pointing to a small but neat room with bunk beds. She carried our new baby brother, Breland, who was only a few weeks old, in her arms. He was named after the man who married Mama and Daddy.

"I got top bunk," I yelled.

Neenah and I put our bags of clothes in the room.

"Julene and Dinky have this room," Mama continued, "and your Daddy and I have the big room."

We were all excited to have a real house in a real neighborhood like real people.

After we settled in, I went outside to toss the baseball to myself. It was two days before my ninth birthday. Whitey played with me.

Whitey was our dog that lived with us on Sand Mountain. Someone had dropped him off when he was a puppy, and I took him in. I had had him since I was three. That's how it worked on the mountain. You didn't have to find a dog; a dog would find *you*.

Whitey was a stocky pit bull, white in color with a brown spot over one eye. He kind of resembled Petey from the *Little Rascals*. He was a big teddy bear, and I loved him dearly. I had taught him how to sit and shake.

I had never lived in a city before. It was certainly different. Cars drove by every few minutes. Then, a familiar car drove by and stopped in front of the house. It seemed kind of odd seeing them here. I didn't know what to do, so I waved. The men in black suits waved back. I continued playing.

A young boy my age walked up to me. He must have seen me tossing the ball up and down, and he had a baseball glove too.

"Hey, y'all just move in?"

"Yeah."

"You play baseball?"

I nodded. "I played last year."

And what a year I'd had. Daddy had taken me to Sylvania to sign up, and they told him that I would have to play T-ball. Daddy wouldn't hear of that. Not his son. He tried to get them to put me on an older team, but they refused. He got angry, called them a few names, and we left.

He drove me to Rainsville and got me on a real team under the tutelage of Coach Bethune. I rode the bench most of the year, but at least I wasn't on a sissy T-ball team. I was only put in one time. We were way behind in the top of the ninth inning, so the coach put me in left field. I guess he figured I couldn't screw up a lost game.

I was just happy to finally be playing. With two outs, nothing had yet come my way. The next batter connected and hit a fly ball that would land right between me and the infield. I ran as fast as I could. My legs were always proportionately too short for my body, but I had that speed gene or a part of it from my daddy and grandfather.

I could see the ball falling and ran faster, and then I tripped. I slid face-first in the grass. I stood up looking around for the ball and couldn't understand why everyone was cheering until I looked in my glove. That was a fluke. I ran in with a big grin.

"Good catch, Wooten." That was the only time the coach ever used my name.

I started throwing with my new neighbor. "I'm Neal."

"I'm Joe."

That should be easy to remember. "Like Joe Namath."

He laughed. "Yep. Everyone calls me Broadway Joe."

After about thirty minutes, the black car drove on.

It was a good first day, and that evening, we sat down for supper in our beautiful house. As we ate, we suddenly heard the most horrible commotion.

"Whitey!" I said and jumped up.

Daddy followed me out the kitchen door, and when he saw what was happening, he had to grab me. Three large neighborhood dogs were apparently not as welcoming as Broadway Joe and were attacking Whitey.

"Don't move," Daddy instructed and rushed back inside the house.

Tears rolled down my face as I screamed at the other dogs. Whitey was the most lovable dog I ever knew, but he was holding his own and giving as good as he got. Several times, he pinned one of the large dogs, his teeth around their throats, but the other two were always on him too fast.

Daddy ran out carrying my big wooden baseball bat and rushed at them screaming and swinging it wildly. The three dogs fled.

Whitey turned to look at me, his white face dripping with blood. He came casually trotting toward me but collapsed when he got to the carport.

Daddy and I rushed to him. He was breathing hard and panting.

"Oh Lord," Daddy said. He saw it before I did. Whitey had a gash in his stomach a foot long.

Mama made him a bed on the kitchen floor, and Daddy carried him inside. He knew not to leave him outside all night. We were all surprised because Daddy hated the idea of dogs inside a house. Even when people had tiny dogs inside, Daddy thought it was the stupidest thing ever.

"Is he going to be okay?" Mama asked.

Daddy shook his head. "I don't know. We'll see in the morning."

I stayed by Whitey's side all night, bringing him water and just providing emotional support, until I fell asleep beside him.

Daddy woke me early the next morning. "Come on. You can go with me."

"Where?"

Daddy lifted Whitey and told me to open the door. He carried him to the car and told me to open the back door. He placed him on the backseat. "You ride back here with him."

ABOVE: My great-grandparents, Van and Della Wooten. BELOW: My great-grandparents' shack in Blake, Alabama, with some of their kids and other relatives.

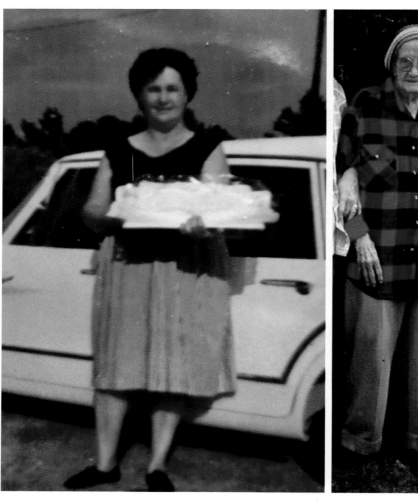

LEFT: My paternal grandmother, Elsie Wooten.
RIGHT: My maternal grandmother, Lela Jackson (aka Granny).

My granddad, Pete, with my dad, Travis.

‑JOURNAL

THURSDAY

10c Per Copy

JURNAL and THE TIMES-NEW ERA

...MA THURSDAY, AUGUST 23, 1962

TEN PAGES THIS ISSU...

Sand Mountain Man Kills Son-In-Law Wednesday

Assailant Also Shot; Now In Critical Condition

A young DeKalb County man was killed Wednesday morning by a single blast to the heart by a 16 gauge shotgun. The fatal shot was reported to have been fired by the man's father-in-law, who then turned the gun on himself. The shooting was said to have resulted from an argument over some potatoes.

The dead man is Raymond Styron, 35, of Fort Payne and the father of three children. He was shot by Peat Wooten on the farm located some 7 miles from here on Sand Mountain near Wesley's Chapel Church. The shooting took place about 7:45 a. m. yesterday

morning.

Mr. Wooten was reported to have turned the gun on himself after firing the fatal shot, but the sheriff's said yesterday afternoon that investigation so far had not confirmed that Wooten shot himself, that someone else may have shot Wooten.

DeKalb Sheriff W. L. Elawrds said that an investigation by his office was in progress and he hoped to reach some definite conclusion in a few hours.

Mr. Wooten was shot in the upper chest and was taken to a Chattanooga Hospital. County Coroner, Hoyt Wilson, said the man was in critical condition upon arrival at the hospital. Late yesterday no futher report was

78 Year Old Man Lost 14 Hours On Lookout Mountain

A 78 year old Fort Payne, route one man, was found some five miles from his home about 3:00

Spot Where Raymond Styron Died

DeKalb Sheriff W. L. (Buck) Edwards, left, and Chief Deputy Roland Weldon inspect the site where Raymond Styron, 35, died early Wednesday morning after having been shot by his father-in-law, Peat Wooten. Wooten either shot himself or was shot by an unidentified party and is in critical condition in a Chattanooga hos...

The 1963 Spring term of De-Kalb county circuit court, a jury term, convened Monday, March 4, and remained in session for three days. These three days were taken up by the trial of the State of Alabama versus Peat Wooten in connection with the shotgun slaying of his son-in-law, Raymond Styron, late in August, 1962.

Wooten was tried and found guilty by the jury. His charge, murder in the first degree, was reduced to manslaughter and his sentence was set at ten years imprisonment by circuit judge W. J. Haralson.

ABOVE: The article from when my grandfather shot and killed his oldest son-in-law. LEFT: The article from the trial.

ABOVE: Kilby Prison in the 1960s.
RIGHT: My grandfather when he was a convict at Kilby.

My dad visiting my grandfather in prison
with my two sisters, Julene and Neenah.

My dad on another visiting day at the prison, my two sisters a little older this time.

The original Blake Elementary School.

Uncle Doodle Jackson.

My dad in the U.S. Army.

My mom, Hazel Jackson, in high school.

ABOVE AND BELOW: Me and my two older sisters, Julene and Neenah.

ABOVE: My dad when he drove a truck. BELOW: Uncle Roy Helms and wife Helen.

Boots, Esther, and Ilene in the back row. Talmadge, Uncle Roy, and Dad in the middle. Jerry in the front.

Me and my three sisters: Julene, Neenah, and Dinky (I couldn't find the original without the silly text bubbles).

ABOVE: Dinky, Dad, Breland, and Mom in front of our little shack (only nine years since construction, the shack wasn't holding up well. The bicycle wheels were used for a TV antenna for the rare times we had electricity). BELOW: The only picture of me and my dad together.

LEFT: Mom and I are still close to this day (Christmas 2020). CENTER RIGHT AND BOTTOM: Wild animals still like me.

No one else in our house was even up yet as we drove away. Maybe we were going to a veterinarian. I couldn't imagine Daddy spending money on an animal, even one as great as Whitey, but I really didn't know the plan.

I kept my attention mostly on Whitey, but I noticed Daddy keeping an eye out in the rearview mirror a lot. We drove for over an hour until I recognized the old store in the curve. I finally knew where we were going. Daddy pulled up to the house, and Uncle Roy came out.

"What in the world are y'all doing here?" He seemed worried.

Daddy took Whitey out of the car and explained what happened.

"Get him up here on the porch," Uncle Roy said. "Helen, get me some cloths and hot water."

Daddy lay Whitey on the concrete porch, and Uncle Roy took over.

"It's gonna be okay," he said stroking Whitey's side. He took the cloth and water and washed away the blood stains.

There were parts of his innards protruding from the wound. I didn't know what those parts were, but I was sure they should stay inside. Uncle Roy carefully put them back in, took rubbing alcohol, and dabbed it over the wound.

Whitey whined but lay still.

"I know it stings," Uncle Roy said. "Believe me, I know."

Helen was standing ready with a needle and thread. Uncle Roy sewed him up right in front of my eyes. He was so gentle and caring. Daddy definitely made the right decision to bring him here. It was clear that Uncle Roy cared about all life.

I gave Uncle Roy a hug, and Daddy and I drove back to Rome.

❖

The next morning, I woke, climbed down out of the top bunk, and made my way to the bathroom. All I could think about was Whitey. I sat on the couch and turned on the television. One by one, everyone else got up and came into the living room as well, each smiling at me. I guess they were trying to comfort me.

Mama made breakfast, and we all ate. Finally, I got up, went outside, and just walked around the neighborhood exploring. I got back home around eleven, and it finally dawned on me why everyone was smiling. With being so worried about Whitey, I had totally forgotten.

"Happy birthday!" everyone yelled as I walked into the kitchen from the carport.

I grinned as I watched Mama light the nine small candles atop the orange cake. I'm not sure why, but when I was four, Mama asked me what kind of cake I wanted for my birthday. I thought a second and said, "I want an orange cake with orange icing and orange ice cream."

That became the tradition, and every year since, that was what I had. No matter how bad times were for us, no matter how little money Mama had, she always made sure to celebrate each of our birthdays with our favorite cake and ice cream.

"Make a wish," Julene said, "and blow out the candles."

I could only think of one thing to wish for—that Whitey would be okay. I blew out the candles, and we all ate orange cake with orange icing and orange sherbet.

After we ate, Mama gave me two wrapped presents, and my sisters all brought me a handmade birthday card. Dinky's card just had scribbles, and I was not sure if it was in English. Neenah's had a big heart with the words: "Happy Birthday. Love You." Julene's card was made from thicker paper and actually folded like a real greeting card. On the cover was written "Happy Birthday" with each neatly printed letter in a different color.

"It's kind of a cross between a birthday card and get-well-soon card," Julene said.

I opened it and saw a short stick figure standing beside a dog with stick legs. The dog was white and had a brown spot on one eye. Above the art were the words "Happy Birthday, Neal" and "Get Well, Whitey."

I looked it over carefully. "So, the kid with the hole in the swollen hand is me?"

Julene popped me on the back of my head. "That's a baseball and glove."

I chuckled and rubbed my head. "Oh, okay." Sitting there looking at all those smiling faces and those homemade birthday cards, I felt there was one thing that was abundantly clear—I was definitely the only artist in the family.

❖

As the days passed, we got to know a lot of the kids in the neighborhood. One day, the gang took me and my two older sisters to their clubhouse. It was through the woods in a small meadow. It was basically a wooden shed weathered gray by Father Time and smelled of burlap sacks. The flat roof served as a deck, and there was a ladder fixed onto one side. It was awesome.

Among the group was a set of brothers, five in total, by the name of Butler. Ronnie was the oldest at fifteen, and they were all wild as bucks. All of them had long blond hair that was almost white and ghost-blue eyes, and I never saw any of them wear a shirt.

"We're going back to the house," Julene said as she and Neenah walked away.

"Okay," I said. I was enjoying being on the roof. It felt forbidden and powerful.

Soon, others left and only three of us remained standing there on top of the clubhouse: me, Ronnie, and a boy my age named Marty. We were the same age, but very different by personality. Every kid I ever met not from Sand Mountain seemed more worldly and knowledgeable than me but somehow weaker. I just figured it was a tradeoff.

"I have an idea," Ronnie said. "Let's play a game."

I noticed Marty's eyes lower.

"Neal, you can go first. Follow me. Marty, you wait up here, and no peeking."

I followed Ronnie off the ladder and into the clubhouse. Sunlight squeezed through the cracks in the ceiling. I had a strange sensation but didn't understand why. I just stood there staring at the older boy. Having my Mama's facial features, I tend to look angry and my mouth droops when I'm concentrating, and I think that worried Ronnie.

"You're not goanna tell anyone about our clubhouse, are you, like your dad?"

What an odd question. Was this part of the game? I hardly ever talked to Daddy about anything, but I didn't answer.

Ronnie looked unsure. "You don't know what we're doing, do you?"

I shook my head.

"That's okay. Just pull your pants down and make groaning noises."

This game was getting stupider. But I pulled my pants down after he did and tried to mimic his sounds. We did this for five minutes before we pulled our pants back up.

"Okay, go back up and send Marty down. And remember, no peeking."

I did and watched Marty climb down and enter. A moment later, I heard them making the same noises. This game made no sense at all. Never one to follow the rules, I quietly knelt down and peered through one of the cracks.

They both had their pants down, but Marty was lying face-down on the dirt floor and Ronnie was facedown on top of him. His naked buttocks were the only things moving, repeatedly and quickly going from a normal rounded appearance to both cheeks sinking into huge concavities. What the heck was I witnessing? I had no idea but decided this game was no fun, so I climbed down and went home.

❖

The summer passed, and Neenah and I started school at Coosa Middle School. It was huge compared to Sylvania. And I was shocked to learn that, unlike Sylvania, everyone was not white. There were a lot of Black students. I was deliberate about using the word "Black" because I could never bring myself to use the word Daddy used. In fact, none of the things Daddy had told me about Black people seemed to be accurate.

Not long after we started school, we packed up and said goodbye to the mansion. Apparently, rent, like utilities, is expected to be paid every month. Tyrants.

We moved into a trailer only a few blocks from the middle school. I liked it too, but a few months later, we lost electricity. Nothing we weren't used to.

One day, Uncle Jerry came to visit by himself and hugged us all. We never knew when he would show up, where he was currently living, or what he was currently doing. But we were always glad to see him. Then, he and Daddy sat at the table.

"Dark in here, isn't it?" Uncle Jerry asked.

Daddy gave him the pissed-off look.

"Oh, okay," Uncle Jerry said. "Hey, let me show you something."

I followed Daddy and Uncle Jerry around to the side of the mobile home where the electric meter was located. Uncle Jerry took a lighter and heated the little plastic lock until he could work the thin wire loose. He opened the glass shield. "Watch this."

Daddy and I both watched.

Uncle Jerry moved some wires around and closed the shield. "See that?"

"What?" Daddy asked.

Uncle Jerry pointed to the little flat disc that rotates in conjunction with your power usage. "It's running backwards."

It really was. Instead of going in a clockwise spin, it was going counterclockwise.

"And the numbers won't move," Uncle Jerry added.

We walked back inside and saw that all the power was on. We were all very happy. Uncle Jerry knew how to do everything.

❖

Time passed, and Christmas morning came. Julene did her duties and woke us all up very early. She handed me a long, heavy wrapped present from under the tree, which I eagerly tore open. It was an awesome gift: a Bear bow with a set of arrows. It was a large fiberglass recurve bow, thirty-pound pull, and bright yellow. I had never seen anything so magnificent.

"Nice gift," Julene said. The sarcasm was not subtle.

For some reason, my Christmas and birthday gifts were always superior in scale and cost compared to the ones my sisters got. It embarrassed me a little and made me feel bad. The only thing that could have made nine-year-old me feel worse was being somebody not getting the best items.

I was still trying to get the string on when Mama and Daddy got up.

"Let me show you how." Daddy placed one end of the bow between his legs and behind his left calf, bent it into a curve, and slipped the string on easily. Then, he removed the string and handed the bow to me. "Now, you do it."

You would think with clear instructions and a live demonstration, I would have been able to do it easily. You'd be wrong.

Daddy snatched it from me and did it again. Then, his eyes lit up as if he had thought of the cure for cancer. "Come on, kids. I'll show you something."

Julene, Neenah, and I followed him outside. He had us stand at the base of a tall poplar tree in the front yard. There must have been a thousand arrow blockers—uh, I mean limbs on this tree.

"Watch this," Daddy said. It's amazing how many of his sentences began with those very words. He placed an arrow in the bow, pointed it straight up, pulled it back, and released. "Wow! It's almost out of sight."

We had to take his word. We couldn't see anything from our position.

The arrow came down about twenty feet away by the side of the road. Daddy gathered it and took his position to go again. I'm pretty sure Daddy did this with every bow he ever held. He pulled back and fired another wooden missile into the air.

Suddenly, the front door to our mobile home flew open and Dinky came running out, smiling and eager to join in on the fun. The sight of our little sister running through the live firing range sent chills through our bodies.

"Stop!" we all screamed in unison.

It must have scared that little five-year-old half to death, because her smile disappeared and she froze in her tracks, even her arms stopped mid-swing. A nanosecond after she came to a stop, the arrow came back to earth a mere inch in front of her little pug nose and stuck in the ground right between her feet.

We all stood there in disbelief at what had just happened and, more importantly, what had almost happened.

Daddy was furious. His quick glance to those of us under the tree told us everything we needed to know. In short, this was the second time we almost killed our sister. Daddy marched straight toward us clutching at his belt buckle.

Neenah started crying. Dang, she was smart.

For the most part, however, life in Rome wasn't bad. The trailer we lived in was old and smelled like sweaty socks, but at least it still had one of those special rooms with a commode. We had to learn all of Daddy's new hiding places from where he liked to pounce and yell out a blood-curdling scream, which would then be matched by our own version.

By the time baseball season came around, we had been in Rome about eight months, so I had plenty of friends. I joined a team called the Dodgers. They used pitching machines over here, which was really neat.

For some reason, the coach tried me out at shortstop, and it was a fit. I was having a banner year, and Daddy was very proud. The coach's son, Brady, played third base. My neighbor, Broadway Joe, played second base.

My entire family, even my baby brother, came to all my games. On the way to one game, I had the strangest idea. I'm not sure if it was because the coach had one or because I had seen some movie stars with one.

"Daddy?" I asked. "Will you grow a mustache?"

Daddy laughed. "Why?" He always stayed clean-shaven. I had never even seen him with a five o'clock shadow. He didn't go in for facial hair or hair over his ears. You know, hippie stuff.

"I just want to see how it looks."

"Me too," Neenah said.

"Can you even grow one?" Julene asked.

Daddy laughed, but it was a valid question. Besides getting the Native American features like dark eyes, dark hair, and darker complexion from his Mama's side, Daddy had no hair at all on his chest. We all knew that well, because he rarely wore a shirt around the house, even when we had relatives over.

"I'll tell you what, Neal. You hit a home run tonight, I'll grow one."

I smiled really big. "Deal."

We were playing the Bulldogs at their field, which was right beside their school. Like a lot of the fields we played on, there was no fence across the outfield. But at this field, left field joined up against a very tall chain-link fence that went around the school building.

I came up to bat for the first time and stared down the pitching machine, I guess, to intimidate it. A player played the position of the pitcher, but he simply stood beside the machine. The coach for the team at bat put the baseball in the machine each time.

The ball came speeding toward home plate, and I connected. Much to my and everyone else's surprise watching the game, the ball soared way over the head of the kid in left field and dropped into the schoolyard. I repeated that feat twice more during the game for three home runs.

Daddy kept his word and grew a mustache. It was a good time for all of us. As long as I played well, Daddy seemed content, because that was a reflection on him, and he made sure everyone in hearing range knew that I was his son.

After the last game of the season, the coach shared some news. "What a season. We finished tied for first place with the Bears. That means we will have a playoff game next week to see who will be number one."

We all knew that was important because the team in first place got to send more players to the all-star game.

"Neal won't be able to make it," Daddy said.

I don't know who was more devastated, me or the coach.

"My company is holding a convention in Knoxville."

I was confused. Daddy's company held a convention every year, and he never went. I knew I couldn't say anything though. Luckily, my coach did.

"Neal can stay with us."

Mama and Daddy agreed. So, when the rest of my family was headed to Knoxville, they dropped me off at my coach's house. I was more than a tad nervous. I had never stayed overnight anywhere except at a cousin's house. But I surely didn't want to miss the playoff game, so here I was for the next three days and nights.

No one ever knows what goes on behind closed doors of any family, and I was in for the shock of my life. Brady was an only child, and that first night at supper, the weirdest thing happened.

"How was your day, son?" Coach asked.

"It was great, Daddy. Me and Neal rode bikes and played basketball."

"That's great. Hey, why don't I take you fellows fishing tomorrow?"

"Yes!" Brady was so excited that he knocked over his glass of milk.

I cringed, waiting on the inevitable. But it didn't come. Coach laughed. He laughed.

"Don't get too excited," his mama said while also laughing and cleaning up the mess.

All three days went like that. Coach had real conversations with Brady and never once raised his voice and certainly never whipped him, not even a spanking. Even when I wet the bed every night, just like I did at home, it brought no repercussions.

I never told any of the guys about the bizarre thing I had witnessed. I liked Coach and didn't want anyone thinking less of him.

CHAPTER TWELVE

TRIAL AND ERROR

1963

W ell, someone's feeling better," Boots said as she and Esther walked into Travis and Hazel's house in Rainsville and saw the checkerboard set up on a wobbly table beside the small bed in the living room.

Pete was staying with them after leaving the hospital. He sat upright, his legs dangling over the side of the bed. A recent shave left his face fresh and clean, but he looked thin. An open button on his flannel pajama top revealed a protruding collarbone.

"How are you feeling, Daddy?" Esther asked.

"Still weak," he replied, studying the board.

Boots nodded. "That's what spending a month in the hospital will do to you."

Travis sat back down at the board. "Did you touch any of my pieces?"

Esther laughed. "Y'all take this game too seriously."

Boots wasn't laughing. "Travis, can we talk to you outside?"

He got up and followed them out on the porch. "What is it?"

"We talked with the sheriff," Boots said.

"And?"

"He said the prosecutor is charging Daddy with murder."

"What!? That's a load of shit." He turned and looked off into the distance. "Hell, Buck was there. He knows Raymond had a steel rod. It was self-defense."

Esther nodded. "Still, he says we need to get a lawyer."

Travis shook his head, ignoring that part. "Have either of you talked with Ilene?"

"Some," Boots answered.

"You call her and tell her we need to have a family meeting." He looked at Esther. "See if she can be at your house Saturday at noon."

"Okay, Travis," Esther said.

Travis walked back into the house and continued the game, never letting on to his daddy about the pending murder charges. He understood his father's temper all too well and had a pretty good idea that killing Raymond was, in the moment, his intent. But still, he felt like it was his duty as a son to try to protect the old man from prison.

Saturday, he drove down to Fort Payne and went to Esther's house. Esther, Boots, and Ilene were sitting around the kitchen table, each with a cup of coffee. Travis grabbed a chair and joined them.

"How's Daddy?" Ilene asked. She had not seen him since the day of the shooting.

Travis nodded. "He's doing well. Healing fast."

Several seconds of silence passed. The three sisters stared into their drinks, twirled the mugs slowly, and waited for their brother to explain why he brought them together.

"I've been thinking about the best way to move forward," Travis said. "And I have thought of a way to make this go away."

The sisters' heads snapped up. They looked at each other with confusion in their eyes.

Travis continued. "This is going to trial." He looked specifically at Ilene. "When you get on the stand, you tell them that the gun belonged to Raymond."

Ilene's eyes opened wide. "What?"

"Yes, tell them it was Raymond's gun and he had it in the truck. When Daddy went down to talk to him, he took the gun and shot Daddy. When he realized Daddy was still alive, he tossed the gun in the dirt and took the steel rod to finish the job. That's when you picked up the gun and shot Raymond."

"But I already told them the truth," Ilene said. She slid her chair back from the table, stood up, moved over to the sink, and looked out the window. The yard behind the house was nothing but crab-grass and dandelions, but she couldn't help but replay the scene in her mind's eye. She saw Raymond again with the rod marching toward her daddy and then on the ground and her daddy with the gun at his chest. She closed her eyes tight against the memory as Travis kept talking.

"I know. But you'll explain that you were afraid you were going to get in trouble." He turned his attention to Boots and Esther. "Y'all will testify that Ilene called you before the sheriff got there and told you the same thing, but she was scared. Y'all came up with the other story because y'all were also worried about Ilene. So, y'all told her to tell them Daddy shot Raymond and himself. We all thought Daddy would die anyway, so the story makes sense."

There was a deafening silence in the room. All the sisters, especially Ilene, felt betrayed, and they couldn't believe what was being asked of them. They felt defeated, as if they had been kicked in the gut. None of this made sense to them.

"I will make sure Daddy tells the same story," Travis added to reassure everyone. "If we all stick to this story, there's not a damn thing they can do about it."

No one said anything for a full minute. Boots got up, walked over to Ilene, and put her hands on her shoulders.

"Okay?" Travis asked.

All three half-heartedly nodded. They knew their brother's commitment to their father, and though they all understood the impossibility of Ilene hurting a fly, they also knew better than to start an argument with Travis.

Travis drove back home, knowing his sisters would comply. He was satisfied his plan would work. When he arrived, he found Hazel and Etta sitting on the couch holding each other and crying.

"Where's Daddy?" He asked, looking at the freshly made empty bed.

Hazel stood up. "They came and got him."

"Who?"

"There was a local officer and two DeKalb County deputies," Hazel answered.

Travis flew into a rage. "And you let them?" He knocked the checkerboard off the little table and chips flew everywhere. Everyone was silent as several pieces wobbled themselves to a stop.

Hazel put her hands on her hips and stood her ground. "They had a warrant. What could I do?"

Travis left the house, slammed the door behind him, drove back to Fort Payne, and went to the sheriff's department. He ignored the woman at the front desk and grunted as he marched back to the sheriff's office.

He opened the door without knocking and screamed, "What the hell have you done with my daddy?"

Buck looked up from his desk, a bit startled but not surprised. "We arrested him. You knew we were going to have to."

"I want him out," Travis insisted, slamming his fist on Buck's desk.

Buck nodded, crossing his arms, remaining calm. He knew the family and the history. Travis had a bark *and* a bite, but he was also smart enough not to get too aggressive here and now. "You just have to post bail."

"How much?" Travis asked.

"The judge hasn't set it yet, but we should know by tomorrow." Travis left the sheriff's office and drove home, furious.

His mood did not improve the following day when he learned the bail had been set at ten thousand dollars. He sat down in his kitchen and called all the brothers and sisters. No one had enough cash to put a dent in that, and none seemed willing besides. He cocked his head, looked at the paint chipping in the corner where the wall met the ceiling, and decided to try a different approach. "Do you think your daddy will help? He has land and can sign for the bail."

Hazel, who was busy at the stove, turned around fast, caught off guard. "I don't know." She knew her daddy hated Travis. They hadn't spoken in years.

Travis spent the next several minutes convincing her to try, explaining that eventually her father would be off the hook, when Pete was surely acquitted. He needed her help. His daddy needed her help. Something in his eyes, the way they softened as he pleaded, made her feel sorry for him and relent. So, the two of them went to ask.

Harley Jackson sat in his big chair listening to Travis's pleas and couldn't have cared less. He was tall, lean, and as backwoods as they came. He scratched at his white stubble on his burly jawline. He pulled a toothpick from between his teeth and said, "This has nothing to do with me. Leave me out of it."

Lela, Harley's wife and Hazel's mother, sat across the room without saying a word, but her eyes betrayed her thoughts as they bore right through Travis. Her son-in-law, as far as she was concerned, was as no-account as anyone on the mountain. He always had something up his sleeve, and it was rarely the truth.

"Please, Daddy," Hazel pleaded. "We're not asking for money. You just need to sign."

Harley shook his head. "I don't think my property is worth that."

"I know," Travis said, sitting forward on the couch, "but we thought you could ask your brother too."

Hazel pulled in a quick and quiet gasp. Travis had never mentioned that part of the plan.

Harley was shocked as well, and he scoffed at Travis's audacity. The only person in the world he hated worse than Travis was his own brother, Harvey.

But Travis was nothing if not a smooth talker. Somehow, after a few rounds about how this favor would ultimately be helping Hazel, he convinced Harley, and he and his brother signed to get Pete out.

❖

Travis picked up his father when he was released. "We're gonna need a good lawyer," he said after getting in the car.

Pete nodded and pointed through the windshield. "Let's go see William Beck. He's the only one I trust."

Mr. Beck had been a lawyer in Fort Payne for several years and was grooming his son to join and eventually take over the firm. He was soft-spoken but knew the law as well as anyone.

Travis drove there, and after a brief meeting, they hired Mr. Beck and he began working on the case.

❖

Eight months later, he called them into his office. Travis and Pete each took a seat in a faux leather chair across the desk from Mr. Beck. "The date has been set for the trial and the jury selection is going on now."

"What's the date?" Travis asked.

"March fourth." He removed his glasses and set them on the stack of papers in front of him. "The prosecutor is seeking a conviction of murder in the first degree."

Pete shifted nervously in his chair. "That's not good."

Mr. Beck shrugged. "Maybe. Maybe not. It is harder to prove. He has to not only prove you did it, but that it was your intent. Fortunately, it does leave us with the possibility that they'll offer a plea deal."

"Plea deal?" Pete asked.

Mr. Beck nodded and leaned back. "It's not uncommon for a prosecutor to offer a deal before the trial starts or even after the trial. But this needs to happen before the jury comes back with a verdict. If you plead guilty to a lesser offense—say, manslaughter—the main charge is dropped and the prosecutor still gets to chalk up a win."

Travis sat there with his arms folded across his chest. "Daddy is not pleading guilty to anything." He was sure the plan of action he set in motion with his sisters would get his father off.

❖

The day of the trial arrived. The two-story DeKalb County courtroom was packed with spectators, including the balconies overlooking the room. A hum of movement and chatter echoed off the walls. Pete sat at a table with his lawyer and the prosecutor, Matthew Hardeman, and his assistant sat at the other table. Twelve men sat in the jury section. Two of them were younger, Travis's age, cleaned up, and wearing ties. The rest were older and rugged. Pete's peers.

The bailiff spoke. "Hear ye, hear ye. This court is now in session. The honorable Judge W. J. Haralson presiding." The courtroom grew silent. "All rise."

The judge entered, took his seat, and straightened his robe. His black hair had one white streak running away from his forehead. He looked down his pink nose through a pair of thin wire-framed glasses and read from the papers in front of him. "You all may be seated." He turned to the jury. "Good morning, gentlemen. You have been selected as the jury in the matter of State of Alabama versus Pete Van Wooten. Mr. Wooten is charged with first-degree murder. He has entered a plea of not guilty to these charges. The defendant is presumed innocent until proven guilty beyond a reasonable doubt, and that burden of proof is always on the State. You must all agree on a guilty or not guilty verdict."

The members nodded in unison.

"Is the State ready to make an opening statement?"

"Yes, Your Honor." The prosecutor walked over and stood before the jury. Mr. Hardeman was young for a prosecutor, slender with slicked back hair but sharp as a tack. "Good morning, gentlemen," he began, placing his hand on the wooden rail. "We intend to prove that on the morning of August 22nd of last year, Pete Wooten willfully and deliberately shot his son-in-law, Raymond Styron, in the chest with a 16-gauge shotgun, killing him dead." He paused and let the words "killing" and "dead" sink in. "Now, you're going to learn that this was over a farming dispute. You're probably even going to hear stories about how bad a man Raymond Styron was. But in this country, we don't settle our disagreements by killing people, no matter what kind of person we perceive them to be. When everything is said and done with this trial, no matter what you think personally of the victim, one fact will remain clear, and it's a fact they won't dispute: Pete Wooten walked all the way down to where Raymond Styron was working in the field, and he carried with him a loaded shotgun, and he shot and killed Mr. Styron. We will ask you to return a verdict of guilty of murder in the first degree. Thank you." He turned and walked back to his seat, the soles of his shoes clicking against the tile floor.

The judge looked at Mr. Beck. "Sir, are you prepared to make an opening statement?"

"Yes, Your Honor." Mr. Beck stood and began speaking immediately. "Mr. Styron was not a good man. But the prosecutor is correct, that's no reason to kill a man." His arms were wide, his hands open. He looked around the room, as if arguing to the public as well as the jury. "What you're going to learn during the course of this trial is how much Mr. Wooten had already endured, how much he had already let slide from a man outright stealing from him from one hundred acres that Pete had rented himself.

"When Pete came home on the morning of August 22nd and found Raymond Styron on his own property now stealing from his personal crops, he did what any one of us would have done: he went down there to run off a trespasser and a thief."

He moved over and stood directly in front of Pete. "Yes, he carried a gun, but for protection. And it was a good thing he did. You'll learn from the sheriff's report that Raymond Styron came after Pete with a steel rod." Pause. "Ask yourself what you would have done if you found yourself in a similar situation. Would you have let a man beat you to death on your own property? Would you let a man who was trespassing on your property and stealing from you simply beat you to death with a steel rod? Or would you have done what any man in the same circumstance would have done—defend yourself? Thank you."

The judge waited for him to sit. "Is the State ready to call its first witness?"

"Yes, Your Honor. The State calls DeKalb County Coroner Hoyt Wilson."

Mr. Wilson took the stand and testified as to the nature of the wounds on both the victim and Pete.

Next, the prosecutor called the sheriff. "State your name and occupation."

"W. L. Edwards. I'm the sheriff of DeKalb County." He then told the court what he found when he got to the scene.

Mr. Beck then rose to cross-examine. "Had Mr. Wooten filed a complaint with you the morning of the incident?"

The sheriff confirmed the conversation Pete had with him that very morning.

"So, according to the defendant, Mr. Styron had already taken all the potatoes in the main field, although he hadn't kept his end of the bargain, and had not even given Mr. Wooten any money from the sale of these potatoes."

The sheriff nodded. "That was the nature of the complaint, yes."

"And did Mr. Wooten mention the ten acres behind his house?"

"Yes, he said that Mr. Styron had told him he could harvest those and keep the money."

"I see," Mr. Beck said. "And Sheriff, when you arrived on the scene, how far apart were the two men, Raymond Styron and Pete Wooten, when you found them?"

"About eight feet."

"And was Mr. Styron holding anything in his hands?"

"No."

"But there was something lying beside him, correct?"

"There was," the sheriff said. "There was a steel rod about four feet long and an inch and a half in diameter. It looked like it had come off the harvester."

"Did it appear to you that he had been holding this rod when he was shot?"

"That was my assessment, yes. And the witness, Ilene Styron, backed it up."

"No further questions, Your Honor."

After that, the prosecutor called Ilene.

Ilene walked slowly to the stand. She did not make eye contact with Travis. There were whispers in the gallery. A few members of the jury shifted in their seats.

"State your name for the record," the prosecutor said.

"Ilene Wooten Styron."

"You are the widow of Raymond Styron?"

"Yes."

"How long were you married?"

"Twelve years."

"Did you know about the agreement between your father and husband?"

"Yes. I knew they agreed to plant one hundred acres of potatoes in a rented field and the ten acres behind Daddy's house and split the profits."

"So," the prosecutor said, "the ten acres behind your father's house was part of the deal?"

Ilene paused. "Uh . . . yes, I believe so."

"That morning, you went to the field behind your father's house with your husband. Is that correct?"

"Yes."

"Did you think you were doing anything wrong?"

"I didn't at the time."

The prosecutor paused. "Okay, tell us exactly what happened that morning." The only sound heard was a soft rain falling outside.

Travis held back a smile. He couldn't wait to see the look on the prosecutor's face when Ilene told him she was the one who shot Raymond.

Ilene took a deep breath. "I was standing by the truck while Raymond was on the tractor. Daddy came out of his house with a shotgun."

That wasn't the story. Travis almost jumped out of his seat.

Ilene continued. "He walked down to where Raymond was plowing and told him to leave. He pointed the gun at him. When Raymond got off the tractor, he grabbed the rod, and that's when Daddy shot him."

"And what happened after that?" The prosecutor turned and stared at the jury.

"Daddy turned the gun on himself and fired the second shot."

The prosecutor let that sink in. "Was it to make it look like self-defense?"

"Objection, Your Honor," Mr. Beck said. "The witness can't possibly know what another person is thinking."

"Sustained."

"Very well," the prosecutor said. "Why do you think he shot himself?"

"I don't know," Ilene said, shaking her head. "Maybe he felt remorse."

"No further questions, Your Honor."

Travis tightened his fists in his lap.

Under cross-examination, Ilene admitted to learning that Raymond had cheated her dad.

Travis became more incensed when Boots and Esther both testified that Ilene had told them exactly the same story right after it happened. His temples pounded. He couldn't believe they had all betrayed him, betrayed their own father. Never mind the truth; his story would have worked.

After the prosecutor rested his case, the judge adjourned until the following day.

The next morning, the judge brought the court to order and called on Mr. Beck. "The defense may call its first witness."

Mr. Beck called several witnesses, anyone who had firsthand knowledge of the agreement between Pete and Raymond: the guy who rented Pete the land, the neighbor where Pete went several times to call Raymond, and the guy who had loaned Pete his tractor to do all the work Raymond was supposed to do. He was successful in painting a picture of Raymond not keeping his end of the bargain when it came to the work or the money.

After lunch, Mr. Beck called Travis.

Travis, angry he was left to try to undo the mistakes his sisters had made, told story after story of Raymond being a liar and a cheat. The prosecutor objected many times, saying it had no bearing on this case, but the judge allowed it.

Mr. Beck continued. "When you first spoke to your father in the hospital, what did he tell you?"

"He said he just wanted to scare Raymond off, but that Raymond jumped off the tractor and grabbed the steel rod. He rushed Daddy, yelling he was going to kill him."

"He said those words, that he was going to kill your father?"

"Yes." Travis was lying through his teeth. He looked over at his sister, who was sitting in the first row behind the defense table. "Ilene told me the same thing the next day, that Raymond yelled he was going to kill Daddy."

"What did your father say when you asked him why he shot himself?"

Travis lied more. "He said he felt so bad for having to shoot his daughter's husband in self-defense, he couldn't live with it."

"Thank you. No further questions."

"Would you like to cross-examine?" the judge asked the prosecutor.

He was dying to. He stood up and straightened his tie. "Are you sure Ilene told you that Raymond shouted what you claim? Because she never said anything like that to me during the deposition or here on the stand. It's not in the sheriff's report either."

"I'm sure."

"You realize you're under oath, sir?"

Travis's face turned red. Well, redder than normal. "Are you calling me a liar?" It was well known on Sand Mountain that you did not call Travis Wooten a liar. It's not that he was honest by any means. In fact, his motto in life seemed to be "why tell the truth when a lie will do." But he still didn't cotton to being called a liar.

After Travis testified, the judge adjourned until the next morning.

The next day, against the advice of Mr. Beck, Pete took the stand. He was still angry about the whole situation. He wanted the opportunity to tell his side of the story, how badly he had been wronged, how he had to take matters into his own hands.

"What were your intentions when you walked down to where Mr. Styron was harvesting potatoes on your property?" Mr. Beck asked.

"I just wanted to scare him off," he said to the men of the jury. "He had already cheated me out of my money on the big field, and he had told me I could have this small field."

"And when you told him to leave, that's when he grabbed the steel rod and came at you?"

"Yes."

"Did he say he was going to kill you?"

Pete hesitated before answering. "I don't remember, but I was certain I was about to die."

After Mr. Beck finished, the prosecutor took over.

"Mr. Wooten, do you keep loaded guns in the house?"

"No."

"So, you had to load both barrels before you went down there. Is that correct?"

"I guess."

"Why?" the prosecutor asked. "If your plan was simply to scare him, the mere sight of the shotgun would have sufficed, don't you think?"

"I don't know."

"You were angry that morning when you saw Mr. Styron in that field, weren't you?"

"Yes."

"You say he rushed you?"

"Yes, he did."

The prosecutor shook his head. "What kind of a person rushes a man with a shotgun?" He didn't give Pete time to answer. "Would you rush a man pointing a shotgun at you?"

"I don't know."

"Did you yell for him to stop?"

"No."

"Did you fire a warning shot?"

"No."

"After you shot him dead, you panicked, didn't you? Is that why you shot yourself?

"I . . . I don't . . . It happened so fast. I was upset."

The prosecutor continued. "This man had, according to you, made you do all the work and then stole from you. Right?"

"Yes." His face began to flush.

"You were angry about that, weren't you? You were angry enough to go to the sheriff to lodge a complaint, right?"

"Yes."

"What did the sheriff do to get you your money?"

Pete was becoming more and more agitated. "Not a goddamn thing."

"So, you decided to take the law into your own hands, didn't you?'

"No, I—"

"If this man was as bad as you say, do you think scaring him off for one day would end it?'

"I don't know," he yelled.

"You didn't want him scared, did you, Mr. Wooten? You wanted him dead."

Pete sat there breathing heavily but didn't answer.

"We're waiting on an answer. You wanted this man who had conned you and cheated you dead, didn't you?"

Pete looked down and shook his head. "No . . . no."

"No further questions, Your Honor."

After the prosecutor and Mr. Beck delivered their closing statements, the jury was excused to go to the deliberating room. It was eleven A.M.

"We'll recess for lunch," Judge Haralson said.

Travis looked around for his sisters, but they had all left. He and Pete went to Mr. Beck's office and waited there.

"What now?" Travis asked.

"We go back after lunch," Mr. Beck answered, "and hope the jury is not sitting in there."

"Why?" Pete asked.

Mr. Beck explained. "The rule of thumb is, the longer a jury takes to make a decision, the better for the defense."

Travis's heart sank when they returned to the courtroom and saw that the jury was present.

The judge brought the court to order. "Has the jury reached a decision?"

The foreman stood. "We have, Your Honor."

"What say you?"

"We, the jury, find the defendant, Pete Van Wooten, guilty of murder in the first degree."

A wave of noise moved around the room, skirts ruffled, people coughed, tongues clicked.

Judge W. J. Haralson dismissed the jury. "Will the defendant please rise?"

Pete and Mr. Beck stood.

"You have been found guilty by a jury of your peers," the judge said. "We'll meet again in one month for sentencing."

Pete stayed incarcerated for that month. His children couldn't swing the bail this time. A month later, he stood in front of the judge again.

"Do you have anything to say before sentencing, Mr. Wooten?"

Pete looked genuinely contrite, possibly for the first time in his life. His eyes were sad; his shoulders sagged under the weight of his arms. "Just that I'm sorry, Your Honor. I wish I could turn back the clock. I never meant for any of this to happen."

"I'm inclined to believe you," the judge said. "I'm not sure what your intentions were that morning, but I'm convinced you did not plan this out before then. With that in mind, I'm reducing the charge to manslaughter and sentencing you to serve ten years in the state penitentiary."

CHAPTER THIRTEEN

RAISING CANE

1975

Y ou're not even trying!"
   Ah, yes, it was good to be back living in our tiny house on Sand Mountain where the neighbors were too far away to hear Daddy yelling. Rome was okay, but the houses seemed so close together. It seemed interesting at first, but for a mountain boy used to the wide-open spaces, it became smothering. I guess Daddy felt the same. So, after a year, we moved back home. Of course, I knew I would forever miss that indoor plumbing.

The shack was not holding up well to time at all. Daddy had never added trim around the eaves, leaving the house open to weather and varmints. The cheap plywood and cheaper roofing were deteriorating quickly. But like our automobiles, maintenance was never forthcoming.

I'm not sure why Daddy kept trying to teach me how to play checkers. I mean, I could play with other kids for fun, but for

Daddy, it wasn't meant to be fun. When you see those old-timers in front of the mom-and-pop stores or in the park staring at a checkerboard, it's not for fun. It's not a game to them. It's an exercise in strategic warfare.

"You have to look four moves ahead," Daddy said, getting more and more angry.

He must have told me that a hundred times over the years. What a joke. I didn't know what my next move was going to be, much less my next four.

Daddy could never understand how I couldn't pick up on things easily and do them exactly like he did. In his mind, my lack of skill was intentional, a slap in the face. He was from the old school of management and *knew* that the longer and louder you yelled at someone, the faster they would catch on. It didn't matter if it was throwing horseshoes, playing checkers, splitting wood, hammering a nail, or whatever. And I dare you to say "hit me" during a game of blackjack when you have a face card and a three and he, as the dealer, has a five turned up. Seriously, I dare you.

I knew this would pass, as it always did, after I would screw up enough for him to realize that something wasn't suddenly going to click and put me instantly on his level.

"Just forget it." He got up and walked away.

Whew. That's life, though. You take the good with the bad.

Later that day, we were due for some good times. Julene, Neenah, and I went with our Jackson cousins to go swim in the coal mines. This was one of my favorite things to do.

Unlike in West Virginia, coal on Sand Mountain is shallow enough that you can just dig down to it. After the bulk of the coal is removed, they simply leave these huge dugout pits in the ground, which eventually fill with rain and turn into beautiful little lakes with crystal-clear sapphire water. That didn't take long, since Sand

Mountain, with the exception of the Gulf Coast, gets more rainfall than any other part of Alabama.

Older people on the mountain often warned us the water wasn't safe and could cause brain damage, so of course that made us want to swim there even more.

These areas were called "reclaimed coal mines," because after the valuable coal was gone, the land reverted to the owners. The Tennessee Valley Authority would send reps to all the landowners with an offer to buy the mineral rights. That gave the power company the ability to test your property for coal. If they found any coal, or gold, or uranium, or whatever, they owned it. If they found nothing, you kept the free money.

Daddy couldn't sign fast enough. They drilled in several places around our thirty acres but only found a few inches of coal, which wasn't worth the expense to dig out. Daddy laughed all the way to the bank. Free money. What could be better?

A few days later, we did one of my other favorite things. We all piled into the car, including my little brother, Breland, who was now over a year old and walking, and headed to Uncle Roy's. I was ready. We had not been since we took Whitey, and since they had no phone and apparently no mailbox, I had no way to know if he even survived.

I'm not sure why we never visited when we lived in Georgia. This was the longest we had ever gone between visits. I assumed it was because Rome was twice as far away from Rising Fawn as our home on the mountain.

It was a typical trip with Mama and Daddy enjoying the panoramic view of the countryside, constantly scanning the scenery all around. This trip we drove through Henagar and off the mountain into Trenton. I guess Daddy could never figure out which was his favorite route.

We went off the mountain on the curvy road and stopped at a small store so Daddy could buy cigarettes and gas. My sister Neenah and I walked inside. We never had money to buy anything, but we always enjoyed seeing the sights.

As Neenah and I walked down one aisle, someone suddenly whistled. You know, *that* whistle guys make at attractive women. We spun around, but no one was there. Looking at each other, we started to walk on, but it happened again. We spun around again.

The only living thing we could see was a crow in a birdcage.

"Do you think?" Neenah asked.

"Can't be."

We walked over to the big black bird and stared at it. I could tell by the beak and small markings on the head that it wasn't a crow. It whistled again. We laughed so hard.

"That's a miner bird."

We looked around and saw the store owner.

"A miner bird?" Neenah asked.

"Yep. Sounds like a person, doesn't it?"

We both nodded.

"Let's go," Daddy called out.

We got back in the car and couldn't stop talking about that crazy bird. I wasn't sure if it was called a miner bird because it wasn't a grownup or because people used them to work in the coal mines. But it sure was neat.

As we passed the little store in the curve a mile from our destination, Daddy was staring intensely at the rearview mirror. "Goddammit. Can you tell?"

Mama looked in her sideview mirror, then turned and looked out through the back. "I can't see."

I poked my head up and looked too, although I knew this went against road-trip etiquette. I could see a black car far behind us.

Daddy was concentrating so hard he missed the turn.

"Daddy, you missed the road," Julene said.

"Hush."

Daddy continued a mile down the road and pulled off to the side into a graveled area. The car passed. It was a family with three kids in the back seat. Daddy mumbled under his breath and turned back.

As we pulled into Uncle Roy's yard, I saw him. He looked healthy and fat. I jumped out of the car and ran to the porch. "Hey, Whitey. How are you doing, boy?"

Uncle Roy came out with his normal big smile. "He's doing just fine. He healed up well."

Whitey was almost bouncing he was so happy. It was obvious he remembered me, but did he remember everything?

"Sit."

He sat.

"Shake."

He extended a paw.

Uncle Roy patted me on the head. "I didn't know he could do that."

We spent the better part of the day there, and as always, it was great. Whitey wasn't the only thing that had grown. My tree, and Neenah's and Julene's, had grown a lot. Dinky was now six, so it was time to initiate her to the tradition of walking around the large rock structure in the woods beside Uncle Roy's place.

"Don't fall inside," I said, giving her the same talk Julene had given me. "There's monsters under the leaves in the middle waiting for kids to fall in." I looked back to see her scared reaction, but she was already halfway back to the house screaming and yelling. Oh, crap. I knew what that meant.

I hopped off the wall and waited. I didn't have to wait long. Daddy came walking at a brisk pace taking off his belt as he strolled.

Dinky wasn't yet familiar with the code. Julene and Neenah would walk through hot coals to fight a giant fire-breathing dragon with a thumbtack to keep Daddy from whipping me. Little Dinky would sell me out in a heartbeat.

Okay, so other than a few hiccups, it was a great visit.

When I went back inside, Uncle Roy was sitting at the kitchen table wearing weird glasses. I had never seen him wear glasses before. I walked up beside him.

"Uncle Roy is working," Mama said. "Come in here."

"It's okay. He can stay." He smiled and nodded his head toward the seat beside him.

I sat and watched quietly. On the table was the gold casing to a pocket watch, the insides were sprawled out in front of Uncle Roy like puzzle pieces. Little cogs and springs lay everywhere. He had a small set of tools also on the table and carefully picked up each tiny piece and inspected it closely; he then straightened and cleaned it, meticulously putting the entire thing back together, situating it back inside the frame, and clicking the glass back into place.

"This is the crystal," he said. The light coming from the windows refracted off the clear covering and made the watch shine like new.

I was mesmerized.

He wound the clock and placed it to his ear. "Perfect."

"Where did you learn to do that?

He pointed to the side of his head. "Where I learned how to do everything."

"I wish I could do that."

He smiled. "You can do anything you put your mind to, son. You're smart and very coordinated."

I grinned. Uncle Roy was a big BS-er, but you had to love him.

❖

On the way home that day, Daddy saw something at an old farm that caught his eye. It was a FOR-SALE sign in front of what appeared to be a pile of rusted scrap.

The next day, he took me back over there and bought all the stuff. It took us several trips with Daddy's old pulpwood truck to haul it all home. On the way back home with the last load, I asked the obvious.

"What is all this stuff?"

Daddy smiled. "It's from an old syrup mill. This is how they used to make syrup in the old days. I worked at one when I was a little older than you. This is a moneymaker."

That's another phrase I had heard from Daddy many times over the years. Daddy could make some good money doing just about anything from selling cookware, pulpwood, or tomatoes and okra, but it came in spurts and never lasted long. But it wasn't enough for him to make a bunch of money here and there; he was always looking for the big score. That ever-elusive, life-changing pot of gold.

If Mama had not always kept a steady job at the hosiery mill, we would never have had lunch money every day at school. Julene told me once that we qualified for free lunches, but Daddy was too proud to let us sign up for them.

I never understood why we didn't take advantage of things we qualified for, but he was that way with everything. Granny Jackson, who lived on the same dirt road as we did, got the subsidy cheese every month, cut about two inches off for herself, and gave us the rest. Man, that cheese was good.

At least Mama could use coupons. I went with her to Finley's Grocery one day, the little store in Sylvania, and she paid with this funny-looking money. I first thought it was Monopoly money.

Pete Finley, the cashier and owner of the store, actually gave her real money back. Pete was a pleasant man with thinning hair and small wire glasses. He was probably too nice for his own good, often extending credit to local farmers beyond what he should.

"What kind of money is that?" I asked confused.

"Oh," Mama said, "it's . . . uh . . . coupons."

On the way home that day, Mama mentioned them again. "Don't tell anyone about the coupons, especially your daddy. Okay?"

"I won't." And I never did. I also never told anyone about seeing Mama put a pack of cookies in her purse instead of the cart. But I understood. Cookies were an important item. Daddy didn't like it when Mama came home from the store without them.

We arrived at home with the wonderful syrup-making equipment and unloaded all that junk way back at the edge of the woods behind the house.

"This is where we'll build the mill," Daddy said.

I nodded.

That evening at supper, Daddy couldn't stop talking about it. "Do you know how many people eat sorghum syrup? Just about everybody. When we get the mill going, we'll start bringing in so much money. We'll probably have to buy trucks just to ship it all."

"That sounds great," Mama said. She had learned the hard way to not even ask logical questions like "Where will you plant the sugarcane? Who will do the work? Have you done any market research?" Questions like that were perceived as doubting the validity of the plan, and Daddy didn't care for having his brilliance critiqued.

Mama's brother, Doodle, owned a stretch of land that ran beside and almost the length of our dirt road. He had cleared it years ago but had never yet planted anything there. Daddy secured that land for his sugarcane.

I had hoped our farming was over for the year. Daddy always planted fields of tomatoes and fields of okra. Over some years, he would throw in some corn and watermelons too. We would haul it to the Chattanooga Curb Market to sell.

Daddy never really seemed like a farmer to me and was certainly out of place among them. It wasn't just the way he dressed but also the way he talked. The way he thought.

One day at the market, a frail old gentleman in faded overalls was explaining the good old days to Daddy. "In my day, you could work one day and make enough money to buy a brand-new pair of overalls."

"Really?" Daddy asked, never one to simply agree and let it go. "And how long did you have to work?"

The old farmer beamed with pride. "Sunup to sundown."

Daddy nodded. "Well, today you only have to work eight hours and can make enough to buy three pairs of brand-new overalls."

The old fellow was not near the size of my daddy but suddenly seemed smaller still. He couldn't find the words to respond, so he slowly turned and walked away, I assumed in search of a more understanding conversationalist.

Daddy certainly didn't shy away from work, just supervised work. I guess that's why farming appealed to him.

Me, I hated every second of it, especially okra. The only thing worse than picking it was eating it. Most people on the mountain will argue that you cut okra, you don't pick it. But that was too slow for Daddy. He taught me how to pinch the stem behind the spear and snap it quickly. The best okra, or so I was told, was the small tender spears, so picking it when the plants were still small made for the best crop. It also made for the most pain as bending over all day was murder on the back.

But I hated all of it. The miracle of nature had long lost its wonder to me.

One Saturday morning, Daddy woke me very early. "Neal, get up. Let's go to work."

I cleared my eyes and looked up at him. School had already started back, and I only enjoyed waking on Saturday mornings to the smell of breakfast. But I knew better than to argue.

We walked to the field. Daddy already had the turning plow hooked up to the tractor. "You plow, and I'll go pick up the cane sprouts."

"Okay."

He pointed to the horizon, which was a mixture of morning pinks and blues and dark ominous clouds. "Let's get it done before the storm gets here."

Thunderstorms were as common on the mountain as sunshine. Sometimes, the rains came soft and lasted for days. These were called ground-soaking rains. More often than not, however, the rains came with angry clouds, pounding the ground violently and packing the dirt so hard you couldn't hoe it. Every ditch transformed into raging rapids, and these storms would disappear almost as soon as they began. At 1,500 feet above sea level, we never worried about biblical-type flooding on the mountain, but flash floods were a constant threat. And every kind of rain, soft or hard, retained the option of bringing their tornado cousins with them.

I actually liked plowing. Daddy had a large H-model Farmall tractor with all the plows and even a bushhog. It was the first tractor we ever owned with hydraulics. I did not miss the days of getting to the end of a row and having to grab a long arm and pull with all my might to lift the plow. How he ended up with such a valuable piece of machinery was a feat in itself.

Daddy was a master at trading. Believe it or not, it all started with a small fiberglass boat he bought for two hundred dollars. It was dark pink, and even the seats were fiberglass. It had a thirty horsepower Johnson motor.

He traded even for a 1949 Chevrolet ton-and-a-half truck, which had a starter button on the floor where the light dimmer switch was on our car. He took the back off and added metal runners and wooden poles on the corners so we could haul pulpwood to town.

He traded that in an even trade for a 1959 two-ton flatbed.

Next, he traded even for a small A-model Farmall tractor with all the attachments.

Then, he met an old widow whose husband had died recently. The H-model he owned was too large for her to handle, and she loved Daddy's little A-model. They traded evenly.

That's how Daddy ended up with two hundred dollars in five thousand dollars' worth of farming equipment.

After we got the field turned, disced, and the rows plowed, Daddy showed me how to plant sugarcane.

"Take a clump of sprouts and break away three or four stalks like this. Then, lay them down in the row on their side. Lay the next one at the end of this one and keep going."

"Okay," I said. "Sounds easy enough." And it was. It was a lot easier than throwing horseshoes or playing checkers correctly.

It took us all weekend to lay them all out. By Sunday evening, I was ready to go back to school. And I hated school.

The months passed, and the sprouts began to grow. I was glad to learn there was nothing to do until time to harvest. I stared at the field every day as the school bus drove us past it watching those green stalks getting taller. But it worried me too. I knew we'd have to start building the mill now. I kept waiting for Daddy to wake me one weekend morning to start on that, but he never did.

❖

Christmastime came, and I *loved* Christmas. Daddy woke me one morning to go cut down a tree. I carried the ax. It had snowed the night before, a rarity on the mountain, but we loved it.

"Look at that," Daddy said pointing to the ground. "You know what that is?"

I looked at the tracks. "Bobcat?"

Daddy nodded. "Yep. And here's some deer tracks."

The snow was like a road map of all the creatures living in the woods. We saw deer, bobcat, rabbit, possum, and I think bear, Bigfoot, and alien tracks.

"We'll try to find a nice pine," Daddy said as we walked.

That was our MO every year. We'd try to find a small pine tree with only one naked side, which we could turn toward the wall. If we couldn't find one, we'd cut down a small cedar, although they were less fun to decorate, with their prickly foliage.

"How's this one look?" Daddy asked.

I nodded. It was a decent-looking pine tree. We cut it down and drug it back to the house.

Daddy carried it inside and set it up using the old tree stand with four screws to hold the trunk; he then stood back to marvel at his own accomplishment.

Mama popped popcorn, and Julene took three needles and threaded them. We always strung popcorn to decorate the tree. Mama pulled out the box of old ornaments she'd had for years. I hadn't really picked up on the fact that we didn't have as many fruits, nuts, and candies as we normally did each year.

But at least the snow added a bonus. Even though it was only about an inch deep, Mama was able to scrape enough off the cars to make snow cream. Mama would pour milk in a bowl, add sugar and vanilla flavoring, and rake in snow until it was a creamy mix of heaven. I loved ice cream made from snow.

That night, it was tough to leave the comfort of the main room to go to bed. I wore two pairs of sweatpants and two sweatshirts and crawled under six layers of quilts and blankets. My breath billowed out a white mist as I stared at the ceiling monsters.

I fell asleep but woke sometime in the wee hours of the morning. It was still dark outside, but the pale moonlight highlighted rough edges in my room. As I lay there somewhere between consciousness and sleep, I slowly became aware of a presence. I felt something by my leg and realized I wasn't alone. Our cat had crawled under the covers with me. Oh well.

Suddenly, I had a most distressing revelation: we didn't have a cat. I could make out the bulge under the covers, feel the warmth against my calf muscles, feel the fur, feel the breathing as the creature's lungs expanded and deflated. I wanted to pull back the covers and look, but I decided this was one of those cases where ignorance really was bliss. Whatever it was just wanted to be warm. I understood that all too well. I decided to be a Southern gentleman and let it stay.

Well, to be honest, I was scared half to death.

Actually, I'm not sure which was scarier: being awake or being asleep. My nightmares were far more frightening than whatever was currently seeking refuge in my bed. I had nightmares every night. Some had become legends in my family, and they got a kick out of them like the huge, round, furry demons that chased me and a cousin up a tree in the pasture. They had huge gaping mouths with giant sharp teeth, and when we wouldn't come out of the tree, they started eating away at the trunk. They had a name—Coconuts—and I believe that as much as anything else led to my family's laughter.

I finally did drift back off, and when I woke the next morning, the critter was gone.

❖

Finally, Christmas morning came.

"Neal, get up. Hurry." Julene woke us every year before the sun came up, and we rushed to the living room, not only to see what Santa had brought but to be back in the room with heat.

I opened the flue, tossed in a couple more pieces of firewood, and made the room nice and cozy.

Julene dug under the tree and found our presents. We never had a lot of money, but every year, we got at least one decent gift.

I sat on the couch and tore away the wrapping paper on the first of two presents. It was a set of checkers, a cheap set with plastic pieces and a fold-up paper board. I had seen similar sets at the flea market for fifty cents.

I figured the expensive gift was in the larger present. I ripped away the paper. It was a denim cowboy hat. A used denim cowboy hat. In all the Westerns I had ever seen, I couldn't remember one hat made of denim. I was certain it had come from the thrift store. Plus, I only wore baseball caps. I felt like I had been kicked in the gut. I looked up to see Julene, Neenah, and Dinky with the same reactions to their equally crappy gifts.

Neenah asked the question we all were thinking. "Is this it?"

I felt so ashamed. I felt ashamed because I was so upset. I knew there were kids a lot worse off than us in the world who would have been happy with such gifts, but I still hated it. And when I say there were kids much worse off, I wasn't one hundred percent convinced of that, but that's what grownups love to say. I had seen those commercials of starving kids in Africa, so I guess it was true. I remember one that said you could clothe, feed, and educate a child in Africa for only fifty cents a day. I worried that Daddy might take advantage of that deal and send us there.

"Merry Christmas."

We all looked up to see Mama standing watching us. She seemed to force a smile. No one moved for several seconds.

Julene broke the tension. "Thanks, Mama. We love it."

That was our cue. We always looked to Julene to set the example. We followed.

"Thanks, Mama," Neenah chimed in. "It's wonderful."

"How do you like your hat?" Mama asked.

I placed it on my head and smiled really big. "It's perfect."

The rest of the day was great. None of us ever let on that we were heartbroken. Even when we had pintos for Christmas dinner instead of ham, turkey, rolls, dressing, deviled eggs, and more desserts than you could shake a stick at, we feigned contentment. But, to be honest, pintos, cornbread, fried potatoes, buttermilk, and raw onions were like heaven to me.

❖

After the holidays, we started back to school. Every day, the school bus rode by that field of sugarcane. One day, something clicked. There had to be a connection. Daddy had spent all our money trying to get his latest goldmine venture going on the old rusty equipment and an entire field of sugarcane, and I had never really been enthusiastic about it at all. In fact, I had secretly been happy that Daddy never went ahead with the project. We never built the mill, and we never harvested the cane. I never knew why. The equipment was still sitting and becoming overgrown with weeds and kudzu down by the woods. And there was the answer: somehow Santa knew my heart and punished us for it. Every day, I watched that sugarcane grow until the next spring when it started to die. It was a fitting metaphor.

CHAPTER FOURTEEN

KILBY PRISON

1963

It took less than three hours for the bus to make the trip south from Fort Payne to Kilby Penitentiary near Montgomery. Looking out the dirty window and watching the world pass by gave Pete time to reflect on everything, not just the shooting but also his childhood, his ex-wife, and his children. He wasn't angry anymore. He wasn't anything but numb.

The prison, known as Alabama's Alcatraz, was built in 1923 and named after Governor Thomas Erby Kilby, who was the governor when construction began. There were only six inmates on the bus, although it could easily carry twenty. They sat apart from each other, some with a look of nervous anticipation, others with abject fear, and still others were aloof and unflappable.

The big fenced gate pulled open, and the bus rolled inside and stopped. A tall fence ran around the entire perimeter; rolls of razor wire ran along the top and on the inside. A guard walked around the bus looking underneath, while another climbed in, looked at everyone, never spoke, and got off. Both were dressed in guard uniforms—brown slacks, tan short-sleeve shirts, name tags RHODES and MILLER, and holsters with flaps snapped up around revolvers. It was like being in a library and everyone knew the rule, without being told, that there was no talking.

The bus continued down a small, recently paved road and circled around a lookout tower that looked more inviting, like a lighthouse, than what it really was. It pulled alongside a long one-story structure that had an entrance in the middle and barred windows that ran down both sides to the ends. A longer, four-story building with more of the same windows sat parallel behind this one. Twenty-six huge round exhaust vents adorned the top of that building like giant mushrooms.

Pete counted them.

Additional buildings stood behind those, and they were spectacular steel and concrete structures with a beautiful redbrick veneer. Webbed cracks all along the beautiful façade revealed the toll that decades of time and weather had already taken. After the bus stopped at the walkway leading to the entrance of the smaller building, a tall guard stepped onto the bus. His hair was sheared close to his scalp. He didn't bother taking off his mirrored sunglasses.

"Everybody off."

Pete stood up and followed the rest down the middle aisle and off the bus.

"Line up and follow me," the guard said sternly as he started toward the entrance.

Pete was the last one in line. He looked around and noticed the armed guards on the tower, guns cradled.

Once inside, they were processed one by one. Pictures were taken and numbers assigned. Each inmate was given prison-issue clothing and told where to change. The uniform consisted of white pants, a white T-shirt, and a white button-up with ALABAMA DEPARTMENT OF CORRECTIONS stenciled on the back.

After they dressed, they were made to stand in an empty room. There too, the prison showed its age. The honey-colored paint on the walls was chipped and bubbled. A spot on the ceiling betrayed a leak of some kind, a patched water pipe, perhaps, or a broken toilet in an upper floor. An older guard came in. He was short and stout. The buttons on his shirt struggled to hold on.

"I'm Alfred Cummins," he said in a clipped, no-nonsense tone. "I'm the captain of the guards. You will refer to me as Mr. Cummins or Boss, whichever you prefer. We have over nine hundred inmates, and we operate a smooth prison here at Kilby, and we intend to keep it that way. You will learn the rules as you go. My advice—keep your head down, obey the rules, do your time, and go home."

Another younger guard led them to a room where they were issued a single gray wool blanket, one set of white sheets, and a pillow that had seen the dreams of many inmates who had come and gone. From there, they were taken directly to their assigned bunks.

Pete was surprised to see two dozen wooden bunkbeds in one large room. Men sat around on the bottom bunks and talked or played cards. He was expecting to be in a cell with bars. The room had an odor that was familiar to Pete and not unpleasant. It reminded him of the crappy shed housing at the tobacco fields. There was food cooking somewhere nearby and coffee brewing.

The guard stopped by a bed and pointed to the lower bunk. "That's you, Wooten."

Pete noticed the number painted in block letters on the side post matched the number he had been assigned. He put the sheets and blanket on the bed and sat on the edge.

A young, fresh-faced man came and sat beside him. "Hey, man, we were on the bus together. You're Pete Wooten, right?"

Pete nodded.

"Cool. My dad used to do some work for your dad. He told me once that you were the fastest man he ever saw."

Pete smiled. It seemed like a lifetime ago. "There was a time when I was fast."

Another young man came over and sat on the other side of Pete. He had that long hair like some young people were wearing now. "I was on the bus too. What are you in for?"

"He killed a man," the first guy said.

"Really?"

Pete didn't answer.

An older guy walked up. "Don't mind these idiots. That's a standard question here. Hell, we love to hear about other peoples' misery to take our mind off our own."

They all laughed. And just like that, prison didn't seem quite as scary anymore. Heck, it seemed friendlier and easier than the tobacco fields.

"They call me Miles," the older man said. "You'll get the hang of the place."

Pete nodded. "How long you been here?"

Miles laughed. "Hell, I can't count that high."

"My dad also said you were the funniest guy he ever knew," the young fellow said. "Tell us a joke."

The older man sat on the lower bunk across from Pete. Apparently, live entertainment was rare, and he didn't want to miss out.

The owner of that bunk, a very large man with a long beard, walked over. He stood over six feet tall and was as broad as a horse. His wavy brown beard came halfway down his white shirt.

He didn't look like a pleasant person, but looks can be deceiving. "What's the powwow here?"

The old man looked, smiled, and motioned for him to sit too. He did.

Pete searched his memory. He knew thousands of jokes, but they were all eluding him at the moment. Finally, he thought of one. "Okay. A man was visited by a ghost in the middle of the night. The ghost said, 'In the morning, your son's grandfather will die.' The next day when he woke, his wife's mama called to say his father-in-law had died. He couldn't believe it. The next night, the ghost came back and said, 'In the morning, your son's grandmother will die.' When he woke, his wife told him the news that her mother had passed. Now, he was getting worried. The ghost appeared on the third night and said, 'In the morning, your son's father will die.' The man was scared to death. He didn't want to die. He tried to stay awake all night, but he fell asleep. He woke with the sun coming through the window. He was still alive. He was so happy, he ran out of the house to celebrate and tripped over the milkman."

Everyone laughed but the bearded man.

"I don't get it."

The old man looked at him and shook his head. "The milkman was dead. The boy's father was the milkman, not the man. Get it? His wife had cheated."

The bearded man doubled over with laughter. "That's good. Tell us another." He wasn't one to miss out on the entertainment either.

"Okay," Pete said. Looking at the big guy, he asked, "What's the proper pronunciation of the capital of Florida? Is it My-ami, or Me-ami?"

"Oh, shoot," the big guy with the beard said. "Even I know this one. It's My-ami. I ain't never been there, but I sure know how to say it, and I ain't never heard anyone say it the other way. Am I right?"

Pete shook his head. "No."

It was hard to tell from all the facial hair that the big guy had been smiling, at least whatever expression he had that passed for a smile. But whatever it was, it quickly ran away from his face. "What?"

Pete smiled. "The capital of Florida is Tallahassee."

"Oh, shit," the guy said while slapping his leg and laughing. "You got me good on that one."

A loud buzzer sounded and startled Pete. "What's that?"

"That's lunch," Miles said. "Come on."

Pete followed the others. The big guy with the beard walked behind him.

"Hey, man," the big guy said. "They call me Brutus. What's your name?"

"Pete."

"Well, Pete, do you like good country cooking?"

"Sure."

Brutus patted him on the shoulder. "Then you're gonna be very disappointed." He laughed at his own joke.

Pete followed the others, grabbed a tray, and went through the line. He watched as they dumped stuff onto his metal tray, most of which he couldn't readily identify. Afterward, he stood looking over the large, crowded room. Tables were lined up wall to wall, and there were at least a dozen rows. He wasn't sure where to sit.

"Follow me," Brutus said as he walked past him.

Pete followed and sat at the same table. Six other inmates, including Miles, who were already there, greeted Brutus.

Several guards strolled among the tables. Several other armed guards stood watch from elevated walkways. It was almost like the lunchroom of a high school with people sitting with their close-knit friends and talking and laughing.

"Guys," Brutus said, "this is Pete."

They all nodded.

One younger inmate spoke with food in his mouth. "Whatcha in for, Pete?"

Just like Miles had explained, this was a common question.

"Murder." Pete wasn't sure why he lied. Perhaps, it sounded better. And it was almost true. He was convicted of murder, but he saved in the eleventh hour by a lenient judge.

Everyone at the table looked confused.

"Murder?" the young inmate asked. "How come you ain't in cell block D?"

Pete looked around at all the faces staring at him. He suddenly realized he had made his first error and knew he had to say something. "I promised them I wouldn't do it again."

Everyone laughed.

"This guy's funny," Brutus said before devouring the entire plate of the stuff in front of him.

Pete took a bite of something that resembled meat with gravy. It wasn't bad. He wasn't sure what it was, but it wasn't bad. He hadn't realized how hungry he was and was able to eat all of it. Of course, now he was craving a cigarette but was afraid to ask anyone. He knew cigarettes took on a whole new meaning on the inside.

After lunch, they were allowed to visit the yard for several hours. It was a nice day; the sun was shining, and a soft breeze managed to find its way through the fence and into the yard. Pete loved the outdoors. Whether he was surrounded by walls or surrounded by tobacco, it didn't matter, it made him feel trapped, claustrophobic. Somehow, he felt at home being touched by nature, even if it was only a caress. There was a basketball court with an asphalt floor, exercise equipment, and several tables where men played cards and checkers. Off to both sides, men sat in bleachers, shooting the bull and passing the time.

Pete closed his eyes and lifted his head, letting the sun soak into him. He decided to just spend the first few days getting the feel of the place, not getting involved in anything, until he felt more comfortable. But the checkerboards became too hard to pass up, so he wandered over. At the table, he stopped to watch as the two guys concentrated on the board and never looked up. He realized right away that they were decent players, but they were really just passing the time of day more than anything else.

All the other activities in the yard faded away as Pete became more focused. He watched intently, becoming impatient, as the game played out way too long. Finally, the game ended, and the players began setting up for another.

"Can I get in on a game?" Pete asked.

The loser looked up. "Sure. Take my place." He got out of his chair.

Pete took the seat. "Winner goes first."

His opponent slid his first piece one spot diagonally forward.

From there, Pete dominated, quickly humiliating the other player.

The man looked up for the first time. His eyes were set wide and dark brown. "Who the hell are you?"

Pete laughed. "Pete."

The man shook his head in disbelief. "Let's try again, and let me actually focus this time."

It didn't help.

Pretty soon, a crowd gathered and watched as Pete beat each contender who sat across from him.

"How do you do that?" his last opponent asked while leaning back in the chair and staring at the board.

"You have to look four moves ahead," Pete answered.

The guy laughed. "Right."

Every day, when Pete went to the yard, he walked straight to the checkers area. It gave him a sense of normalcy, of belonging. But as he tried to teach the other players how to play like he did—you know, correctly—he became more and more frustrated that they couldn't catch on. Several guys simply moved on to other activities less stressful than checkers. Of course, they had never considered checkers to be stressful before Pete came along, but back then, they could play for fun.

The nights were the worst as Pete lay awake, longing for sleep. It wasn't just the dozen or so inmates snoring out of unison that kept slumber at bay; it was the mental anguish, the thoughts spinning inside his mind like a witch stirring her brew, the devil whispering in his ear all night, teasing him, taunting him, and laughing at him.

He replayed that fateful day over and over. Why could he not just walk away? Why hadn't he simply driven back to the sheriff's office? Why had he not heeded Travis's advice in the first place? The more these thoughts consumed him, the angrier he got, and the further away sleep stayed. The odd thing was, he didn't even know who to be angry at. It was just his nature. He had to stop thinking of the past and focus on his current lot in life just to get his pulse back to normal.

His mama used to tell him that when he let his temper take control, he was no longer Pete Wooten. She didn't know who he was anymore.

Some nights, he found himself still struggling with these ghosts until the bell sounded for breakfast. The days became a mundane blur as his routine never changed, and soon, he felt like he too had become just another white dot in a sea of white. For a man who loved to live by his wits, to go where the wind and the money took him, to have an audience of free people watching him run or listening to his jokes, this dull existence was his true penance. His prison was not constructed of metal, bricks, and fences; it was in the depths of his very soul.

Finally, the first visiting day came, and Rhodes, the guard he saw when he arrived, made his way over to Pete's bunk and told him he had visitors.

He followed the guard to an outdoor area and saw Travis and Etta sitting at a wooden table with round seats anchored to the ground. He hugged Etta, and she and Pete each took a seat. Travis stayed standing, arms crossed, chin against his chest.

"How are you?" Etta asked.

"I'm fine. It's not bad at all."

"The food okay?" Travis asked. He was still upset over the whole affair.

Pete nodded. "Have you talked with your sisters? Do you think they'll come visit?"

"No, I haven't talked to them, and I don't plan to."

Pete shook his head. "Don't be upset with them. They did nothing wrong."

"They didn't do what I told them to do. That makes it wrong."

Pete sighed. "Sit down, son."

Travis slid onto one of the seats and set his hands flat on the table in front of him.

"I've had a lot of time to think in here. A lot of time." Pete searched for how to begin.

Whatever this was, Travis wasn't comfortable with it. He pulled his hands back and stuffed them into his pockets.

Pete decided to come at it from another angle. "You know what I remembered the other day? I remembered that time I took you to the creek fishing. You were only about four years old."

Travis smiled. He couldn't help it. He knew the story well. It was the only story, at least the only good story, in his memory of he and his daddy doing something fun together.

Pete continued. "We were sitting on the bank, which was very high off the water, and you hooked this little mud cat. As soon as you got it on the bank, it came off the hook and started flopping back toward the water. It went right over the edge, and you went right after it. If I hadn't grabbed you by the foot, you'd been in the creek. You remember that?"

Travis laughed. "Yeah, I remember. I wanted that fish."

Pete laughed and then stopped. "I know I wasn't around a lot when you and your brothers and sisters were growing up. It was a hard time, and I had to go where the money was to make a living. I just want you to know I did the best I could for y'all."

Several seconds of silence passed. Etta let tears sprout up in her eyes and roll down her cheeks.

"Is this your way of apologizing?" Travis asked.

Pete looked up sharply. "Apologize? For what? I'm just explaining because you and your sisters seem to think the world owes you something, that maybe you got the short end of the stick for not having a father who could be around all the time."

Travis laughed and shook his head. "No, you're not apologizing; you're making excuses, like always."

"Let me tell you something," Pete snapped, lifting his finger and pointing it directly at his son. "Don't ever apologize for nothing in life. You hear me—nothing. That means you're not man enough to stand by your own decisions, and that makes you weak."

It was Travis's turn. "Let me tell you something." He leaned forward. "Van and Della were the only parents I knew. They were good and hardworking people. And the day I take advice from a lying, murdering piece of shit like you will be a cold day in hell."

Pete sat there staring at the table. He couldn't say anything. The lump in his throat felt like disbelief, betrayal, and loneliness at once. Family was family, right? Family stuck together no matter what.

Travis wasn't finished. "I intend to be there for my kids and give them what they need and treat them right. I will be a real father."

Pete swallowed hard and stared at his son. He could see Elsie. Travis had her features: dark hair, eyes like coals, and a darker complexion that instantly took on a reddish tone when anger took hold. But it wasn't Elsie he heard when Travis talked. It was himself. Finally, he found his voice. "If I was so horrible, why did you stand by me through all this?"

"Because I knew no one else would. You've hurt people for so long, and it came back and bit you on the ass. I took care of my sisters and little brother when you were God knows where doing God knows what. I was the one who did what was right. I stood by you through this whole thing, because you're my father, and I was doing what was right. That's the only reason. It wasn't because you were right. You're never right about nothing. I'll continue to do what's right. I'll bring Etta every week to see you, because I gave you my word that I would. It's not me trying to fix something you broke a long time ago, because that can't be fixed. But know this, if you ever get out of here alive, don't call on me. I'm through. I will never help you do anything ever again."

"Fine," Pete said, standing up. "I won't ever call on you. You can believe that."

CHAPTER FIFTEEN

TAKE THIS JOB . . .

1976

The first day of sixth grade came, and nothing had changed since fifth grade. I still hated school. I hated everything about it. I hated when the summer ended. I hated the mean teachers. I hated the nice teachers. I hated staying here for seven hours. In Daddy's day, it was better. He left school after second grade. Had it not been for the crazy laws today, I could have done the same. Daddy wouldn't have cared. He saw no benefit to a formal education. He had never needed one.

In early elementary, teachers looked at me with pity. But things had changed. Fewer looked at me with pity, while more and more looked at me with contempt. I'm not sure which was worse. I didn't know what I had done to elicit such emotions, but they were there and quite obvious. But looks of contempt and suspicion were common outside of school as well and from just about everyone, especially policemen and store owners.

What made this year even worse was that we were getting to that awkward age of being social. Kids became boyfriend-and-girlfriend in my class, which was weird. Kids had parties at their homes: birthday parties, pool parties, and even dance parties. They invited half the class to come.

I never went. If I felt like an outsider before sixth grade, I really did now. We weren't allowed to bring people to our house because Daddy was embarrassed for people to see how we lived. Only a few close relatives had that privilege.

But school was a fact of life, like death and taxes, so I stuck it out and waited for the few good moments.

"Okay, everyone," Miss Edwards said. "Let's go to break."

We walked out single file, marched down the hall, and out the back door of the school. The store was in the concession building by the football field. Mama gave us one dollar a day for lunch. The lunches cost ninety cents, leaving me one dime for break. The only thing there for ten cents were those six-inch-long candy sticks, but luckily, there were several flavors.

As we followed Miss Edwards toward the store, I heard a commotion and noticed a group of high schoolers in a circle behind the back of the gym. I could tell by the way they were yelling and focusing on the center of the circle that there was a fight in progress.

"Let's go," one yelled.

"Get her," another yelled.

Her? I stepped out of line and let the ones behind me pass. I walked over to the circle and squeezed between the bigger kids until I was on the inside. I wasn't surprised to see what I saw. It was Julene fighting another girl. I looked around, knowing Neenah was somewhere. I found her standing there innocently, tears soaking her face.

This made up a big part of Julene's school days—defending Neenah against some other girl or girls who had made fun of her, insulted her, or were just plain mean to her.

"Come on, rush her," one of the other girls called out to Julene's opponent.

Easier said than done. I looked at the other girl and felt sorry for her. I understood all too well. I had stood exactly where she stood now. It's normal for siblings to fight, and Julene and I had had several bouts. It usually happened when Mama and Daddy were on a dinner, and Julene had to babysit all of us. Without Daddy around, I often pushed the envelope. Unlike the normal scuffling, headlocks, rolling around on the ground, and so on, Julene simply punched me in the head until I saw things her way.

The poor girl stood there; her hair was a mess, her face red with blood streaming down from both nostrils. She was possibly in shock.

Julene, on the other hand, stood there poised, her feet wide apart with one foot in front of the other, her fists in the correct positions in front of her face, the left slightly ahead of the right. She didn't go in for swinging wildly and hair pulling; she came to fight.

Just like poker, checkers, and whatever Daddy taught us or tried to teach us, repetition was the key. I, too, had stood toe to toe with him in the front yard many times as he provided proper boxing instructions. He had boxed in the army and was undefeated.

The girl finally got up the nerve to rush Julene again, head down, arms flailing, screaming like a banshee. Mistake. Never take your eyes off your opponent. Julene caught her flush with an uppercut that made her head snap up high and her hair go even higher, the sound of the contact echoing off the cinderblock wall.

I could never understand it. Neenah was the sweetest person. You needed no qualifications, no special skills, and no social status to be her friend. She was gentle and kind to everyone, which made her a little different, and I guess that's all that was needed for some people to treat her poorly.

And that's where Julene came in. It didn't matter what grade the offender was in, how big they were, or how many of them there were, it was Julene's job to take up for Neenah and enact revenge. No, really, it was her job. Those were Daddy's exact words. The first time he learned that someone had been mean to Neenah at school and Julene had done nothing about it, he beat her so badly that her backside, from her lower back to her knees, was black and blue for a month.

"Break it up," someone yelled loudly.

I looked around and saw two male teachers. They grabbed Julene and her foe by the arm.

"Let's go to the principal's office."

That was a scary fate for most, but something told me the other girl was glad it was over. And I knew that whatever punishment awaited Julene was nothing compared to what she would have gotten at home if she hadn't fought.

It wasn't fair. Life seldom is. Julene should have been able to go to class, have a few friends, and enjoy school as much as possible without this added responsibility. I think a part of her resented Neenah for it, but to her credit, she never let on. I was never bullied, but she would have defended me too. She was our ringleader. Whatever strength and security we gained from being part of the ragtag trio came from her.

After school, Dinky sat between me and Neenah on the dark-green, vinyl seat for the long bus ride home. We were the first ones on the bus every morning and the last ones off in the afternoons, so we had an hour-long trip each way.

I think it's safe to say that Julene, Neenah, and I were fairly grounded in reality. Dinky, however, had quite the imagination.

"I can speak Chinese."

Neenah and I laughed. "Let's hear it," Neenah said.

"Chiy shen yuk woy ling struct tol."

We laughed again.

Dinky didn't care for the doubt. "Hey, I know what I said."

"What else can you speak?" Neenah asked.

"German. Chiy shen yuk woy ling struct tol. I know what I said."

Dinky went on to regale us with several languages: French, Italian, and Swahili. All of them sounded amazingly alike.

After we got off the bus, we picked up our little brother from our aunt's house and walked the rest of the way home. Even when Daddy was home, he couldn't be bothered to watch his two-year-old son for a couple of hours between the time Mama left for work and we got home from school because he stayed too busy. Usually, playing solitaire or plotting his latest get-rich-quick scheme.

"You need to burn the trash," Daddy said as I walked in.

This was one of my chores. We used the paper bags from the grocery store as trash bags. I threw on my favorite ball cap and carried the bags to an old rusted fifty-five-gallon drum a hundred feet behind our house and set it on fire. I always watched it burn a while. The flames mesmerized me.

Afterward, I decided to check my rabbit traps. I had worn a trail through the woods all the way to the creek and had a dozen wooden traps I had built. They were boxes about two feet long and eight inches high and across. A forked stick protruded from the top middle where a longer stick was attached to a trap door in the front and a notched stick poking through a hole near the rear. I checked the traps every day before school and every day after I got home and added a fresh slice of apple.

I caught rabbits, opossums, raccoons, and even one skunk. I never hurt them; I just wanted to see them up close then let them go.

When I got back, Neenah had made supper. I quickly and half-heartedly washed my hands and sat at the table. I never saw it coming. I only felt the impact as I went flying backward, my chair flipping over, my back slamming the floor hard. I reached over to grab my ball cap, which had landed away from my head, and then it became clear.

"Leave it!" Daddy shouted.

I wiped the blood from under my nose and sat back at the table sans cap. It wasn't the first time Daddy had backhanded me for sitting at the table wearing a cap. It was his pet peeve for sure.

The weird thing was, we were instilled with very few lessons in manners and etiquette at all. I never had a curfew. If I was gone for several days, no one cared. Mama might ask where I've been, but that was the extent of it. But there was something about the disrespect of wearing a ball cap at the table that Daddy loathed. I assumed his granddad must have hated that as well, and it stuck with him.

That and a weak handshake were about the only two things that bothered Daddy in that area. Don't hand him a dead fish when you shake his hand.

After everyone went to bed, I stayed up to wait for Mama and Julene to come home. Julene didn't ride the bus in the afternoons. Mama picked her up an hour early from school, because they both worked second shift in the valley at Cooper's Hosiery Mill in Fort Payne, where Mama was a boarder and Julene was a knitter.

They came in about eleven o'clock. "What are you doing up?" Mama asked.

"Waiting on y'all. There's some leftovers from supper."

After Mama and Julene ate, Julene pulled out one of her schoolbooks. This was her routine. She let Mama sleep a little later in the mornings, and she woke us all and got us ready for school. She'd do her homework late at night after working a full shift at the mill, go to bed late, get up early, and do it all over again. On top of that, she gave almost her entire paycheck to Mama for groceries and bills.

"Don't stay up too late," Mama said as she disappeared down the hallway.

I sat watching my oldest sister. I was always in awe of her. "Whatcha working on?"

Julene smiled. "Algebra." The pencil glided effortlessly across the paper. She didn't even use a calculator. Her left arm was hairless and red from halfway down her forearm to her wrist from turning newly knitted socks inside out for eight hours. Her knuckles still bore the rawness from the fight earlier in the day.

I don't know if she noticed me during the fight, but I said nothing. She said nothing. She never did. She simply suffered in silence. This, she definitely didn't get from Daddy.

When Daddy was sick, which was often, he made sure the entire world knew. Besides having a perpetual headache, he got heartburn and indigestion often. For this, he relied on his home remedy, the most horrible elixir to be invented. He'd add vinegar to a glass of water, mix in a tablespoon of baking soda, and then quickly drink down this foaming volcano as it erupted. An extremely long and loud belch later, he was good as new.

Many times, when I had a tummy ache, he tried to force me to drink this deadly concoction, but I never could. Boy, would that make him mad. I finally learned as well that it was best to just keep being sick to myself and not share it.

Julene closed her book. "Done. Let's get to bed."

Things had gotten better at home. Daddy had also gotten a job. A real job. Well, as real as it gets for Daddy. He became a truck driver for Southwest Motor Freight in Chattanooga. He drove as a team with his cousin, Early Ray Wooten, who had gotten him the job, and they ran the California route. I think he made pretty good money, but unlike Mama's and Julene's, his paycheck didn't find its way to necessities and seemed to evaporate as fast as he got it.

I often wondered what that was like for Early Ray, a gentle, quiet, devout Christian man riding in the same truck with my daddy, who was loud and obnoxious, cussed like a sailor, and avoided church like the plague. Daddy often told me that he would most likely burst into flames if he ever entered a church. I believed it.

This job, however, was a blessing for all of us. Not the money per se, since we didn't really benefit from that, but the fact that Daddy would usually be gone for a couple of weeks and sometimes a month at a time. I never knew things could be so peaceful. Daddy would come home in between runs for several days and make up for lost time, I assure you. But those stretches of normal-level voices, no objects flying across a room, and no belt whizzing through beltloops was like heaven.

We all had our jobs. Apart from being the defenders of all things Neenah and working full time at the sock mill, Julene helped around the house a lot. She'd always go with Mom to do laundry. Neenah cooked, and Dinky translated if any foreigners came to our house, and we all chipped in to wash and dry dishes. My task list, being the eldest son, was pretty extensive: cutting and splitting firewood, cutting pulpwood, mowing, bushhogging, working the fields, going to the farmers market, and so on. But hey, there was always room for more, right?

Daddy was forever the aspiring entrepreneur, keeping his eyes open for an opportunity. It began simply enough. Daddy bought two small hogs to fatten up to kill. They were both white. We built a small fenced-in area behind the house and kept them in there. We fed them slop from the leftovers and grain feed we bought from the Pendergrass feed store in Powell. With no room for exercise, they grew quickly. A couple of months before we took them to the meat packing place to be slaughtered, we only fed them grain feed.

When the time came, we hauled them off and went back and picked up so much meat it was incredible. Boxes and boxes of meat wrapped in plain white paper with magic marker writing on all of them: ham, bacon, sausage, pork loin, etc. We had to buy a large freezer to hold it all. I must admit, other than the bacon being thick and too salty, it was all very good.

It was also a good sign that we might have power for a while, since we couldn't afford to let all that meat ruin. In the seven years we had lived in this house, we could count the number of months we had electricity on both hands. We still had to go down to the hollow to retrieve water, but at least we could put the kerosene lamps away for the time being.

One day, the inevitable happened. Daddy was home and sold a lot of the meat from the hogs we had killed. That's all it took. That evening at supper, he shared his thoughts, as he always did. "With me driving a truck and not planting, we got all this land here not doing anything. There's a lot of money in pigs."

I glanced around and saw all the expressions, especially on Mama's face. I could read her thoughts. *Oh God, here we go again.*

"I'm gonna buy some pigs while I'm home and get us started."

Mama took a brazen leap. "How are you going to raise pigs if you're gone most of the time?"

Daddy kept eating and never looked up; he simply pointed at me.

Figures.

The next day, I went with him to buy seven piglets. Three were black, and the other four had black, white, and light-brown markings. We put them in the small pen where we raised the hogs to eventually kill. It was late October and already getting cold.

The very next morning, we went down to feed the pigs, but only six came to the trough.

"We're missing one," I said.

We entered the little pen and looked around.

"Here it is," Daddy said.

When I saw it, I almost cried. It was one of the black ones. It had been trampled down in the mud and was barely alive. I think it was alive, because its head was moving like it was having convulsions. I'm not sure it wasn't just reflexes.

Daddy picked it up by its hind legs. "We can't just let it suffer." He walked over to a tree and stood there.

I couldn't watch and turned away. I waited for the horrible sound. It didn't come.

"Here," Daddy said. "You do it."

"What?" Was he serious?

He walked over and handed me the pig. "Just hit its head on the tree. Do it hard so you make sure you kill it."

I walked over to the tree with a sickening feeling in my gut like I'd never had before. At first, I thought this was just another one of Daddy's life lessons. But standing right there on that cold morning holding that cold pig, the cold truth dawned on me—he couldn't do it. With a tear rolling down my cheek, I swung with all my might.

Daddy grabbed the pig and tossed it down into the woods, and we started walking back toward the house.

Then, I had a thought. "How are they going to have room in here when they grow?" Note to self: don't ask questions you don't want to know the answer to.

"I'm glad you asked," Daddy said. He pointed to the cleared eight acres behind the house. "We are going to fence in this area and on down into the woods."

I knew Daddy only had two days before he had to leave out again and was pretty sure what "we" meant. I was right.

He stared out over the imaginary fence with that distant look in his eyes I had seen before. Slowly waving his right hand across in front of him in reference to an invisible billboard, he said, "Wooten's Pig Farm. It's gonna be huge. I'll be the president, and you're the executive officer. We'll have trucks running all over the country."

I never understood Daddy's obsession with owning a fleet of trucks, but I think it had to do with being able to show people how successful you were without having to tell them. Knowing Daddy, though, he would still tell them. "See those trucks over there with my name on them? Those are mine."

Daddy had bought an old chainsaw, and the next day, he cut down a lot of posts, bought a raggedy pair of posthole diggers, and rolls of barbed wire. When Early Ray came by to pick him up, he left me with these parting words: "I expect you to have the fence complete when I get back."

So, every day after school, and all day on the weekends, I dug holes twelve feet apart and planted posts. It didn't take many holes to understand why it's called Sand Mountain. Not far below the rich topsoil is a bedrock made of sandstone. Many times, to get to the proper depth, it required posthole diggers and a hammer and sharpened steel rod to use as a chisel.

After the first day, I had blisters filled with fluid at the base of each finger and on the tips of each thumb. The second day, they burst and soaked my gloves. I was so glad when I finally got to the pine thicket and there were enough trees that I didn't have to use one post in the wooded area. Mama helped me string up three rows of barbed wire.

When Daddy got back home, the fence was complete. "Looks good," he said. "Let's move the pigs over."

I'm not sure they were pigs anymore. At thirty pounds, they're considered hogs. Before he left out again, he went and bought ten more full-grown hogs, which included a six-hundred-pound boar and two large sows. The sows were mean as hell and the only ones we named. We called one Biggie and the other Meanie. If you got within twenty feet of them, they tried to kill you.

Raising hogs soon became an on-the-job training experience. Mostly, I learned that barbed wire was not the right way to go. Daddy wouldn't or couldn't splurge for hog wire for the big fence, and Mama and I paid for that daily.

"Hello?" Mama said when she picked up the receiver. "Okay, we're on our way." She looked at me as she hung up. "Some pigs are out."

This became a common call. We'd go find them and herd them back home.

"You got to ring their noses to keep them from rooting," Uncle Doodle told me one day. Uncle Doodle knew a lot about farming.

He showed me how to do a couple of the smaller ones. I did the rest, including the huge boar, Biggie, and Meanie. I had to tie those two up to do theirs. They stopped rooting, but they didn't stop getting out.

"You really need hog wire," Uncle Doodle explained, "but since you don't have that, you need to add some electric wire."

So, we bought a used charger box, and I ran two strands of electric wire between the three strands of barbed wire. It didn't help. The hogs would push right through, squealing in pain as they were being shocked.

When Daddy came home in February, I was ready to kill every hog we owned . . . and him.

"How's the hog business?" he asked one morning at breakfast.

I had no words to offer.

He laughed. "Anything worth doing takes effort, son."

I loved his words of worldly wisdom.

Thank goodness he had a solution. "Come on, go with me."

We drove our pickup with side rails to a farm about ten miles away.

"What are we doing here?" I asked.

"Buying more hogs."

Of course.

After we unloaded ten more hogs, we talked shop.

"I see we have a few litters now," Daddy said as we walked around the pasture.

"Yep."

"You know you have to castrate all the males, right?"

"No, I didn't know."

Daddy nodded. "Yeah. We can only have one boar. If another male threatens him, he will kill them."

"I don't know how."

Daddy had the answer for that too. "Ask your uncle."

After Daddy returned to the road, Uncle Doodle helped me castrate all the male piglets.

"You want to save these?" Uncle Doodle asked while holding up a set of pig testicles.

"Are you serious?"

He spit a large slew of tobacco juice on the ground and laughed. "Yes. Lot of people eat these. Haven't you heard of mountain oysters?"

"Yeah, but I thought that was a joke."

It wasn't. But I knew if Uncle Doodle didn't eat it, it had to be weird. I watched him pick the birdshot out of tiny chunks of squirrel, quail, and doves. And he loved frog legs and snapping turtle. We even had some relative who ate possums, which broke my heart. I loved those little critters.

There were dozens of cow pastures around, which meant dozens of ponds. It was easy to catch massive snapping turtles, a little harder to get them off the hook without getting bit. It was said that if a snapping turtle bites you, it won't let go until it thunders. I think it was an old wives' tale. I don't think they would ever let go.

Sometimes, I'd go with Uncle Doodle or my cousins to these ponds in the middle of the night. We'd take a frog gig, a stick twice as tall as I with a miniature devil's trident on the tip. Shining a spotlight to the opposite bank, the eyes of the giant bullfrogs would reflect across the murky water. While they were blinded by the light, one of us would sneak around with the gig, ever vigilant for the water moccasins, who also called the ponds home, and ram the gig through the frog's body. We'd fill a bag in no time.

Frog legs and turtle necks actually have a great flavor. They taste like chicken.

❖

When spring came around, things got worse as the hogs that got out of the pasture sought out our neighbors' newly planted gardens. That added a level of urgency.

Biggie was expecting another litter, and one day, I couldn't find her. I looked all over thinking she must have gotten out. I finally found her in the woods laying on her side. I walked up very slowly. "Hey, big girl. You okay?"

I had watched enough sows deliver to know that something was wrong. Her breathing was very fast, and she seemed to be in a lot of pain. She didn't even care that I was near her. I ran back to the house and called Uncle Doodle. "She looks bad. She's been like that for hours and hasn't had her piglets yet. I'm afraid she's going to die. What do I need to do?" I listened intently as he told me exactly what to do, which left me with only one more question. "Are you joking?"

He wasn't.

I just wanted to know one thing—why me? I would much rather be swimming or fishing. But I went back to the woods and walked slowly up behind her. "Hey, it's me. Everything's gonna be okay." I knelt behind her and started scratching her belly. Hogs loved that.

She didn't react.

I started scratching her hind quarters.

She didn't react.

I took a deep breath and proceeded to go on a treasure hunt. I slid my right hand inside of her and kept going until my elbow disappeared. Nothing. I pushed farther. I felt one. I wrapped my fingers around it and pulled it out, cleaned it off, and put it around to her belly.

It found a teat and went to town.

I continued until I had pulled out eight and could feel no more. The afterbirth released, and Biggie finally started breathing right. She reached her head back and began licking the piglets. Then, she looked at me and growled.

"Hey, just doing my job."

CHAPTER SIXTEEN
JUST WALK AWAY
1965

Pete was always the life of the party, and he loved being the center of attention. Even in prison, he was able to hold an audience.

"My first night here, I noticed everyone seemed so depressed. So, I decided to tell them my best joke. After I finished, no one laughed at all. Then, someone down the block yelled 'Eight,' and everyone burst out laughing. Someone yelled 'Ten,' and everyone laughed. Someone yelled 'Twelve,' and everyone laughed.

"The next day out in the yard, I asked an old man who had been here a while what all the numbers were about. He said, 'Here in prison, we don't always have time to tell a full joke, so we've numbered our jokes.'

"'Oh, I said. That makes sense.' The next night I was ready. Someone yelled 'Eight,' and everyone laughed. Someone yelled 'Ten,' and everyone laughed. I yelled 'Twelve.' Nothing. Someone else yelled 'Twelve,' and everyone laughed.

"The next day in the yard, I told the old man what happened. He said, 'Well, some folks can tell them; some folks can't.'"

All the prisoners and a few guards standing around laughed.

"You crazy, man," a tall inmate said.

"That's a good one, Wooten," Tony said. Tony Wilbanks was a young man, mid-thirties, who had been a guard at Kilby for ten years. He had dark hair with a buzz cut and was fairly athletic. He had taken a liking to Pete from the beginning.

Pete lit up a Pall Mall cigarette.

"Your wife coming this weekend?" Tony asked, leaning against the wall and resting his thumbs in his belt.

Pete nodded, a tendril of smoke curling into his eye. "Yeah, my son Travis is bringing her. They come every weekend."

"That's good."

Pete decided to broach a subject weighing on his mind. "Hey, Tony, I see those inmates who get to work outside cutting grass and stuff. How do I get a job like that?"

Tony laughed. "You can't. You have to be a trustee."

"So?" Pete asked. "How do I become a trustee?"

Tony shook his head. "I don't think you can. That's usually for nonviolent offenders."

"Ah, hell, you know I'm not violent. I've been here a year now. You know me."

"I don't think you're violent either, but those are the rules."

Pete smiled. "You could probably pull a few strings."

Tony laughed and walked away.

❖

Pete had settled in at Kilby. He didn't have a choice. He had a group he played cards with. Several even knew how to play his favorite game—tonk. They even had a few checkerboards, but the other inmates didn't like to play Pete. He was too good.

Pete considered himself one of the lucky ones. He had visitors every visiting day, always Etta and Travis, and sometimes Boots, Esther, Jerry, or some of his brothers and sisters. His father, Van, had passed away one year before the shooting, and his mother, Della, never came. When they told her the news of Pete being convicted and going to prison, she had no expression at all and hasn't spoken of it since.

In all, prison life wasn't too bad. On the outside, Pete had never held a real job, simply because he hated the idea of someone being in charge of him. But now, he had a lot of people in charge of him, so getting to work on the outside away from eyes and guns had appeal. It could also break up the monotony. He really wanted to be able to step outside these walls even for a moment, and being a trustee seemed like the only way that was going to happen.

A few months later, while eating dinner, he overheard a conversation between Tony and another guard, Bert.

"Come on," Bert, the other guard said. "Auburn's looking good this year."

"Forget it," Tony said. "My wife almost killed me when she found out I lost fifty dollars to you last year."

"Don't you want a chance to win your money back?"

"Oh, I'm gonna win it back somehow. You'll see."

Bert laughed.

Later in the day, Pete seized the opportunity and walked up to Tony, who was sitting behind a small metal desk at the guard station. "How did you lose fifty dollars to Bert?"

"We had a bet on the Alabama-Auburn game last year. He gave me Auburn and twenty points."

"And?"

Tony laughed. "And they lost thirty-eight to nothing." He leaned back and put his hands behind his head.

Pete went for the kill. "I know a way you can win your money back."

Tony was intrigued. "How?"

"It's a sure thing," Pete said. "You just have to bet on me."

Tony squinted. He wasn't sure whether to trust him or not. "What's your angle?"

"If I win you your money back, you put in a word to make me a trustee."

Tony thought for a second. "Okay. But only if I win my money back. If I lose more to Bert, I'll make your life a living hell. You understand?"

Pete grinned and nodded. "Follow me."

Tony got up and followed Pete as they walked over to the basketball court, where two teams were in the middle of a game that looked more like combat. Pushing, shoving, and no one dared call foul. A young Black inmate, whom everyone called Smokey, was watching from the sideline and waiting for his turn to play. Pete walked right up to him. Pete was taller, a good six inches.

"Hey, Smokey. How'd you like a chance to win a pack?" He pulled out a new pack of Pall Malls.

"What you talking about, old man?" he asked, looking straight into Pete's eyes.

"A foot race," Pete said. "Me against you. Loser pays the other a full pack."

Smokey laughed. "Hey, guys. Y'all hear this? This old man wants to race me."

The game stopped as everyone gathered around laughing as well.

"We got a deal or not?" Pete asked.

"Sure, man. That's easy money."

"This is your plan?" Tony asked, looking at Pete in disbelief.

Pete winked. "Trust me."

"Go get Niles," someone yelled out.

Niles was an older inmate who had been there for twelve years. He was the self-appointed prison bookie. He walked up to the group. His head was slick, bald, and shiny. He wore a constant mischievous smile that revealed tobacco stains and a missing top-right incisor. "What's the game?" he asked, rubbing his hands together.

"Me and this dude gonna race," Smokey said.

Niles looked at Pete and raised an eyebrow. "You sure you want to do this?"

Pete nodded.

"Okay." Niles acknowledged. "Someone draw a starting line and mark off about forty yards."

Bert walked up. "What's going on here?"

Tony explained.

"You got to be kidding me. How old are you, Wooten?"

"Fifty-six."

This brought about more snickers.

"Okay," Niles said. "Anyone want to bet on the old white man?"

Nobody said anything.

Niles adjusted the stakes. He knew his crowd. "Two-to-one?"

Nothing.

"Any takers at five-to-one?"

Silence.

"Final offer: ten-to-one."

An inmate standing three deep spoke up. "Hell, I'll risk a pack on the old man for the chance to win a carton."

"Covered," another inmate said.

Another spoke up. "I'll bet a pack on the old man just to watch this."

Pretty soon, several others were placing bets.

"You believe this?" Bert asked Tony.

Tony smiled. "I'll put ten dollars on Wooten."

Bert laughed. "You're on."

"That's ten-to-one, you know?" Tony said.

"I know," Bert answered. "Doesn't matter. This is gonna be easy money."

"Okay," Niles said. "To the starting line."

Pete and Smokey walked over. Pete took off his shoes and rolled his pants legs up to his knees. He walked to the starting line, his footprints in the dirt showing off the full impression of his flat feet. Pete felt alive again as his memories drifted back in time to all those races from when he was young. He felt the energy from the other inmates and remembered how he thrived off the crowd. The only difference was that, back then, he was sure he would be victorious.

Overhead, birds hovered under a cloudless sky, perhaps to watch as well. A slight breeze trickled across the yard.

Another inmate chimed in. "Y'all might be in for a shock. In case y'all didn't know, this old dude survived a shotgun blast at point-blank range in the chest. Hell, he might be Clark Kent."

"Is that true?" Smokey asked, taking his stance.

Pete smiled and shrugged. He placed his left leg back and his strongest leg to the front.

"Okay," Niles said. "Let's do it. On your mark . . ."

Pete tightened his hands into fists.

"Get set . . ."

Pete leaned forward.

"Go!"

All the people watching that day, the few guards and several dozen inmates, would surely talk about this race for the rest of their lives. Smokey jumped out to an early lead, about three feet, but it was short lived. Pete's long legs moved faster and faster as the muscle memory came back to them. He crossed the finish line five feet in front of Smokey.

Smokey handed Pete a pack of cigarettes. "You sure surprised me."

"Me too," Pete said breathing hard. "I'm a lot slower than I used to be."

Smokey laughed.

The others gathered around cheering, laughing, and patting Pete on the back.

The inmate who had mentioned Pete being shot spoke again. "What kind of drugs did they have you on in the hospital?"

"I want some of them," another said.

After everyone disbursed, Tony walked over wearing a conspiratorial smile. "Impressive."

Pete grinned. "You get your money?"

"On payday, he said. But he'll pay."

"And our agreement?" Pete asked.

Tony nodded. "I'll put in a word for you, but there are no guarantees."

"Fair enough."

❖

The months passed. Pete had made a lot of new friends, especially those he helped win a carton of smokes. Several inmates challenged him to races after that day, but Pete told them his racing days were over. But one thing the other inmates had learned for certain was that Pete was no ordinary man. In addition to friendship, he had gained their respect. In prison, he was able to put his money where his mouth was. He was a bullshitter like the rest of them, sure, but somehow, he was able to back his up when it counted. Guys liked that.

❖

The new year rolled around, 1965, but there was little celebrating in the prison. On January 15, William Bowen was executed in Kilby's electric chair, known as Yellow Mama or sometimes Big Yellow Mama. The US Supreme Court put a stop to those executions immediately after to determine if this method was constitutional. But there was a cloud of darkness engulfing the entire facility for several days after the execution. It was a feeling of loss, a solemn reminder of their incarceration, of remembering that no matter what kind of life they had behind these walls, they were, without a doubt, not free.

On March 4, exactly two years after the start of his trial, Pete got the news he had been waiting on.

"Hey, Pete, come here."

Pete walked over to Tony, who was standing alone in the corner of the yard. "What's up?"

Tony smiled. "It's done."

"What?"

"You're now officially a trustee."

Pete smiled. He couldn't believe it. "Thanks, Tony. Really, I do appreciate it." They exchanged a quick private handshake.

❖

Over the next three months, Pete often cut the grass and trimmed the hedges outside around the prison walls. He felt free on those days. The strange thing was, Pete never cared for lawn work before, but now, he loved it. Like most things taken for granted, once the sense of accomplishment and self-worth came back, Pete was able to look at actual work in a new light. A couple of times, he had even been driven over to the warden's house to cut the grass there.

In June, he had a visitor. The guard led him to the same area in the yard that was walled off with a high metal-wire fence for this purpose. It was Travis with his two daughters, who were three-and-a-half and one-and-a-half years.

"Oh my," Pete said, placing his hands together in a prayer-like pose. "Who do we have here?"

Travis smiled. "These are my daughters, Julene and Neenah."

Pete squatted down to get on eye level. "Wow. Julene looks like me, and Neenah looks like you."

Travis agreed with a smile, and then took on a serious expression.

Pete looked up. "What is it?"

"I spoke with Mr. Beck."

"And?"

Travis shook his head. "No appeal."

"Figures."

"But," Travis added, "you might be up for parole in a couple of years."

Pete didn't want to dwell on that. "How old are you, Julene?"

Julene held up three fingers. Neenah stepped forward.

"Hazel's pregnant with our third," Travis said.

"Maybe you'll get you a son this time," he said as he lifted Neenah onto his knee.

"Hopefully. So, how you holding up?"

Pete smiled, bouncing Neenah. "Good. I get to go out and work now. You get used to it, you know."

Travis nodded. "I guess so."

After Travis and the girls left, Pete moped around for a week. It was great having visitors but very hard when they left. In addition, he was upset about the appeal. It wasn't surprising news, so he couldn't quite understand why it bothered him so much. He guessed the visit and news coming all at once made freedom seem that much further away. A couple days later, he sat on his bunk reading a letter from Etta when a guard walked up.

"Let's go, Wooten."

Pete got up and followed. "Where to?"

"Warden wants his lawn mowed."

The guard took him to a pickup truck with a push mower in the back. He drove him to the warden's house and dropped him off. Pete took the lawnmower and gallon of gas out of the back.

"I'll be back in a couple of hours," the guard said. This was the normal routine.

Pete waved. "Okay."

There was still a little dew on the grass as Pete began his first lap across the large yard. He looked at the sun hanging over the eastern tree line. It was beautiful. It was a beautiful day. It reminded him of the day long ago at the community event in Blake when he met Elsie. He wished he could be back there now, foot racing and pitching horseshoes. It was just too nice a day to be working. It was just too nice a day to be captive. Pete cut off the lawnmower, looked around, walked to the road . . . and just kept walking. It was not planned.

He made his way to the interstate and stayed inside the woods just far enough off the road to not be visible to the traffic and headed north. He removed the button-up shirt with the writing on the back and buried it in the dirt underneath a pile of sticks and twigs. The leaves covering the ground padded every step, but Pete began to worry that he was leaving a scent behind and expected to hear the howl of hound dogs any second. He wasn't even sure if they still used dogs to track escaped convicts, and he didn't want to find out. When he came to a creek, he waded in and walked downstream about a hundred yards before crawling out of the murky water and continuing on his journey.

As the moon replaced the sun in the sky, he continued walking for hours until he was too tired. He hadn't eaten since early that morning, so he found a place to bed down. But slumber didn't come easy, as his paranoia made every noise, every cricket, every car in the distance, every plane in the sky sound like the authorities closing in on him.

The next morning, he woke up with the first bird chirp. He got up and trudged ahead as his thoughts of being captured consumed him. He walked all day again. As night made its way across the land once more, he came across a road. By now, he had wandered well away from the interstate. He needed his bearing. He needed to find a phone. So, staying out of sight, he followed the road to his right back toward the interstate.

As he neared the entrance to I-65 south, he saw a gas station and, more importantly, a pay phone. He wasn't sure what time it was, but he knew it wasn't too late. The lights were off. The station looked closed. He took a deep breath and ran to the phone.

He heard a crackle and then, "Operator."

"I need to place a call and reverse the charges."

"What number?"

Pete gave her Travis's number.

Travis and his family were just getting ready for bed. They happened to be living only about twelve miles away from Pete's hometown of Blake in Chavies, a small community near Rainsville. He answered the phone.

"I have a collect call from Pete Wooten. Will you accept the charges?"

Travis was confused. "Yes."

"Go ahead," the operator instructed.

"Travis?"

"Daddy, what's going on? They let you call from the prison?"

"Listen, I can't stay on the phone long. I need you to come get me."

"What are you talking about?"

Pete looked around nervously. "I'm at a station somewhere above Clanton, I believe."

"How did you get there?"

"I left."

Travis was getting tired of the cryptic conversation. "Just tell me what the hell is going on."

Pete took a deep breath. "I walked away yesterday morning. Do you understand? I escaped."

Travis pulled the phone away from his ear and stood there looking at it in disbelief. "Where are you?"

"I'm on a road. Uh . . . I saw a sign that said FORTY-TWO. I'm at a gas station that says THOMPSONS. There's a big 76 sign. You can't miss it. I can't stay on the phone. I'll be in the woods across the road. Bring food." He hung up and ran back across the road to the woods.

Travis hung up and grabbed his car keys and stuffed them in his pocket.

"Where are you going?" Hazel asked.

He threw some food in a bag, filled a jug of water, and looked at his wife. "You don't want to know."

Travis took the I-59 to Birmingham and picked up the I-65 toward Montgomery. Twenty miles out of Clanton, he kept his eyes peeled for a sign that might display the road he was looking for. He found it at the Jemison exit, got off, and found the station.

Pete ran out of the woods and got in the car. "Let's go. And don't take the interstate. Did you see any roadblocks?"

"No." Travis tossed the bag on his daddy's lap.

Pete opened a box of crackers and munched away. "This all you could find?"

"You prefer prison food?"

Pete laughed. "No, this is fine."

"There's some peanut butter and potted meat in there. I just grabbed what I could."

Pete used crackers to scoop peanut butter out of the jar and drank water right out of the jug.

Travis drove the backroads all the way to north Alabama as Pete recounted the events of the last two days. Travis didn't know whether to be impressed or angry.

"Where are you taking me?" Pete asked as they neared home.

"I'm waiting for you to tell me."

Pete said nothing for a minute. He felt both nervous and excited. It had been a while since he actually had a decision to make for himself.

"I guess we'll go to my house."

"Are you crazy?" Pete asked. "The police are probably there right now."

"Well, you better figure it out quick."

Pete looked out at the darkness. "Just take me to Mama and Daddy's old place."

Travis knew it well. It's where he had spent most of his childhood. "The house is gone, you know?"

"I know. I'll just hide in the woods. Come back for me in the morning."

Travis was too tired to argue. He drove up Sylvania Gap Road, turned left past Cunningham Bridge, and stopped just short of

Jackson Road, the short dirt road where Hazel's parents, Harley and Lela Jackson, lived. He could see their house from his grandparents' house, and this was how he came to know Hazel, a shy, plain country girl.

When Travis joined the army at age eighteen, she was only eleven. But each time he came home to visit, he watched as she grew. While still in the service, he got a tattoo of a heart with her name in it. He had not even spoken to her yet. After six years in the army, he courted her and married her on her eighteenth birthday.

At the end of Jackson Road was the thirty-acre wooded parcel Harley had given them as a wedding present, and Travis had been clearing an area to build his own home.

He pulled the car over where the entrance to his grandparents' home once was, but now, it was overgrown with normal roadside growth. A fence now separated the pavement from where a pasture full of cattle now grazed.

Pete got out with the bag of food and the water. "Be back bright and early, and I'll have a plan by then."

"A plan?" Travis laughed. "Well, better late than never."

CHAPTER SEVENTEEN
THE KEY TO HAPPINESS
1977

There were only seven days left before the summer break. I was very excited. All the boys in gym class were. Next year, we would be in seventh grade, which meant we would finally be taking classes in the upstairs part of Sylvania School.

Coach Kirkland had us all line up on the gym floor. I'm not sure who was pushing, but the surge came from far behind me making the entire line react like a wave. Several times, I had to catch my footing to keep from falling.

The coach was a big man, over six feet tall, with curly brown hair, a thick mustache, and a barrel chest. He was the assistant varsity football coach and believed in the old style of coaching, getting the most out of your players by keeping them under an iron fist of fear. And, like all coaches at schools this small, he doubled as a teacher, applying the same principles to his history and PE students.

"Stop pushing!" the coach yelled.

It didn't stop. He yelled again but to no avail. He took off his belt, doubled it over, and walked up and down the line, I guess, thinking that would scare everyone into standing straight. That didn't work either. He stopped right beside me, took his belt, and struck me in the chest. The resounding pop made everyone immediately stand at attention.

I gave it no thought at all.

That evening, I sat in my room reading. I got this from my mama. Daddy could read very well, but I never saw him read for pleasure.

Mama, on the other hand, if she was at home and not eating, cooking, or being yelled at by Daddy, there's a good chance she had her face planted inside a Harlequin romance novel. She had boxes of them and went through one a week for years, decades even. I tried reading one once, but there were a lot of words and scenes that either eluded me or embarrassed the crap out of me. But if they were a refuge for her, then I was happy.

I, on the other hand, found my escape in Louis L'Amour books and read every one I could get my hands on. I knew more about the Sackett family than my own. I also read many other Westerns, including the *Longarm* series, which also contained two or three scenes that would have fit into the Harlequin genre. I quickly skipped over those paragraphs. And I learned the hard way not to read them when some of Daddy's Holiness relatives were visiting after looking up from the pages one evening and blurting out to anyone in hearing range, "What is incest?"

I didn't get the definition, but Daddy explained later, without using words, not to ask that specific question in front of company.

It was when I found a set of H. G. Wells's books at the thrift store, however, that my world would change. Wow, could that guy write! When he described the premise behind time travel, I was solidly convinced it would work. The *War of the Worlds* and *Food of the Gods* were equally intriguing.

I was almost twelve and must have read five hundred books in the last five years. It's easy to understand why. It was a great escape. Just knowing there were people out there living different lives, even fictional ones, gave me hope for the future, which I often needed, since the present sucked big time.

"Supper!" Mama called out.

Thank goodness. I jumped off my bed and ran to the table. I had no shirt on as usual. It was always too warm in the house this time of year.

Daddy was home from driving a truck and took his seat beside me at the head of the table, as Mama set stainless-steel pots of food in the middle of the table. All my siblings were there too. My little brother was now three.

"What is that?" Daddy yelled.

Everyone jumped, including me.

Daddy was staring at my chest. "Who did that?"

I looked down. I hadn't even noticed there was a welt across my chest. "Oh, Coach Kirkland got upset with all the boys in gym class today for pushing."

"And he hit you?" Mama asked.

"Yeah," I answered. "Just to get everyone to stop."

Mama looked concerned. "What did he hit you with?"

"His belt."

"Were you the one pushing?" Daddy asked.

"No."

Daddy went back to eating, and that's all that was said about it. I didn't think it was a big deal either.

The next day at school, an hour before lunch, the speakers came to life. "Neal Wooten, come to the principal's office."

Everyone looked at me. I was confused. I searched my memory, but I couldn't think of anything I had done this time. I had been called to the office more times than I could count, and math was my best subject. Each time resulted in a paddling. Three licks. I wasn't a bad kid, mind you, but it was tough staying inside the lines of all the rules. I walked the all-too-familiar path and entered the main office.

The lady behind the counter looked up and smiled. "Go on in."

I walked into the principal's smaller office, and Weldon Parrish sat at his desk. He motioned for me to sit on the cold leather sofa. Coach Kirkland stood behind him.

"Neal," Mr. Parrish began, "I understand there was an incident yesterday in gym class."

I nodded. "I wasn't the one pushing."

Mr. Parrish smiled. I knew he believed me, because I never lied when he asked me if I had done something wrong. If I had, I never denied it. He was a fair principal, always calm and collected. Having been a college basketball player, he could still swish the net from the corner of the court at will and often did so to the joy of the students watching. "I know, but Coach Kirkland has something to say to you."

I looked at the coach.

"Neal, I'm sorry I struck you with my belt. I was just trying to get everyone's attention."

"I know. It's okay."

Coach Kirkland smiled. "It was still wrong, and I wanted to apologize for that."

I didn't know what to say. A teacher had never apologized to me for anything.

"That's all, Neal," Mr. Parrish said. "You can go back to class."

"Okay." I walked back to class with a strange sensation. I had never had a pleasant visit to the principal's office before.

After the last bell, I was headed to the school bus when a boy in my class, who was also a baseball teammate, walked up. "Hey, man, what's going on?"

I shrugged. "Nothing. Why?"

"Boy, your dad sure was mad this morning."

I was lost. "Where did you see my dad?" I realized he knew him from our baseball games.

"I saw him here . . . at school."

Daddy had never come to school for anything, not the Harvest Festival, school plays, parent–teacher nights, or anything. "What was he doing here?"

The boy became animated as he told his story. "He was talking to Coach Kirkland. I was too far away to hear the words, but it was clear he was chewing him out. He was poking him in the chest really hard and yelling in his face."

"Really?"

"Yeah. The coach just stood there and didn't do anything."

Suddenly, the visit to the principal's office made more sense. Daddy never spoke of it, so neither did I.

That evening, I decided to get Julene's opinion. I wanted to at least tell her about it, tell someone. I always went to her for advice or questions about life. She was book smart for sure, but she had a worldly wisdom about her too. I knew she would know. "So, you think Daddy going to school and confronting the coach was over what happened to me?"

"I have no clue," she said.

I knew she'd figure it out. Julene was my only connection to the outside world other than books and Daddy's boring army stories. She was a true child of the seventies. Her long, straight blonde hair came down past her glowing cheeks. She wore bell-bottoms and butterfly collars. At home, she had a small record player and a box of 45s. She turned me on to the Eagles and Credence Clearwater Revival.

"I guess Daddy figures no one hits you with a belt but him."

I nodded. I think that was it. He was just being stingy.

It could have been worse. Coach could have called Daddy a liar. For some reason that I never understood, you could call Daddy just about any name in the book, and it wouldn't matter. But calling him a liar was fighting words . . . literally. Maybe it was because that hit too close to home, because being honest was never Daddy's first choice.

One day, our cousin Mandy left her husband, Joe, who was a notorious bad boy, having been arrested many times for alcohol, drugs, and assault, among other things. After he tried to run her over with his car, Mandy fled and hid out with friends. Naturally assuming she had come to our house for refuge, as she had done several times already, Joe called, and Daddy answered.

Daddy informed him that she wasn't there. And she wasn't. But Daddy's face suddenly took on that look I had witnessed too many times when Joe replied, "I know you're lying, Travis."

It's difficult to describe the look on Daddy's face when he's called a liar, but it doesn't look human. I was just glad it wasn't directed at me this time. He already despised Joe because he sold and used drugs and drank like a fish. Daddy was a teetotaler. He never drank—not even beer—and certainly never did drugs. Mama said he got that from his father, Pete. Both men looked down on this as a weakness.

It wasn't easy to be a heavy drinker on Sand Mountain, since DeKalb County still embraced Prohibition. Sure, the rest of the country was glad when Prohibition was repealed in the 1920s and new laws were quickly passed to make the selling of alcohol legal. Not us. We clung to Prohibition like it was a Bible. So, if you wanted a beer or something stronger, you had to drive twenty-five miles to the Georgia state line or the same distance to the Etowah County line—or just ask the bootlegger sitting beside you in church.

Most bootleggers on the mountain had abandoned their stills and just made runs to Georgia, stocking up on the favorites and selling them at exorbitant prices. Everyone knew who they were, including the law.

Daddy got into the car; drove off the mountain into Fort Payne, where he knew Joe would be; walked in; and hit him in square in the face. Joe went down hard but jumped back up. Daddy's next punch knocked him all the way through the front screen door. Once outside, Joe tried boxing with him. It didn't go well. Joe was much younger and a mean cuss for sure, but he was nowhere near as mean as his opponent. He lacked Daddy's size, strength, speed, and actual boxing experience. And one thing I knew for certain—he couldn't have outrun Daddy. Swinging wildly, he never landed a shot as Daddy beat that poor guy to a pulp. Even when he was on the ground begging for him to stop, Daddy wouldn't . . . or couldn't.

When the police got there, Joe got up and ran to them for protection. It marked the only time in his life he ever ran toward the police. The police officers, who seemed giddy about the whole ordeal, never charged Daddy with anything.

Daddy's hands were swollen for several days from hitting Joe so many times, but even Mama seemed proud and openly bragged on him. You have to give the devil his due I suppose.

❖

A few nights later, Mama called everyone to supper. As we ate, she talked about the Fourth of July. The mills always closed for the week of the Fourth. That was the only vacation the employees got. "Guess where the company picnic is going to be this year?"

We were all excited by Mama's excitement but could not guess.

"Lake Winnie."

Wow! We had all heard of Lake Winnepesaukah amusement park but had never been. We had planned twice to go, but once, Daddy decided we couldn't afford it, and the other time, he got angry about something and called it off.

Neenah looked at Daddy. "Can we go?"

"The tickets will be paid for," Mama said as if also trying to convince him. "And they'll have food for the employees and families."

We all looked at Daddy.

"We'll see."

At least it wasn't a no, and that was enough to get our hopes up.

When school let out for the summer, we all tried to be as good as we could be when Daddy was home. We were practically zombies. We didn't horse around and did whatever we were told to do quickly and with no complaining. We didn't want to do anything that might upset Daddy and make him change his mind about going to Lake Winnie. He had already put in to be off that week, so it looked like we were really going.

The week came, and Daddy was off work and in a great mood. Sure, he and Mama still had several yelling spells each day, but that was normal. In the verbal department, Mama had begun to give as good as she got. On July 3, it seemed all but certain we had succeeded when Daddy decided to grill hotdogs and hamburgers, something he often did on the Fourth of July. But this was a day early, a Sunday, which was more evidence of our real vacation.

Daddy's grills were disposable as well. He bought only the cheapest, smallest ones, about fourteen inches in diameter and two inches deep. We used them once, and then afterward, they lingered outside in the rain and elements for a year, usually with the old charcoal still in them. When we were ready to use them again, they were always rusted through, so we'd get another small cheap one.

"Y'all ready for some burgers and dogs?" he asked as he dumped the entire small bag of charcoal into the round grill atop a flimsy tripod.

"Yes." Julene, Neenah, and I stood around the marvelous circular outdoor cooking contraption with our mouths watering.

Daddy turned up the plastic jug of lighter fluid, the large one, and squirted half of the flammable liquid all over the coals. He immediately took his lighter and lit the pile. Poof! Flames jumped six feet into the air as a nuclear bomb-shaped mushroom cloud of smoke rose above us.

Me and my sisters stood there grinning, most of our eyebrows withered away and slightly smoking.

"Go get me the meat," Daddy said as he positioned the little grill rack on top.

Julene rushed inside, the black marks on her face making her teeth look whiter. She came out with the patties and raw wieners.

Daddy threw the meat right on. As the flames began to die down, he squirted more of the combustible cocktail on the coals, and we had another semi-explosion. This he repeated until the wieners and patties were almost black.

It didn't seem an efficient process to me, but that's how Daddy did it, so I know it had to be correct. We all went in with the blackened burgers and scorched hot dogs and sat at the table where Mama had the buns, onions, tomatoes, lettuce, and condiments waiting.

"Boy, you'd think we never feed you," Daddy said smiling at me. "Slow down."

I swallowed quickly, as I realized I had forgotten protocol. Before we ate, we were supposed to give thanks for the food we were about to receive. "Thanks, Daddy. You outdid yourself this time."

"Yeah, Daddy, it's great," Neenah added.

Julene and Mama chimed in with their compliments to the chef.

Daddy was happy.

I took another huge bite. It was hard to tell what my favorite part was: the crunchy, crispy black exterior of the patty or the soft, moist, raw interior.

"You won't get anything this good at Lake Winnie tomorrow," Daddy said.

We all stopped eating and looked around at each other, our silly grins betraying our excitement of that confirmation. We had succeeded. Tomorrow, we would experience something few people in this area ever got to do, something only rich people enjoyed—go to a real amusement park.

After we ate, we helped Mama clean up. It was the least we could do, since Daddy had done the hard part.

"I'm going to run to the store and get some groceries."

We all looked at Daddy in disbelief. Mama as well, because Daddy never did the shopping. He would occasionally go to the store for cigarettes or ice cream, but not actual groceries. For those, he preferred to wait for Mama to get home with them, so he could complain about her not getting cookies or ice cream sandwiches. But this was another sign of how great things were going.

An hour later, Daddy pulled in front of the house in our car, a 1970 burgundy Cutlass, and came inside. He handed me the keys. "Go get the groceries out of the trunk."

"Yes, sir."

There were only two keys on the keychain: the one with the rectangular head was for the ignition and the one with the round head was for the trunk. I slid the round one into the keyhole at the top of the trunk lid and turned. It didn't budge. I wiggled it a little and tried again. Nada. I took it out and looked at it. It seemed fine. I slid it in again, and again it wouldn't turn. I tried harder. It was stuck good. I put more pressure on it. It turned, or at least the head did. The part inside the trunk didn't move at all, and the head twisted right off in my hand. I just stood there staring at it. I felt like I had been bucked off a horse into a mud puddle and kicked in the head. How could this happen? Why did it have to happen today of all days?

"What's taking you so long?"

I looked up and saw Daddy standing in the open door to the house. I couldn't speak. I couldn't move.

Daddy walked out and saw what happened. To say he lost it would be an understatement. I'd never seen his face get so red so fast. "You goddamn sorry piece of shit bastard son of a bitch!"

It was an impressive sentence.

"I didn't mean to."

"That's your whole goddamn vocabulary." He grabbed for his belt but wasn't wearing it.

Normally, when he wasn't wearing his belt, he would send me to the woods to cut a hickory switch, and it had to be a sizable limb or I was sent back. It was akin to asking a man sentenced to a guillotine to pick out which blade he preferred. It was truly adding insult to injury.

This time, however, Daddy couldn't wait on that. He grabbed me around the neck and continued his assault on me and the English language. "What the hell is wrong with you, you stupid little shit? Why can't you pay attention to what the hell you're doing? You're the most useless stupid goddamn idiot in the world. You're so goddamn . . ."

I could keep going, but you get the gist. He continued for twenty straight minutes. This is not an exaggeration—twenty minutes. Even the neighbors a mile away must have heard him.

Mama rushed out of the house. "What happened?"

Daddy held up the broken key. "This stupid son of a bitch broke the goddamn key off in the trunk."

"Can't you get another one made?" Mama asked.

Daddy stared at me for the longest time, his face so red I was afraid something was going to rupture. He let me go and got into the car, backed up, and sped away.

Mama looked at me and broke down crying. She always referred to it as "browbeating." I wasn't sure if that was a real phrase or something she made up. The only thing I knew for sure was that it hurt a lot worse than a belt.

What hurt even more was the knowledge that I had ruined our vacation for everyone else. I walked past Mama and kept walking. I walked past the house to the fence and jumped over. I walked straight toward Biggie and Meanie, but they simply moved out of my way. Great, even the hogs felt sorry for me. I came to the other side of the pasture deep in the woods, jumped over, and kept walking.

I passed the remnants of the old still, the rusted fifty-five-gallon drum half filled with pine needles, the swirls of copper tubing still scattered about the site. Making moonshine is remarkably easy. Just fill a drum with water and add about any produce, such as sugar beets. But corn whiskey was preferred on the mountain. After it ferments—or rots, actually—it creates alcohol. Then, you heat it. Alcohol boils at 173 degrees and water at 212 degrees, so if you simply keep the temperature between those numbers, only the alcohol boils. The rolls of copper tubing cool the steam and convert it back to liquid, so what drips out is pure grain alcohol.

I kept going. I knew these woods like the back of my hand and knew exactly where I was going. At the very back of our property was a ridge where the land rose up high above the creek below. Dirt gave way to rock at the edge of the cliff. I had stood there many times staring out in awe at the splendor of God's creation. But at this moment, I wasn't thinking about God, or the beautiful scenery, or of anything wonderous at all.

As I stood right on the edge of that cliff for what seemed an eternity, I truly believed it was for the best. I knew in my heart that everyone would be better off without someone like me around. It didn't seem fair. I truly didn't want to be a bad person, but I had come to the conclusion long ago that things like this were beyond our control. Some people were just born bad.

I heard the call of a bird and looked up and saw a redtail hawk sailing overhead. He flew high and free without a care in the world. How dare he? What gave him the right? That made me want to jump even more.

But time kept passing, and still I stood. I couldn't understand why I hadn't jumped. Just when I thought I couldn't feel any lower, the reason dawned on me why I couldn't do it—I was afraid. Great. Not only was I useless, unable to throw horseshoes, play checkers, or open trunks, but I was also a yellow-bellied coward to boot.

I sat down and slumped over in complete defeat. I sat there for hours contemplating life. What kind of future could someone like me ever have? What contributions to society could I ever make?

After the sun ducked below the pines, I got up and headed back. The shadows in the woods projected the perfect metaphor for my thoughts. I assumed Daddy would be back, and I could only imagine how much money he had to spend to fix the car. I knew it would be too much to afford to go to Lake Winnie tomorrow. Maybe he would still be mad enough to kill me since clearly, I lacked the fortitude.

I walked into the house and everyone, including Daddy, was sitting at the table.

"There you are," Mama said. "Supper's ready, so wash up."

I washed my hands and took my place. No one made eye contact; they just talked and laughed like everything was normal. After I ate, I went straight to bed.

❖

Mama woke me early the next morning. "Wake up. Time to get ready."

"Ready for what?"

"Lake Winnie, sleepyhead."

"Did Daddy get the key fixed?"

Mama sat on the edge of my bed. "Yes, it was no problem. They were able to get the broken piece out and make a new one."

"How much did it cost?"

"Oh, I don't know." Mama was a terrible liar. She didn't have the practice that Daddy had.

"How much?"

Mama dropped her head. "Fifty cents."

Fifty cents?

"Now get up so we can get going."

"I'm not going."

"Oh, come on. It'll be—"

"Mama, I'm not going."

She understood. I know it hurt her to leave me that morning. I know it did.

I was glad my sisters got to go. I focused on tending to the hogs and avoided Daddy for the next few days. I think he was happy to avoid me too.

When the time came for him to go back to work and Early Ray came to pick him up, he called me outside. We walked a little piece away from the house. I almost thought he was going to apologize, but he had always taught me that apologizing was a sign of weakness. But I truly believe what he said next was an attempt.

"Uh . . . listen, about that key. I've been thinking about it. I mean, you broke that metal key with your bare hands. That's impressive. I've tried to break that key but couldn't." He patted me on the shoulder and walked away.

I turned and stared in disbelief. That was it? That was his way of telling me to forget everything, that it was no big deal? He really did think I was the biggest damn idiot in the world.

CHAPTER EIGHTEEN
ON THE LAM
1966

Ohio?" Travis snapped. He picked Pete up from Van and Della's old homeplace after dropping him off the night before. He had to scale the pasture fence and walk into the woods to find him sleeping by a pond. He had half expected the authorities to be at his house when he got home last night, but as he drove down the road nearer the house, all was quiet.

Pete nodded. He kept looking over his shoulders and out the windows of the car. "Yes. Morning View. It's a small town. We have to find Clements."

"Who is that?"

"He's a cousin of mine," Pete said. "Clements Helms. I can hide out with him a while."

Travis didn't like it. And he hated the idea of driving all the way to Ohio without knowing who this was. He couldn't believe his daddy had escaped from prison when he could have possibly been getting out in a couple of years. "Are you sure you can trust this guy?"

Pete nodded. "Yes. He's hiding out from the law himself."

"Perfect. He definitely sounds like a relative all right."

Travis drove all day through Tennessee, through Kentucky, and into Ohio, while his daddy seemed to sleep. He finally found the small town at about three o'clock that afternoon. He stopped the car and looked over at his daddy, who was leaning to his right with his head jammed up against the window. It was obvious he hadn't slept much.

He looked at Travis. His hair stood straight up. His eyes were moist and bloodshot.

"We're here." Travis nodded. "What's the address?"

Pete looked at him like he was crazy. "How should I know? I told you he was hiding out."

Travis's face turned dark red. "Then, how the hell are we supposed to find him exactly?"

Pete took a deep breath and rubbed his hands on his thighs. "Well, it's a small town. We'll ask around."

And that's what they did. All day and into the evening. They walked up and down Main Street in Morning View, asking after Clements Helms at every store, restaurant, and business. The town had two gas stations, one on either end; they asked there too. They asked people on the street, and as they turned corners and found themselves in neighborhoods, they even tried a couple of houses. Nothing. Nobody had heard of Pete's infamous cousin.

At one point, Travis stopped at a phone booth and leafed through the directory. "There's no Helms in here at all. Are you sure this is the right town?"

Pete simply shrugged.

Travis's mood was not getting any better. He thought of calling home to let Hazel know where he was but worried their home phone could be tapped. The day had taken its toll. They were both fatigued from the drive, the walking, and the situation.

"I got to find a motel and get some sleep," Travis finally announced.

They found a small motel at the edge of town. A wooden VACANCY sign hung from two hooks screwed into an eve over the front door. Travis exchanged cash for keys with the manager at the desk, and they checked into a room with two full beds. He lay down, inhaled the scent of tobacco smoke in the pillowcase, and was out like a light. He slept until the next morning.

Pete was sitting on the side of his bed dressed and ready to go when Travis woke. "Let's get going."

Travis raised an eyebrow. "Where to now?"

"I have another cousin who lives just above Trenton. I should be able to stay there a while."

"Trenton? As in Georgia?"

"Yes."

Travis was so tired of this. He plopped himself back down on the pillow, wishing his daddy had never called him. He remembered telling him in prison that he would never help him again, but he never expected him to escape. And he knew no one else would. Finally, he crawled out of bed. "You do realize we were thirty minutes away from Trenton before you drug us all the way up here, right?"

Pete didn't answer. He just kept sitting there with a sense of urgency, wondering why his son wasn't moving faster.

Travis smoked a Camel cigarette to steel his nerves before gathering his belongings and following Pete to the car.

They headed back south, avoiding the interstates, stopping only once for gas, snacks, and drinks. Pete directed him where to go, around Columbus, Springfield, and Dayton. By midafternoon, they pulled up the long dirt driveway of a small house in the country above Trenton. It looked well kept and inhabited for sure. The flowers out front had been recently watered, the small square of grass clipped short. Travis felt a bit of relief knowing they were finished chasing the ghost of Cousin Clements. He wasn't sure what to expect with these cousins, but at least they found them, so it was already a more successful venture.

Pete mounted the front steps and knocked on the door.

"Well, Lordy me. Pete." The old woman who answered hugged him. "Samuel, come see who it is."

"Hey, Martha. This is my son, Travis."

"Hello, Travis. I haven't seen you since you was knee high to a grasshopper."

Travis smiled and shook her outstretched hand. He didn't remember her at all. She had a kind face, one he would have liked to remember. Strands of soft gray hair fell out of her bun and hung around cheeks. Her smile was warm and generous.

Samuel came to the door. "What in the world? Pete, when did you get out?"

Samuel was medium height but skinny as a rail. His light-brown hair existed mostly on the sides with a few strands combed over in a failed attempt to make it look fuller. Martha was short and stocky and preferred pants to dresses, at least around the house out of view of the members of her church. Her gray hair was pulled up into the traditional Holiness bun.

Pete ignored the question. "Travis, this is Samuel, Martha's husband. They're distant kin on my mama's side. Martha used to keep me when I was a baby."

"Meanest baby ever," Martha said and chuckled. "Now, answer the question."

"What question?" Pete asked.

Martha gave him a scolding look. "When did you get out?"

"Yesterday?" Pete said sheepishly.

"A few days ago," Travis corrected.

Martha stared at Pete long and hard. "Did you break out?"

Pete dropped his head and nodded.

"Well, Lord have mercy. Get on in here before someone sees you."

Travis looked over one shoulder, then the other, and saw nothing but trees. They all ducked inside and took a seat at the round kitchen table.

"So, it's okay if Daddy stays here a few days?"

"He'll be fine here," Samuel said.

Travis stood back up immediately. "Good. Now, I have to get back. Hazel doesn't even know where I went. I'll be back as soon as I can."

On the drive home, Travis was jumpy. He still couldn't believe what was going on. Yet somehow, it didn't surprise him either. When he got back to his house in Chavies, Hazel was pacing back and forth on the front porch, chewing her lower lip.

"Where have you been?"

They both stood outside as Travis told her the whole story.

"Oh my God. Is he okay?"

"Yes. For now, anyways."

Hazel suddenly brought her hands to her mouth.

"What is it?"

"Some men came here looking for you this morning."

"What men?"

"They didn't say. Just asked where you were. They were in a black car and wore black suits."

"What did you tell them?"

Hazel swallowed hard. "I told them you went to look at a truck for sale."

Travis smiled. "That's good."

Whew.

"Let's go in," Travis said. "I'm starving."

He sat down, and Hazel made him a bologna sandwich. Before he could take his first bite, however, they heard the crunch of tires on the chert. The black car returned. He looked over at Hazel, motioned for her to stay put, stood up, and walked outside.

Both men got out and approached him. Other than one being a few inches shorter than the other, they could have been twins. Both had slender builds, chiseled faces, and medium-brown hair cut into crew cuts. "Travis Wooten?" the taller one asked.

"Who wants to know?"

Both pulled out a badge in unison. The taller one spoke again. "I'm Agent Andrews, and this is Agent Thomas. We need you to come with us."

"For what?"

"We think you know," Agent Thomas said.

"Well, you're wrong. I'm not going anywhere with you without a warrant."

Agent Andrews reached in his inside pocket and produced a warrant.

"Well," Travis said, reading it over slowly, intentionally very slowly. He handed it back to the man. "I don't mind taking a ride."

He got in the back seat of their car, and the three of them drove off the mountain to the Fort Payne police station. They politely opened the back door of their car to let Travis out, opened the door to the station, and motioned him inside. Apparently, the strange men had been here before, because an officer led them straight to an interrogation room. It was small and square with no windows and a metal table in the middle. The men sat down on one side and Travis on the other.

Travis looked around. He was no stranger to jails, treating laws pretty much like he treated monthly rent and utilities, as gentle suggestions. He had even run moonshine for the family at Happy Hollow in Ider on Sand Mountain, pronounced "Happy Holler," of course, known as the Hillbilly Mafia. But this was his first interrogation room visit. As his eyes scanned his surroundings, he was surprised to not see a two-way mirrored glass or a big bright light. Perhaps he had watched too many movies.

Agent Thomas took a recorder from his case, put it on the table, and turned it on. "Would you like an attorney present?"

"No. Why would I?"

Agent Andrews wasted no time. "That's good. More room for us. Besides, you're not in any trouble . . . yet. Just tell us what we want to know."

"And what is that?" Travis asked.

"Where is he?"

"Where is who?"

"Don't play games with us," Andrews snapped. "Where is your father?"

Travis put on his confused look. "He's in Kilby. Y'all could have asked me this back at my house and saved us a trip. Do y'all need directions to the prison?"

Thomas leaned a little forward. "No, he isn't, and you damn well know it."

Travis leaned back and let the front legs of his chair off the floor. "I have no idea what you're talking about. If he's not in prison, then where is he?"

"He escaped," Thomas said. "And he had to have help to do it."

Silence.

"Well?" Thomas asked.

"Well, what?"

Andrews was getting tired. "Tell us where he is, and you won't be in trouble. If you don't tell us, we're still going to find him, and when we do, you'll be in the cell next to him."

Travis nodded. "Okay."

Thomas looked at Andrews and then back to Travis. "Okay, what?"

"Okay. Good luck with that."

"How did you do it?" Andrews asked.

"You know what I think?" Travis began. "I think he was killed in prison, and they're covering it up. Did y'all know about the race where a lot of the prisoners and guards lost a lot of money?"

They didn't answer.

"I didn't think so," Travis said. "He had a lot of enemies there. Have you questioned everyone there? Have you looked into that at all? What exactly is y'all's plan to get to the bottom of this? Do y'all even have a plan besides harassing me?"

Andrews ignored the questions. "We've looked into you. We've questioned your neighbors, friends, and several family members."

"And?"

"And we couldn't find anyone who would admit to being your friend," Thomas quipped.

"That's true," Andrews continued. "Everyone said the same thing about you."

Travis folded his arms across his chest and waited.

"They all said you were the meanest, dirtiest, and most dishonest son of a bitch they ever met." Andrews waited for a reaction. None came. He went on. "Hell, one guy said he was convinced you were the devil himself in human form. I wouldn't even doubt if your father was innocent, and you're the real killer and just let your old man take the blame. That's how I know your whole story is bullshit. If you really believed what you are saying, you'd be down there at the prison threatening everyone there. You'd be calling the prison and probably every politician in Alabama. But you haven't done any of that. You haven't done a single damn thing."

"There's a reason for that," Travis said. "I didn't know he was even missing until you told me a few minutes ago."

Andrews sat back. "This is a waste of time. You're not going to help us, are you?"

"I'd love to. Heck, I like you boys. But I don't know anything."

"Get out of here," Thomas said.

"Y'all ain't gonna give me a ride back?"

Andrews leaned forward again. "But know this. We're going to be all over you like white on rice."

"Both of you?"

Andrews nodded.

Travis stared for several seconds and then let a slow smile creep across his face. "Oh, I see now. I can't believe I didn't pick up on it before. You fellows are lovers."

"Get the hell out of here," Thomas said.

Travis held up his hands. "Hey, I got no beef with it. I don't care what the law says, y'all should be able to have sex with whoever you want to. I'm a firm believer in 'live and let live.' You won't have many friends in this area, but at least I'll be one of them."

Andrews and Thomas closed their folders and walked out of the room, leaving him to fend for himself.

After a minute of chuckling to himself, Travis went to the front desk, asked to use the phone, and called Boots to come get him.

"What in the world is going on?" Boots asked when Travis got into her car.

"Just take me home, and I'll explain everything."

Boots drove and kept looking in the rearview mirror. "Are those men following us?"

Travis didn't even look back. "Yep."

The black car followed them all the way into the driveway. Boots let Travis off and backed up past them and drove away. The black car stayed.

The agents kept their word. For the next two weeks, they trailed Travis everywhere he went—to the hardware store, the grocery store, the filling station, the field where he had planted crops, you name it. They even sat outside and waited while he was at the barber shop. It's safe to say that didn't make Travis happy.

Finally, one day, Travis left Hazel and the three kids at home, which included his new son, Travis O'Neal Wooten II, whom they called Neal, and drove to town, but something felt off. He couldn't put his finger on it right away, but then, it dawned on him. He looked in his rearview mirror and saw there was no black car following. He took advantage and drove straight to the interstate and headed north, keeping one eye on the road behind him. He took the Trenton exit and pulled off the side of the road, got out of his car, and watched the traffic for a long time. Satisfied, he went on. He arrived at Samuel and Martha's house and knocked on the door.

"Oh, thank God," Martha said when she opened the door.

"What's wrong?"

"It's Pete."

"Is he okay?"

She nodded. "We think so. I haven't seen him since the day after you left. I was afraid to call you. I thought your phones might be tapped."

"They probably are. Where is he?"

Martha looked nervous, like she was afraid to answer. "In the woods."

Travis tried not to laugh.

"He's so paranoid," Martha continued. "My daughter called and said she was coming by to visit, and he panicked, starting accusing us of turning him in. I've been leaving bread and canned goods in a bag by the edge of the woods every few days, and it's always gone the next time, so I assume he's still out there. But it's going to be getting cold in a couple of months."

"I'll find him." Travis went around back and walked through their backyard and then the garden toward the woods. It wasn't the first time he had to find his daddy this way. For whatever reason, Pete always took to the trees. Old habits, Travis guessed. He made sure he was deep in the woods before calling out. "Daddy? Daddy!"

"Shut up, you blame fool."

Travis smiled and followed the sound, picking his way over dead trees and fallen leaves. He found his daddy sitting on a log by a small fire, empty cans strewn all around. Pete looked tired. His clothes were filthy, and he hadn't shaved. White stubble decorated his cheeks and chin. His teeth were dull and in need of a toothbrush. Travis sat with his back leaned up against a tree. "Nice place you got here."

Pete looked around and nodded as if he didn't know it was sarcasm. "Were you followed?"

"Of course," Travis said. "Fort Payne police, state police, FBI, and seventeen guards from Kilby. They're waiting for you back at the house."

"This ain't a joke."

"This whole damn thing is a joke."

Pete's face turned red. "Watch it. Don't get too big for your britches, or I'll kick your ass."

Travis's face turned redder. "If you're feeling froggy, leap. I'll break you in half, you mean old son of a bitch. And don't think you can outrun me either."

Pete knew his son was right on both counts. In the old days, Travis would never have been able to outrun him, but Pete was old and tired now. Plus, his bones ached from sleeping on the ground. "I don't know what to do. I'm terrified of being caught and going back. I'll never get out again. Do you understand? They'll add ten years to my sentence or, worse, change the charge back to murder. Either way, I'll die in that godforsaken place."

Travis knew he was truly afraid. He heard it in the way his voice shook. "Well, you can't live like this." He paused and pointed a finger in the air. "I read long ago that the best place to hide is in plain sight."

"What are you suggesting?"

"I'm suggesting you get on with your life. Let me find you a place for you and Etta to live and just get on with living."

Pete wasn't sure. "What if someone recognizes me?"

"*I* don't even recognize you. You won't have to go anywhere. Let's just find a secluded place, and Etta can come live with you. You can grow a garden and never have to leave. All of us will chip in and bring you anything you need. Won't that be better than living like a wild animal?"

"You've talked with your sisters?"

Travis shook his head. "No, but I will. I'm sure everyone will help out."

"I don't know." Pete shifted. He liked this idea, but it also scared the living daylights out of him. He desperately wanted to be back in a house, something he could at least call his own, with a garden, with Etta.

"Well, you gotta do something. For starters, go back to Martha's house and take a damn bath." He waved his hand across his nose. "If she wanted to turn you in, she would have, and hiding out here wouldn't make one bit of difference."

Silence.

"Because let me tell you something," Travis continued, "I'm not coming out in the woods to find your sorry ass anymore."

"I don't have any money," Pete said. "How am I going to find a house?"

"We'll all chip in and pay for it. Don't worry about that."

Pete finally agreed and followed him back to the house.

"Phew," Martha said as soon as they stepped inside. "You smell like the hog that laid the rotten egg. I'll run you a bath."

While Pete was bathing, Travis sat on the couch and talked with Samuel and Martha. "I'm sorry about all this. But thank you for letting him stay here. Hopefully, it won't be for too long."

"He's family," Martha said. "You always look after family. He can stay here as long as he wants to."

"Thank you. Thank you both."

They all decided Pete would stay a bit longer while Travis worked on his plan.

Travis tried to reassure his daddy once again and then said his goodbyes. By the time he got back to Sand Mountain, there was still a little daylight left. As he drew close to home, he spotted the black car parked on the side of the road about a half mile from the house. He sped up, honked and waved as he passed.

The car followed him, and the men got out.

"Where have you been?" Agent Andrews asked.

Travis was too tired and upset to deal with these idiots. He flipped his keys in his hand and made his way toward the front door.

Agent Thomas chimed in. "Hey, we asked you a question. If you don't want to talk here, we can go back to the police station."

Travis stopped and turned around. "I've been doing your job and looking for my daddy, which is more than I can say for you screwups."

"We're going to find him," Agent Andrews said.

"You stupid sons of bitches couldn't find your damn nose on your face. Don't come in my yard again without a warrant." He went in and slammed the door.

CHAPTER NINETEEN
SEASONS CHANGE
1978

I stood there . . . waiting. Waiting for the inevitable. I wasn't scared anymore; I was angry. I was pissed. My teeth were gritted together so hard that my jaw muscles were flexing. My fists were clenched so tightly that the blood was gone, leaving my fingers almost white. I knew I didn't stand a chance. I knew I was hopelessly outgunned. I didn't care anymore. I was almost thirteen years old, and enough was enough.

Daddy stood only inches away in almost exactly the same stance. He was still much bigger, much stronger, much faster, and much meaner. His dark brown eyes, now glowing black, peered into mine. He wanted to hit me. He wanted to crush me. He wanted to kill me. But . . . he stood there.

My friend Michael stood there watching the showdown, fear and guilt emanating from his face.

That was what set Daddy off. I brought a friend home. He was from a poor family too and didn't care about our little house. In fact, he didn't even pay any attention to it. But when we walked into the house that summer unannounced, Daddy went berserk. How dare I bring someone to his house. His rule about bringing people here still stood, so how dare his son defy him.

"What the hell do you think you're doing?" he had asked before jumping up and shoving us out the front door. "I'll beat the hell out of you, you little shit."

I spun around right there on the little concrete porch that had replaced the cinder blocks and stood my ground. "Then do it."

That brought us here to this point. I had never talked back. Never disobeyed. Never stood up to him.

Seconds seemed like minutes. The anticipation was far worse than what I knew to be coming. But Daddy suddenly turned and walked back into the house, slamming the door behind him.

And that was the end of it. Just like every other incident between me and Daddy, it was over quickly and forgotten or ignored even quicker. It was like it never happened. But things definitely changed after that day. For one thing, bringing friends over didn't seem to be a big deal anymore. I began to do it often during the weekends that summer. I think Daddy finally realized he had been cheating himself out of the thing he loved most—an audience.

"What are you fellows up to?" Daddy asked as he walked up on me and two friends one Saturday.

"Playing marbles," one of my friends said.

Daddy laughed. "Y'all are doing it wrong."

I cringed but held my tongue.

"How do you play?" my other friend asked.

Daddy got down on his knees. "First of all, it's called shooting marbles. Draw a circle three feet in diameter."

We did as instructed.

"Okay," Daddy continued, "everyone pick out one of the larger marbles. These are your shooters. They're called taws. Now, dump the rest in the circle. These are aggies."

"What are aggies?" I asked.

"That's the name of these marbles you have here. These are the best ones to use."

Yay. We did something right.

"Hold the taw like this," Daddy said and cupped his fingers, pulled his thumb back into the bent fingers, and placed the taw on top of his thumbnail. "Keep a lot of pressure on it, aim it at a marble in the circle, and flick your thumb hard." Daddy eyed one of the smaller marbles and held his hand right outside the circle, directing the taw toward the target, and flicked.

The large marble shot out of his hand as if it had been fired from a shotgun. It connected with the smaller marble so hard that I was surprised it didn't shatter. The taw knocked that marble out of the circle, ricocheted, and knocked a second one all the way out.

My friends and I knelt there with our mouths wide open.

"Every marble you knock out, you keep," Daddy explained. "Your turn is over when you fail to knock a marble out of the circle."

That point was moot as Daddy continued to knock all the marbles out without missing once.

"Y'all want to shoot again?" Daddy asked.

"We didn't get to shoot that time," one of my friends said.

Daddy laughed. "Okay, you boys shoot the next game, and I'll be the coach."

That worried me more, but Daddy was so patient with those guys, which was amazing, considering none of us could do it like he did no matter how many times he showed us. Pretty soon, we were all tired of trying.

"How about some horseshoes?" Daddy asked.

Oh great. From the frying pan and into the fire we leapt.

My friends quickly learned they couldn't compete in this either.

"How do you make it turn like that, Mr. Wooten?"

"Let me show you," Daddy said and carried the horseshoe over to one of my friends. "Hold it on the side like this, and just release it."

My friend grabbed the horseshoe the way Daddy instructed. *Don't you dare*, I thought. He pitched it, and my friend and I on the other side screamed as the shoe came wobbling toward us.

Whew.

Daddy laughed. Yeah, he just laughed. He enjoyed showing off and telling jokes to my friends. He treated those guys like his sons. Well . . . scratch that.

"Hey, boys, what do you say to a footrace?"

My friends, who played baseball with me, looked at Daddy like he was crazy.

To be honest, Daddy didn't look like he could be serious. He was thirty years older than I was, making him forty-three. He still had a huge chest, shoulders, and arms, although not as toned as they once were. But Daddy loved to eat, especially desserts, and his huge stomach reflected that sweet tooth.

"Let's make it interesting," Daddy said. "If any of you can beat me, I'll pay you five dollars. But if you lose, you owe me twenty push-ups."

My friends jumped at the opportunity.

I marked off a starting line and finish line.

"Hey, Neal?" one of them asked. "You racing?"

I laughed and shook my head. "Pass." I knew better.

All three of them lined up at the starting line. I stayed at the finish line. "On your mark . . . Get set . . . Go!"

Daddy did a trick I had seen him do before, but it was still impressive to watch. He turned around and ran backward. It's hard to describe. You would have to see it to believe it. And he *smoked* them.

My friends were in awe. Daddy laughed as he watched them do their push-ups.

When my friends were leaving that day, one of them said something to me, something I had heard several times before. "Your dad is awesome. Must be great to have a dad like that."

I smiled and returned with my old faithful response. "You have no idea."

❖

It was a good summer. I had my first real job. For the last three years, I had sold Christmas cards every fall. I had seen the ad in the back of a comic book. This company sent you their catalog, and you collected the money for orders and the customers wrote down how they wanted their names to appear. Personalized Christmas cards. What will they think of next? The company would ship the cards directly to the customers.

I would walk many miles every fall and knock on every door. Most people bought, not just because it was a great product, but I think more because they were impressed that a kid would put forth the effort.

I made one dollar for every box I sold, so I had money every Christmas to get my sisters a gift in case Santa got stingy with us again.

I stopped at a doublewide mobile home where I knew our bus driver, Kathy Winkles, lived. The big yellow bomber, old number 207, was parked out front. Ms. Kathy, as we called her, was quite a woman. She was of the Holiness faith and weighed ninety pounds soaking wet. Picture a tiny young woman in a dress with long hair pulled up in a bun controlling a twelve-thousand-pound monstrosity with a stick-shifter almost as big as she was. And all while controlling a bunch of rowdy kids. I don't know why everyone couldn't be a respectable kid like I was.

She came to the door.

"Do you need Christmas cards this year?" Yes, my spiel was on the Knute Rockne level.

She seemed excited to see me. "Junior, come here. This is the kid I told you about."

I wasn't sure if I should run or not. After all, in her own words, she had told me that I set a record for the number of times she had to take a student to the principal's office for acting up on the bus. My personal consecutive stretch was three days in a row.

Junior came to the door. "You're Neal? I've heard a lot about you. How would you like a job this summer?"

I needed no more details. "Yes."

Junior Winkles drove a Coca-Cola truck. His route went all over northern Alabama and northern Georgia. During the summer months, his job was much busier. That's where I came in. Junior picked me up at home in the mornings, Monday through Friday, dropped me off at the Piggly Wiggly across from Union Park in Fort Payne, and went to clock in. The plant was two blocks over from the park. He would swing by and get me in the loaded truck. We had to do it this way, because he wasn't actually allowed to have a helper.

The route ended every day back at the Piggly Wiggly, where we would unload the rest of the truck, usually half a truckload, mostly those heavy thirty-two-ounce bottles, the largest unit Coke offered.

As Junior unloaded with a forklift, I took pallet jacks, wheeled the drinks into the store, priced the tops with a pricing gun, and put them on the shelves. On Fridays, the shelves would hold an entire pallet, and we would leave more pallets in the warehouse to last them through the weekend. I had my routine down pat. Using a pricing gun, I'd slap a price on the lid of every bottle on the top level, grab the bottles with my right hand, toss them to my left, and neatly put them in rows on the shelf. This, I did with lightning speed and accuracy.

One day, I noticed the store manager watching me. "That's the most amazing thing I've ever witnessed. How do you do that?"

Junior walked up holding his clipboard and laughed. "That boy is a miracle. Neal, I unloaded four pallets of regular Coke. How many bottles is that?"

I looked up toward the ceiling. "Uh . . . 2,880."

Junior wrote it down and walked away.

"Unbelievable," the manager said.

Comments from people like this always confused me. How could they see me so differently than how my own daddy saw me? I concluded that either they weren't very experienced in the ways of the world, or perhaps they were just being nice. All I knew was I was making fifty dollars a week. I was rich.

To make summer even better, Daddy decided not to cut pulpwood to sell. That was great, because even having a full-time job would not get me out of that. He did, however, sell some timber to a man-and-wife team, who paid Daddy to cut pine trees for pulpwood from our property.

I do believe this man and his wife were poorer than we were, and I didn't even know that was possible. Perhaps that's why Daddy took a shine to them, and they became friends. I had never known Daddy to have a friend . . . ever.

One day, he decided to have a cookout with them. We killed, skinned, and gutted a sixty-pound hog. That would have been the perfect amount of meat if we'd had, say, a 150 more people coming. We welded a metal rack, complete with a crank handle on one end, and stretched the ribs of the hog over it. Daddy smoked that hog over hickory logs from early that morning until about eleven o'clock that night.

I was *pure* country, but I wanted no part of this event. Watching them cut pieces of meat right off that carcass was the most barbaric thing I had ever witnessed. Not to mention, I had raised this hog from the time it came out of its mother, so it was more akin to a pet than livestock. But the smell was killing me, and I hadn't eaten all day.

At about one that morning, everyone had had their fill, and Daddy instructed me to watch the hog so the dogs didn't get it while he and Mama tried to figure out how to get the rest of it in the freezer. I stood there staring at this cooked hog, ninety percent of it still there. I couldn't take it anymore and cut off a small piece and put it in my mouth. *Holy guacamole.* I had never tasted anything like that before. I started turning the handle and eating right off the hog like a feral maniac. I was a tad ashamed, but I would get over it.

The crème de la crème that summer, however, came not long after that. Daddy sold all the pigs. That made me as happy as a pig in slop. Happy as a pig in the mud. Happy as a dead pig in the sunshine. I'm not sure why Southerners have so many expressions combining "pigs" and "happiness," because those things seemed like polar opposites to me. But I made an executive decision and quickly tore the entire fence down to keep him from getting more pigs, or goats, or llamas, or whatever.

When it came time for him to go back on the road, I rode with him to Chattanooga, so I could bring the car, our only car, back home. He was driving solo now. I never knew why he and Early Ray stopped driving together, but it could have been because Early Ray worried that even being that close to Daddy could ruin his chances for salvation.

I had never known until that summer that Mama had never had a driver's license, or at least had not had one in many years. Of course, at thirteen, neither did I, but Mama hated driving in the city. There were only a few turns to get back on the interstate from Southwest Motor Freight, so it was no big deal.

Our current mode of transportation was another winner: a 1970 AMC Hornet. It was like a small station wagon with a three-speed manual transmission. The tires had zero tread, the same as all the other cars we had owned. Daddy knew, however, that soon the metal wires would be exposed, and voilà, traction again.

Daddy was beginning to mellow a little as he got older, but we all still very much enjoyed the time we had together while he was away.

❖

When fall came around, I began cutting firewood to stock up for winter. I also had two older ladies I cut for in the neighborhood, and they paid me twenty dollars a rick. Most areas don't use that particular measurement and only sell firewood by the cord, which is basically three stacks four feet high and eight feet long. On Sand Mountain, we sold by the cord and the rick, which was one-fourth of a cord.

Anyway, I'd usually sell about six ricks, and it made me enough money to take my sisters to the fair each year.

I walked down into the woods with the chainsaw, and once I had a lot cut, I'd bring the tractor and trailer down to haul it to the house. We still had the same old crappy chainsaw from when Daddy cut the fenceposts. It ran fine, but it had no clutch. That meant that when you let off the throttle lever, the chain never stopped turning.

I was cutting near a pile of brush and raised my right leg to trample it down. My knee bumped the blade. *Oh crap*, I thought and looked down. But all it did was cut a small hole in my sweatpants. That was lucky. I continued working. Thirty minutes later, I realized my foot was soaking wet. I figured I had stepped in a puddle of rainwater. I took off my shoe to empty it, but what poured out was solid red. I noticed my sock was the same color. I pulled up my pants leg and noticed a nice little chunk out of my knee and the blood running down.

I walked back to the house to doctor it, making sure Mama didn't see it. Mothers were so weird about things like that. Of course, if past cuts and gashes were an indication, it meant she would dab a little innocent merthiolate on it, making it feel like the chainsaw had cut all the way through. You could pour a mixture of gasoline, lemon juice, and salt on an open wound and it would hurt less than that reddish-orange drop of Satan's blood. But Mama believed in taking care of most medical issues at home. I could die and she'd tell me to walk it off.

After tying a dirty bandanna around my leg, I went back to the woods. After I had a load ready, I pulled it out with the tractor and trailer and backed our old pickup to where they were bumper-to-bumper. I began throwing pieces over into the truck. Dinky, who was now nine, and Breland, who was four, came out.

"Can we help?" Dinky asked.

"Sure. Y'all get in the trailer and toss me the wood to the truck."

They grinned and got in the trailer. This actually worked out much better, because then, I could stack the pieces as we went.

"Don't worry about those big ones on the bottom," I said. "Just toss me one at a time. Oh, and make sure I'm looking."

Dinky tossed one, and I laid it in the bed. I turned as Breland tossed one, and I caught it and continued stacking. It was working great. We had half the trailer empty in no time. I placed another one of Breland's on the stack and turned around. All I saw was Dinky standing there with her eyes wide open and hands cupped over her mouth. I never saw the five-inch diameter stick of firewood flying through the air . . . but I felt it when it connected to my temple.

"Oh my God," Dinky cried out. "Are you okay?"

I'm not sure if I was dizzy from the impact or from laughing so hard that I was lacking oxygen. That made everyone start laughing.

I got the wood delivered and had money to take everyone to the fair. This was something that I had learned from Julene and Neenah. Whatever money I made was never *my* money. Whatever money they made was never *their* money. It was just part of the collective. Such was the tightknit bond between us. There's nothing like growing up dirt poor to make you appreciate the value of sharing.

Julene drove us in her car, a 1970 Chevrolet Malibu. She had saved enough to buy it over the summer. Daddy had gone with her, so she had perhaps the most experienced car buyer on the mountain helping her. Unfortunately, he was only experienced in buying lemons, like this Malibu that used more oil than it did gas.

Julene parked in the large parking lot across the road from the fairgrounds. We loved going in the daytime when it was less crowded.

I had also entered a drawing in my name and one each under all my sisters' names. That way, we got free passes as well and could save our money for the rides. We had also learned from going to the drive-in that you never spent money on food at these places.

As we entered the big building, we walked to see if we could find all my art.

"Oh my gosh," Julene said waving to all of us.

We walked over, and I stood there in shock. There was my pencil sketch of John Wayne, and there hanging on it was a blue ribbon.

"Way to go," Neenah said.

I didn't know how to react. I had never won anything in my life. I just kept standing there staring and didn't realize everyone else had walked on. I caught up. We walked out into the fairgrounds. The fair in Fort Payne was like another world to us.

"Come on," Julene said.

We left Neenah to look after Dinky and Breland because she didn't crave the dangerous and exciting rides like Julene and I. She was content to ride the safer rides and babysit.

Julene and I walked around and saw something we had never seen at the fair before. It was basically three metal cages painted yellow. They were about seven feet high and four by four feet across and deep.

"How does that work?" I asked.

Julene shrugged.

We watched as two people got into one of the cages, grabbed the middle bar, and started using their strength and momentum. They pushed hard with their legs and pulled with their arms to make the cage go back and forth, getting higher and higher each time.

"That doesn't seem too fun," I said.

But Julene noticed something I didn't. "Wait. I think they go all the way around."

We watched as one pair after another only got the cage to circle up high on each side. Finally, however, two young men that looked to be in their early twenties stepped into one of the cages. They kept pushing with their legs while holding the center bar and the cage got higher, and higher, and higher, until . . . over the top it went. They were able to make it go around three times.

We were hooked. "Let's do it," Julene said.

I nodded eagerly in agreement.

Most of the onlookers, even the guy taking the tickets, laughed as an almost seventeen-year-old girl and a scrawny thirteen-year-old boy stepped up to try. I'm sure they thought it was a waste of tickets. The guy let us in one of the cages and locked the door.

"Ready?" Julene asked.

I nodded, so we began.

Julene was the most athletic of all of us. She played softball and volleyball and held the unofficial welterweight boxing belt. I'm not sure if my years of playing baseball helped, but wrestling pigs and splitting firewood with a mallet surely didn't hurt.

Our cage rose higher and higher as we strained with all our might. It only took us about six passes back and forth with the cage to go over the top. We spun it around a dozen times before the guy sounded the horn. It was good timing since my head was spinning faster than the cage, and I was starting to struggle to keep my breakfast down.

The crowd cheered and clapped as we exited. Turns out having an audience is a super cool thing.

We were all still on top of the world as Julene drove us home. We couldn't wait to tell Mama about the ride and the blue ribbon, but when we went into the house, Mama was on the phone and looking rather upset. For some reason, it seemed normal to go from an emotional high to an emotional low.

"That was Southwest," she said after she hung up. "They're going to radio Travis and tell him to come home."

"What is it?" Julene asked.

"It's Uncle Roy."

Daddy got home the next day, and we all loaded into the car to head to Rising Fawn. Mama and Daddy were clearly upset, and I noticed they weren't even taking in the scenery like they normally did on this trip. All I had been told was that Uncle Roy was very sick.

I hated to hear this. Uncle Roy was the nicest man I ever knew. He made us toys, planted trees for us, and had looked after Whitey after we moved to Rome. Whitey had died last year, but I was always happy that he was able to have a good life.

When we got there, I was surprised to see several other cars. They belonged to Aunt Boots, Aunt Esther, and Uncle Jerry. They were there with several of my cousins. I didn't even know that they knew Uncle Roy.

I stayed outside with my siblings and cousins until I was called in. The old grandfather clocks and guns were still there. Everyone was gathered around a small bed that had been added to the main room.

"Come over here, son," Daddy said.

Uncle Roy was sitting up in the bed. He looked so thin. He saw me and that familiar smile graced his wrinkled face. "Come closer," he said.

I walked right up beside him.

He rubbed my head. "You're growing like a weed. I hear you're quite the baseball player."

I grinned.

"He's fast too," Daddy added.

"I'm sure of that," Uncle Roy said. "Did you see your tree?"

I nodded. "It's really tall now."

It was like one of those family reunions we had at Aunt Esther's house. Uncle Jerry even played the guitar and sang. We played on the old rock fence wall with cousins, and we played hide and seek as well as several other games.

When night came, everyone left but our family.

"We're going to spend the night," Mama said.

I was surprised. We had never spent the night before. Helen took the couch, Mama and Daddy took the big bed, Uncle Roy had his small bed, and blankets were laid on the floor for me and my siblings. Spending the night was a strange feeling. I don't think any of the others would have been comfortable, since Uncle Roy didn't have electricity and running water, but it was par for the course for us.

Their outhouse was even fancier than ours and at the other side of a shorter walk.

But sleep was not easy between Uncle Roy coughing and wheezing and the chiming of the clocks every hour. Morning came, and Mama and Helen made breakfast.

Later in the morning, the cars started coming back with everyone that had been here the day before in addition to Talmadge and Ilene this time.

I was standing out by our trees in the front of the house with several cousins when Mama came out of the house. She walked over to us and asked me to help her get some water. We walked to the well, but there was no bucket. I knew then that she just wanted to get me alone.

She leaned down and looked me in the eyes. "There's something I have to tell you about Uncle Roy."

I nodded. I was pretty sure what she was going to say. "He's dying, isn't he?"

She smiled a weary smile and swallowed hard. "Yes. But there's something else I have to tell you about Uncle Roy." And then she told me a story. Mama was not blessed with Daddy's silver tongue. The gift of gab had eluded her or been returned for a refund. But this time, she had me riveted.

CHAPTER TWENTY

A NEW HOME

1969

Hey," Doodle yelled from atop the roof. "I need a brace twenty-two inches long."

Travis had the front portion of the land cleared that Hazel's dad, Harley, had given them along with the road leading down to it. Hazel's brother and a few other relatives were helping Travis construct his new house. He had drawn it up on paper, and it was coming along pretty well. Travis could do the math in his head to draw up the plans, and his carpentry skills were unmatched. They had used concrete blocks to build columns to support the structure, and so far, the floor frame and wall frames were completed. Then, they were starting on the roof.

Travis's son, Neal, had just turned four. He rushed over and grabbed the tape measure out of the old wooden toolbox sitting on the ground and took it to his daddy.

Travis just smiled. "That's okay, bud. I'll just eyeball it."

Extension cords joined together snaked their way all the way up the hill and into Doodle's house to supply power. Travis took the circular saw, sweat dripping off his brow, and buzzed it quickly through a piece of two-by-four. He held it up to examine it. "Close-ter-nuff." Walking over to the construction, he tossed it up to his brother-in-law.

Despite the heat and humidity, work continued throughout the day. They finished covering the roof with shingles and hanging blackboard on the outer walls. At night, Travis and Neal went back to their home in Chavies. The rising moon brought a cool breeze with it, and they drove with the windows down.

Hazel, who was pregnant with their fourth child, had supper waiting. "How's it coming along?" she asked, wiping her hands on her apron.

"It's looking great," Travis said.

"I'm helping a lot," Neal said.

"I bet," Julene joked. "They're probably using you for a spare hammer."

Neenah looked up from the book she was reading and laughed.

Neal's round little face turned red. He slammed his tiny boot into the floor and said, "I am helping, ain't I, Daddy?"

Travis patted his son on the head. "He sure is." Then, he looked at Julene. "You can help tomorrow too."

Neal pointed at Julene and laughed.

"When do you think we'll be able to move in?" Hazel asked.

Travis let out a dejected sigh. "How the hell should I know? I'm working my ass off. That's all I ever do for you people."

Julene, Neenah, and Neal were all excited about the prospect of living in a brand-new house. They figured they were rich.

The next day, work continued. The layout was pretty simple. The front door opened into a small living room. The kitchen was directly behind that. A back door, which aligned with the front, was placed in the back wall. It was four feet off the ground on that side. A hallway led to three small bedrooms to the left of the building.

Julene had picked a bad day to "volunteer." A constant rain had soaked everything, making the air warm and thick and the work messy.

Travis was in a hurry, though, so construction went ahead as planned. It was just two of his kids and him today, so he knew they wouldn't get much accomplished. But it felt good having his kids be a part of the process. Heck, they might learn something. Because of the rain, he decided they would work inside under the completed roof.

Travis yanked on the extension cord to get a few more inches of slack . . . and his saw died. "Dammit!" He looked out the door and spied the problem. The extension cord had pulled loose from the other one. He looked at his daughter. "Julene, run and plug the cords back together."

Julene was only eight, but a tomboy through and through. She wasn't afraid of anything, especially a little rain. She ran out and picked up the end of the cord and dragged it back a foot or so to the other one. The next few seconds seem to draw out in slow motion. She lifted both arms and lined up the two ends.

As the prongs on the house side began to enter the holes on Doodle's side, Travis yelled out one final instruction. "Watch out for that naked spot."

Getting shocked is a unique sensation. With any other type of injury, the pain is isolated at the point of contact. Electricity, however, simply enters there, and in a split second, it travels to every muscle, every bone, every nerve, and every atom of the body as it frantically searches for a way out.

The moisture in the ground didn't help as Julene shook and screamed in pain and fear, her hands barely able to release the menacing orange tentacles from her grip. Neal's eyes widened as he watched his sister's knees buckle as she dropped the cords and folded herself into the dirt. He didn't quite understand what was happening, but still, he was scared.

Travis was pissed as Julene slowly walked back to the house, her arms crossed tightly around her chest, her heart still racing like a greyhound. He stood firmly in place, gesturing roughly with the saw. "You damn kids have got to be more careful. Watch what the hell you're doing."

He complained the rest of the day, shouting at Neal for hammering a small nail into the wall and telling Julene, who was pale and nauseous, to stay put and not touch anything. It didn't stop on the ride home either. He drove with his left hand on the wheel and right finger pointed at nothing as he whooped and hollered about dangerous tools and "paying attention" and "a good way to lose a finger or an eye." Travis was nothing if not safety conscious.

The next day, after the used doors and windows were installed and the interior walls were added to the living room and kitchen, Travis figured it was "close-ter-nuff." "We're going to go ahead and move in and finish everything else after we get in."

Doodle looked shocked. "I don't think you're quite ready yet."

"You're right," Travis said. "You have some shovels?" Travis knew there was one more most important addition to complete.

They went down behind the house about a hundred yards and dug out a large square hole. On top of that Travis built the outhouse. It was a simple wooden structure with a slanted roof and a plywood door mounted on rusty hinges. But Travis added a little something extra. It was a two-seater. You can't hide money, and he loved being the envy of the neighborhood.

Travis couldn't tell them why he was ready to move in before everything was finished. The fact was, rent was due at their house in Chavies, and he had spent too much on lumber to be able to pay it. Besides, he was confident he could do most of the finishing work himself.

So, the Wooten clan packed up their belongings, piled into the family car, and moved into their brand-new semi-built house. The only things left to do were to add carpeting or some type of flooring, interior walls in the back rooms, a ceiling in Neal's bedroom, wiring, and hopefully some form of heat before winter came.

Hand-me-down furniture they already had. They had even found an old television set at the thrift store one day. It sat in the corner, waiting for electricity. Hazel put several kerosene lamps out to illuminate the rooms at night, and their water came from a spring down in the hollow. That was one of the daily chores the three kids shared, taking old milk jugs to the spring, filling them, and carrying them up to the house.

Several months after they moved in, Travis had run wiring and had the power turned on.

Boots came by. "The place looks great," she lied. It had shape for sure but not much to distinguish it as an actual home, except for the people who lived there. "Travis, can I talk to you outside?"

Travis followed her out. "What is it?"

"Daddy."

Travis exhaled sharply. "Of course."

"I called Martha," Boots said.

"From your home phone?"

"No, I used a pay phone like you told me. Anyway, she said Daddy was back in the woods again."

Travis said nothing. He looked down and kicked the dirt. He had left his daddy there far longer than he planned, but it's easy to forget your problems as long as someone else is handling them. Plus, clearing the land and building the new house had taken a lot of his time.

"Can you go up there and find him?"

He threw his arms up. "Hell, just let him live in the woods if he wants to. I'm tired of dealing with it."

"Okay," Boots said. "Okay. I just wanted to let you know." She turned and walked back toward her car.

"All right. All right. I'll go get him." Then, he paused and cocked his head. "Hey, do me a favor."

Boots turned around, her hand resting on the open car door. "What?"

"Get with everyone and tell them we need to get together some money so we can find a place for him and Etta."

Travis wanted this situation with his father resolved once and for all. And he figured finding Etta and him a place to live was the best way to at least start. He had his own family, his own work, and he couldn't run off to the woods every time Pete got squirrely about being on the lam.

Boots agreed it was a good plan. She went back to town, found a pay phone, and called all the brothers and sisters, including Talmadge and Ilene. Time had healed much, emotions ran softer, and the family had grown up. Everyone saw past Pete being a mostly absent father and now just saw him as an old man who needed their help. They all chipped in what they could. Boots went around and collected, including money wired by Talmadge, and brought the money to Travis.

The agents that were after Pete still came around on occasion, but it was far less frequently. Travis wasn't the only one frustrated.

The next day, after Boots brought the cash, Travis drove to Trenton, making sure he wasn't followed. He didn't bother knocking; he walked around the house straight to the woods and found his daddy in pretty much the same place as before.

"This has got to stop."

Pete said nothing.

"I'm going to find you a house. I'll be back when I do."

Pete sat on the ground, staring at his son. He understood, and he was grateful. He just didn't have the energy to figure a way out.

Travis went back to the house and told Martha the plan. He drove into town and picked up a *Dade County Sentinel*. He sat in his car with a pen and the paper and circled several houses he found that were very cheap. With enough options in the queue, he drove over to a gas station and got ten dimes in change.

Using a pay phone in front of the station, one by one, he called and asked about the places, mostly the locations and surroundings. He went and looked at a couple but knew they were too close to other homes or larger roads and that, for this reason, his daddy would never agree. Finally, he met an older gentleman who had a place for rent.

"This used to be my home," the old gentleman said. His overalls hung loose around his middle. His hands jingled bits of change in his pockets. "I recently moved in with my son after my wife died."

"It doesn't have electricity?" Travis asked.

"No." He shook his head. "Never had the need."

"No running water?"

"No. We did just fine without that too. But the well water is good water, and there's an outhouse out back and it's in good shape." He pulled a piece of long grass out his teeth and pointed with it.

Travis scanned the property. You could see the main road leading to it, but it was too far away to make out people. A smaller road ran right beside it too. "Does it get much traffic?"

"Oh, not at all."

"Did you have a garden behind the house at one time?"

The man nodded. "Yeah, you're welcome to grow one too."

"Well, it's not for me. I'm looking for a place for my parents." Then, Travis saw something in the distance that caused him alarm. "Is someone building a house there?"

"Where?"

Travis pointed. "In the edge of the woods there. Isn't that a foundation for a house?

The guy looked in the direction Travis was pointing and saw the old rock foundation in the woods beside the house. "No. I mean, someone was, but they never did. Years back, I bought that property from them, so you don't have to worry about anyone building on it."

Travis took another three-sixty view. He liked what he saw.

"I know it's not a fancy place," the old fellow began.

"We'll take it."

The old fellow was shocked. "Great. I'll draw up a lease. What name should I put it under."

"Uh. . . ." Travis stuttered. "I don't know."

"You don't know?" The man chuckled and scratched his head.

Travis had to think quickly. "I mean I don't know if it will go under Daddy's name or Mama's name. You know, for credit purposes. They might even want to put it in my name. I'll have to ask."

"Yeah, that makes sense. There's no hurry. If you want to pay the first month's rent, they can move in anytime."

Travis paid the man and drove back to Fort Payne. He got Boots and Esther to help set up some furniture and make the place ready. They also stocked it up with food.

Etta was staying with a relative, so Travis went by to explain what was going on and to bring her to the new place. "We have a house for y'all to live in."

Etta smiled. She was excited but scared. "Is it safe?"

"I think so." Travis nodded. "The good news is y'all will finally be together."

"Thank God," she said, putting her hands together in prayer. "Let me get my clothes." She stood up and hurried off to her bedroom.

Travis drove her to the house. Boots and Esther were there waiting.

Etta walked in slowly and looked around. It was small and plain. Gray paneled walls surrounded the living and kitchen areas. The floor was wood too and needed some sanding and patching here and there, but for the most part, it had been kept well. "I think it's great."

Boots and Esther got her settled in while Travis went to get their father.

❖

"Hey, Travis," Martha said as she opened the door.

"Is he here?"

Martha shook her head.

"Does he have clothes here?"

"Yes."

"Let me get those and put them in the car. I found a place for him and Etta. She's already there."

Martha was relieved. "I'll put his stuff in the car. You just go get him."

Travis nodded and walked back into the woods.

Pete put his hand to his forehead, blocking the sun so he could see Travis. "Didn't know if you were coming back."

"I didn't want to. But I found you a house."

Pete shook his head. "I never agreed to that."

Travis moved a pile of leaves back and forth with his boot. "Etta is already there waiting for you."

Pete was shocked. "Really? Does she think it's safe?"

"Yes. She thinks it will work out well."

Pete stared at the ground for several seconds. "Okay."

They walked out of the woods together and climbed into Travis's car. He drove them to the house in the country outside of Rising Fawn. Etta ran out of the house when they pulled up. Pete got out and hugged her tight. They stood like that for a while, Travis and his sisters watching and smiling.

Pete pulled away, held Etta by the shoulders, and looked her directly in the eyes. "What do you think?"

"It's going to be okay," she said. "We're going to have a home again."

After a look around the house and a short visit, Boots and Esther decided it was time to go home.

Pete, Etta, and Travis settled in around the kitchen table that Boots and Esther had picked up at the secondhand shop in town. Etta slid her fingers back and forth along the seam running across the center, where a leaf or two might slip in to make the table longer. Pete shifted on his wicker seat and asked, "Can you stay the first night?"

"Sure," Travis answered.

Pete was feeling more and more confident about the place. He threw his thumb over his shoulder. "I can grow a garden back there. This will work."

That evening, after Pete got cleaned up, they sat around the table and played several hands of tonk. When Pete found himself down seven games to two, he leaned back in his chair, began shuffling the deck, and said the magic words. "All right, this is where friendships cease in the middle of the west."

Travis smiled. He had heard Pawpaw Van utter those same words when he got behind playing cards, and Travis had already begun saying it to his kids. He wasn't sure what it meant, but it was amazing how many times his luck changed after saying that phrase.

And that's when it finally dawned on him, no matter how many times he got angry at his daddy or frustrated with him, he would never stop helping the old man. He couldn't even if he wanted to. Pete was his father.

Over the centuries, poor people in the Deep South had learned that there was only one constant in life, one reliable source of support. No matter how many years or words or worse had passed between you, you could always count on blood. If you found yourself in bad health, in need of money, or if you decided to leave prison a few years early, this group was always there to have your back. Family.

Travis settled down to sleep that night and felt a sense of peace he hadn't felt in a long time.

Pete, on the other hand, kept getting up to look out the windows in the front and the back. He had become so accustomed to looking over his shoulder, he had a hard time settling in. He felt better when the morning light came.

"There's a lot of room in the living room," Pete said as they ate breakfast. "I can probably make money repairing grandfather clocks and guns for people."

Travis nodded and shoved his last forkful of biscuits and gravy into his mouth. "I don't see why not," he mumbled.

"You sure that's a good idea?" Etta inquired.

"Why?" Pete asked.

"People will see you," she answered. "And I'm sure they will want to know your name."

"Speaking of that," Travis said, "the man who owns this place needs a name for the lease too. There's no way me or either of you can put it in our names. That might not be wise."

"I hadn't thought of that," Pete said. "Well, we're gonna need new names."

"I'll leave you with that," Travis said. "I gotta get back."

Pete walked him to the door. "You are going to bring the kids to visit me, ain't you?"

"I haven't thought about it," Travis said. "If it's safe, I will. But they can never know who you are."

Pete nodded and looked upward as if searching for an answer to a riddle. "Well, just tell them I'm . . . Uncle Roy."

Travis nodded and said his goodbyes. He drove back to Sand Mountain feeling optimistic for the first time in a long time. He smiled at nothing, at the road, or just smiled for the sake of smiling. It was like a weight had been lifted from his shoulders. His daddy was finally settled, in a house. Safe.

When he walked into his house, his small son, Neal, was sitting on the couch in front of the small television, watching cartoons. Travis smiled. He was so proud of this little fellow. He was already smart and strong like his father, and also like his father, he was incredibly honest. Travis picked him up and gave him a big hug. He knew he would always love this little man and take care of him.

Hazel, Julene, and Neenah were in the kitchen.

Travis walked in. "Girls, y'all go watch television with your brother while I talk to your mother."

They obeyed.

"I found them a house," Travis said quietly, "and we got them moved in."

"That's good," Hazel said. "Pete feels good about it?"

"He seems to. When I left, they were trying to come up with fake names to use."

Hazel smiled. "That's probably a good idea. Even Etta?"

"I guess. I'm gonna go work in the garden a while to take my mind off it."

"Okay. I'm going to make BLTs and vegetable soup for dinner. Can you bring back some tomatoes?"

"Sure." Travis got up and walked out.

Julene and Neenah went back into the kitchen to help their mother.

Neal sat there all alone. He couldn't understand why his daddy had just walked in the door and left again so quickly, but he was happy. Had his daddy stayed, he would definitely have had to change the channel to search for a ball game. But now, Neal could watch all the cartoons he wanted. He leaned back; the orange vinyl sofa felt almost like marble to his bare back despite the unrelenting heat in the living room. He cupped his hands behind his head and smiled. Life was good. All was right with the world. Nothing could ruin this day.

Knock Knock.

EPILOGUE

Sometimes, I look back on my childhood and laugh. Sometimes, I don't laugh. But laughter was a big part of my family when I was a kid. When you exist in a violent and unstable environment, humor often becomes a refuge. It's the only thing that makes life bearable.

But this is my story, at least until age thirteen when my mom pulled me aside and said those words: "Uncle Roy is really your grandfather, Pete Wooten." It was both confusing and clarifying. Suddenly, the missing pieces of the puzzle began to fill in. That's why Uncle Roy knew my dad's character and temper so well. That's why we went to see him often, even on Father's Day. That's why Mom and Dad always made sure we weren't being followed. And specifically, I finally understood the presence of the black car with the mysterious men in black suits.

Of course, my story isn't over. I know this because I just turned fifty-five years old, and my mom made me an orange cake with orange icing and orange sherbet ice cream. Seriously. I mostly just write now and help other writers get published. I hold writers' workshops often. I own several residential properties and several commercial properties, including a bank and a church, and my mom still throws birthday parties for me. Bless her heart. And yes, I love it.

But I didn't want to make this book a rags-to-riches story. That would hardly be accurate, and my goal was to tell this tale as authentically as possible. Sure, I wish I could have written that Pete blasted his way out of prison with dynamite and a tommy gun, or that he tunneled all the way to another state and came up inside the Georgia Game Park between the llama with two heads and the calf with three tails, but that would be a bald-faced lie. And I don't want y'all calling me a liar. Them's fightin' words. The fact is Pete simply walked away, but that was something he had perfected long before going to prison.

Let me interject here to say that since I began writing this book, relatives have been pouring out of the abyss like bees from a hive to offer their insights into the shootings. Cousins I haven't heard from in a coon's age have called out of the blue, and every conversation, after the normal pleasantries, has evolved into "I have it on good authority." This is followed by their apparent knowledge as to what really transpired that fateful day in the potato field, passed on by other family members who were alive when this happened but not actually there.

Some say Ilene really shot Pete and Pete took the blame to keep her out of trouble. Knowing my dad and grandad the way I did, the idea of them taking the blame for someone else hardly seems like a valid reality. They never even assumed blame for things they did themselves. I just have to think back to the day that it was everyone's fault but my dad's the day my sister drank gasoline.

One cousin even confessed to me that it was my grandmother, Elsie, who shot Pete and the entire incident was staged just for her to do that. I guess Raymond getting killed was unexpected collateral damage.

I've also heard that the sheriff and his crew did a poor job of investigating and either overlooked or covered up evidence.

I don't buy into any of it. I've always been a fan of the scientific precept known as Occam's razor, which basically states that all things being equal, the simplest explanation is usually the correct one.

The shootings take up one page in this entire book. Regardless of how it played out that day, the things my grandmother, mother, and my siblings and I endured were real. I believe it is the adversity that defines us, that needs telling no matter what someone accomplishes after. Whether a person goes on to become a senator, a doctor, a teacher, or a waitress, the fact that they endured an abusive environment means everything. Just surviving and getting out is the ultimate triumph.

We all got out.

After Julene turned sixteen, she got married and left home.

After Neenah turned sixteen, she ran away from home.

After I turned sixteen, my dad kicked me out.

For inquiring minds, however, I'll provide a condensed where-are-they-now annotation, including an abbreviated version of my life from high school until now.

My oldest sister, Julene, continued to work hard in the hosiery mills until that industry collapsed, at which point she went to college and earned a degree in nursing. Now an LPN, she is still a hard worker, still a fighter, and still the toughest person you will ever meet. Looking back on my childhood, I now know that Julene and my mom are the only real heroes I have ever known.

My sister Neenah quit school the day she turned sixteen. She couldn't wait. As an adult, however, she learned that, outside of the ravages of school, people cherished her kindness and she made friends easily. She went back and got her GED, went to college, and worked in a variety of fields. She died in 2005 at the age of forty-two of complications from surgery. It crushed us all.

Dinky went to Huntingdon College in Montgomery on a softball scholarship, whereupon she told everyone to call her Denise, her real name. After college, she began a career in law enforcement. After fifteen years as an officer and investigator, she moved back to our hometown, where everyone promptly went back to calling her Dinky. She still thinks she can speak all languages.

Breland joined the Marine Corps after high school. He began collecting baseball cards and comic books at an early age and now makes a living selling collectibles on eBay.

My mom, Hazel, finally left my dad after thirty-six years of an abusive marriage. Without telling a soul, one day she simply disappeared. She knew it was the only way. And she was right; Dad searched relentlessly for her until he finally found another woman he wanted to marry. Like father, like son. Only then did he agree to a divorce. At seventy-eight years old, Mom still works full time and is still the hardest worker I've ever known. And she still goes through several romance novels a month.

My dad, Travis, died in 2003 after suffering a stroke two years earlier. As he lay on his deathbed at the hospital in Fort Payne, he had my sisters call me in Montgomery to ask me to rush to get there. I drove the distance in record time. Dad was weak and had wires running everywhere, but he held off dying so he could whisper two words to me: "I'm sorry." I think his tormented soul was finally at peace.

There have now been major advancements in the diagnosis and treatment of mental illnesses, but that was after our time, or perhaps it hadn't yet filtered down to the tiny community of Blake, Alabama. We had never heard the terms "bipolar" or "manic depressive" back then, but I'm convinced that was part of my father's psychological profile. He could quickly go from incredible highs where he was very loving and caring to unimaginable lows where he would step away from the wheel and let his demons drive. In retrospect, I truly believe it would have made for a more stable childhood to have a father who was mean and violent all the time. But I don't believe my dad could control his impulses any more than a man with a gambling or alcohol addiction. I think of him often, not with the hatred and bitterness of my youth, but with sadness and always with awe. I never did learn how to pitch horseshoes or play checkers correctly.

But let me be clear. While I believe the highs and lows were surely caused by a mental issue, not all of my dad's shortcomings were totally unique for the mountain. Back in that day, I knew other mountain men who were very close to their siblings. They adored them, praised them, and would probably take a bullet for them. Yet they treated their wife and kids like crap.

There are certainly people with childhoods far more traumatic than mine. I wonder if it creates a "family" bond so strong with their brothers and sisters that nothing else measures up, not even their own offspring.

My grandfather, Pete Wooten, was never caught. He lived the rest of his life hiding in plain sight as the mild-mannered Uncle Roy Helms. It wasn't just a disguise; he really had mellowed in his later years. Perhaps his time in prison and on the lam had changed him. When the men in the black suits learned of his passing, they issued a final warning to my dad, telling him not to bring Pete back to Alabama to bury him, or they would arrest him on the charge of being an accomplice. Ever defiant, Dad honored his father's wishes and buried Pete in the cemetery at Town Creek Baptist Church in Rainsville on Sand Mountain, where most of the Wootens are buried. The men in the black suits attended, watching from a distance as usual, but we never saw them again. I wish I could have seen Pete run.

All of Dad's siblings are now gone.

Pete's wife, Etta (aka Helen), moved back to North Carolina after his death, and I never saw her again.

My paternal grandmother, Elsie, died when I was two years old. I have only faint memories of her.

My maternal grandfather, Harley Jackson, died when I was five. I just remember him being a stern, no-nonsense mountain man.

My maternal grandmother, Lela Jackson (Granny), lived to be ninety-three and remained just as colorful a character as always. She still tended her own garden and still kept her double-barrel 12-guage shotgun on a gunrack in her bedroom. It was an older gun with rabbit ears. You might have to google that.

She was ornery to everyone in my family except me, even my mom, who embarrassed easily. Granny had no filters and always said what she was thinking and at elevated decibels.

Mom eventually couldn't handle taking Granny to see Dr. Gibson, our family doctor, for her checkups. So, I took over. Granny insisted on getting there an hour early and then cussed loudly every time someone came in after us but was taken back ahead of her. It must have been hard on the staff as well, because it got to the point where they would simply take her back as soon as she walked in. Mom even believes the good doctor retired several years early just so he wouldn't have to go through any more Granny visits. Yeah, I think it's safe to say I loved that woman and miss her dearly.

As for me, I stuck it out in high school and excelled in sports. The things I inherited from my dad—strength, speed, and intelligence—and the thing I learned in his presence—the absolute unwavering ability to do exactly what I was told without questioning—made me a coach's dream.

I also became obsessed with competitions that weren't school sanctioned, especially powerlifting and arm wrestling. In 1983, at the age of eighteen, I won the SEC arm wrestling championship in the 180-pound class.

During my senior year, Sylvania High School announced tryouts for the math team. We were a 1-A school at the time, the smallest school size in Alabama, but we had a devoted math teacher, Tonie Niblett, and she put together a competitive bunch of nerds like me.

I went to the tryouts just to get out of class but scored the highest and earned a spot on the team. I would later win two first-place trophies in competition against much larger schools. Only then did my classmates, whom I had gone to school with most of my life, see me as more than a poor farm boy sitting in the back of class wearing hand-me-down clothes who could at times make a tackle or hit a home run.

Halfway through my senior year, Mrs. Niblett asked a question that caught me by surprise: "Where are you going to college?"

I laughed. I thought she was joking. I truly didn't think I was allowed. Plus, I had always felt out of place at school. I assumed that college was only for rich people and I could possibly be arrested for attempting such an insurrectionist endeavor. I had resigned myself to being a farmer or getting a job at one of the hosiery mills in the valley, renting a crappy mobile home, and getting Uncle Doodle to help me raise anything but hogs. My expectations for myself were lower than what others held of me. "I'm not going to college," I answered.

Mrs. Niblett was furious at this and made no attempts to mask it on her face. She convinced me I was allowed and even explained how she also came from a poor home but went to college. Suddenly, it seemed plausible. I think most of us can point back to one teacher in high school who most influenced us. She was my influence, my inspiration, and the one person who believed in me enough to make me realize I could control the course of my life.

So, after attending Northeast Alabama Community College for one year, I went on to Auburn University. Coming from a town with a population of a hundred farmers and going to a campus of over twenty thousand students from all over the world could aptly be described as culture shock. Did you see the episode of *The Andy Griffith Show* where Gomer Pyle went from Mayberry to the Marine Corps? Yeah, that was me. If I felt I didn't fit in during high school, multiply that by a thousand.

Fresh off Sand Mountain, my hillbilly accent was so pronounced, other students and teachers had trouble understanding me, even when I introduced myself. When I would tell them my name was Neal Wooten, people often repeated, "Leo Whitten?" It happened so often, my friends from college still call me Leo to this day.

While in college and even the years that followed, I seldom came home to visit. As always, Dad acted as if nothing had ever happened between us, but there was still no way to tell what would set him off.

Mom's face usually said it all. There was always something behind her eyes, an invisible code that only her children could see and decipher, but it was clear as day: sadness, frustration, longing, and fear. Perhaps, it was the guilt of leaving that made me visit so infrequently.

College was very hard for me. It wasn't the classes. I struggled financially even with a Pell Grant and small student loans. I tutored math, did art projects for other students, and worked full-time at a gas station, which included a thirteen-hour shift every Saturday, just to pay for rent, utilities, food, and books. While most students were living it up, partying, and going to ball games, I was scratching for every penny I could make. For a solid year, I literally lived on nineteen-cent cans of tomato soup. But I stuck it out there too and finished with a BS in applied mathematics. Math was the only subject that was easy for me.

I owe that to my granddad and dad. That's why they were so good at checkers and could see so many moves ahead. It also had an effect on every physical thing they did. I believe that hand-eye coordination stems from a brain's grasp of mathematics.

While in college, I began performing standup comedy as another way to make a buck and continued doing that full-time after college, traveling the circuit for many years. That could have also been passed down by my dad's love of an audience. It's actually a depressing line of work, requiring a familiar relationship with solitude. But I worked with many big-name comics, had my own television show, and appeared in an HBO special. I still occasionally headline comedy shows to this day.

I created two successful comic strips, *Warp* and *Brad's Pit*, the latter still active in its eighth year and going strong. I have sold several oil paintings at art galleries and appeared in a Danny Trejo movie. I have written for my hometown paper and for the *Huffington Post* for the last fifteen years. I didn't write my first book until I was forty-three years old. Until then, I didn't realize I could do anything but count. My novels have won dozens of awards, and my short stories have been featured in dozens of magazines. I have been invited to speak at many schools, libraries, workshops, and seminars and for different organizations throughout the South and Midwest.

Even when I am the guest speaker at a professional venue, the attendees get more than just information. My presentations are always colorful, as my dad and grandfather's genes sneak in and I summon the spirits of all the great Sand Mountain storytellers.

This is my eighteenth book, and the hardest one I've ever written. It took me over forty years to be able to tell it. I guess I was too embarrassed.

It's amazing how some of the perceptions I had as a kid followed me into adulthood. I didn't want to be different. I think that's a common fear. It took me decades to realize how important it was and how lucky I was to actually be different.

I know now that growing up the way I did, even with the violence, gave me advantages over others. It made me tougher and more resilient. No matter how many times I got knocked down in life, I was never as low as I had at one time been.

And I finally understood that what really set us apart on the mountain was my father's intelligence. Having only completed second grade at Blake Elementary, Travis Wooten was a mathematical genius capable of doing advanced calculus in his head.

Here's an actual example. During a visit home from college, I bragged to my dad about being the only student in my Calculus 4 class to solve a bonus problem. I explained it to him.

"Five men and a monkey are stranded on an island with nothing to eat but coconuts. They decide to gather them all together and divide them into five equal piles. But after they finish gathering, they're tired and decide to divide them the next morning.

"During the night, one man becomes worried he will be cheated, so he divides them into five equal piles. It comes out even with one left over, which he gives to the monkey. He hides his fifth then puts the remaining coconuts back into a pile.

"Throughout the night, the other four, one by one, wake with the same fear. Each time they divide them into five piles, and each time it comes out even with one left over. They give the extra one to the monkey, hide their fifth, and put the remaining coconuts back into a pile.

"So, the question is, what is the minimum number of coconuts needed for this to be possible?"

For the record, I did solve it, but it took me a week and enough paper to put a dent in the rain forest. The next morning as I was leaving to go back to college, however, Dad walked out to my car.

"Here you go," he said handing me a small piece of paper. "I solved that little riddle of yours."

I looked at the paper in disbelief. It read "3,121." And yes, that is the answer.

I often wondered what contributions to the world he could have made if he'd been born to a middle-class or wealthy family who pushed their children to strive for academic excellence and had given him the structure to harness that intelligence instead of always searching for that pot of gold.

I inherited a lot from my father: flat feet, speed, the ability to sweat in a snowstorm, and a knack for math. My IQ was once scored by Mensa at 171, which is 31 points above genius. Unfortunately, I also inherited his temper, but I have successfully locked it away somewhere deep inside of me in a cold dark cell and threw away the key. My sisters, Neenah and Dinky, who got the most physical features from our father, struggled with this much more than me.

It's clear to me that every good physical trait I possess, I got from my dad, and every good character trait I possess, I got from my mom.

At age forty, I met and married my wife, who was from Chicago. Yes, she was a Yankee. When you're from the Deep South, everyone above Tennessee is a Yankee. I think it's safe to say she was amused and bemused at my country relatives. In fact, she would tease me often.

We lived in Milwaukee for ten years. Once, at the lakefront, she watched as a bird landed on my hand and stayed there a long time. She also witnessed me picking up a wild opossum one day and a wild rabbit another day in our backyard. I explained that wild animals have always liked me. She had a different theory. "I think it's because your family has not been walking upright too long yourselves."

We were supposed to move to Alabama in 2016 when she retired, but the closer the time came, the more she was reminded of the stigma she had about the South and couldn't do it. We divorced after twelve years of marriage.

I continued with the plan and, after living away for thirty-three years, moved back to my hometown. It's strange, but no matter where I lived or how long I was gone, this place was still home. It's like a magnet pulling people back.

If you're wondering what's it like living back here after all this time, well, part of it is as easy as pie. Like the saying goes, you can take the boy from the mountain but not the mountain from the boy.

Part of it is hard. People are certainly set in their ways here. I often think people believe that when someone moves away from this area, the location they move to and the citizens thereof are the culprits in tainting a person's personal beliefs. They fail to consider that it could be the person's independent thoughts and open-mindedness that led them to seek out new people and places in the first place.

Regardless, I'm back in the Bible Belt, where it all started. I still have nightmares every night. I thought this was normal until I was in my twenties and all my friends assured me it was not. Is it because of my childhood? The devil inside that my father and grandfather before me had? They never locked theirs away and threw away the key like I did. Theirs was always coming out. Violently so. Could it be that those demons just wreak havoc inside my head at night? Who knows? Maybe it's just my creative brain telling me to write horror books instead.

Do I have regrets in life? Sure, but who doesn't? My main one is this: I never did get to see the paid area at the Georgia Game Park. And for the record, I learned in college that earthworms come up because the vibration makes them believe it's a mole crawling through the ground. Getting to the surface is their only defense. And when people ask me how I'm doing, I still say, "Fair to middlin'."